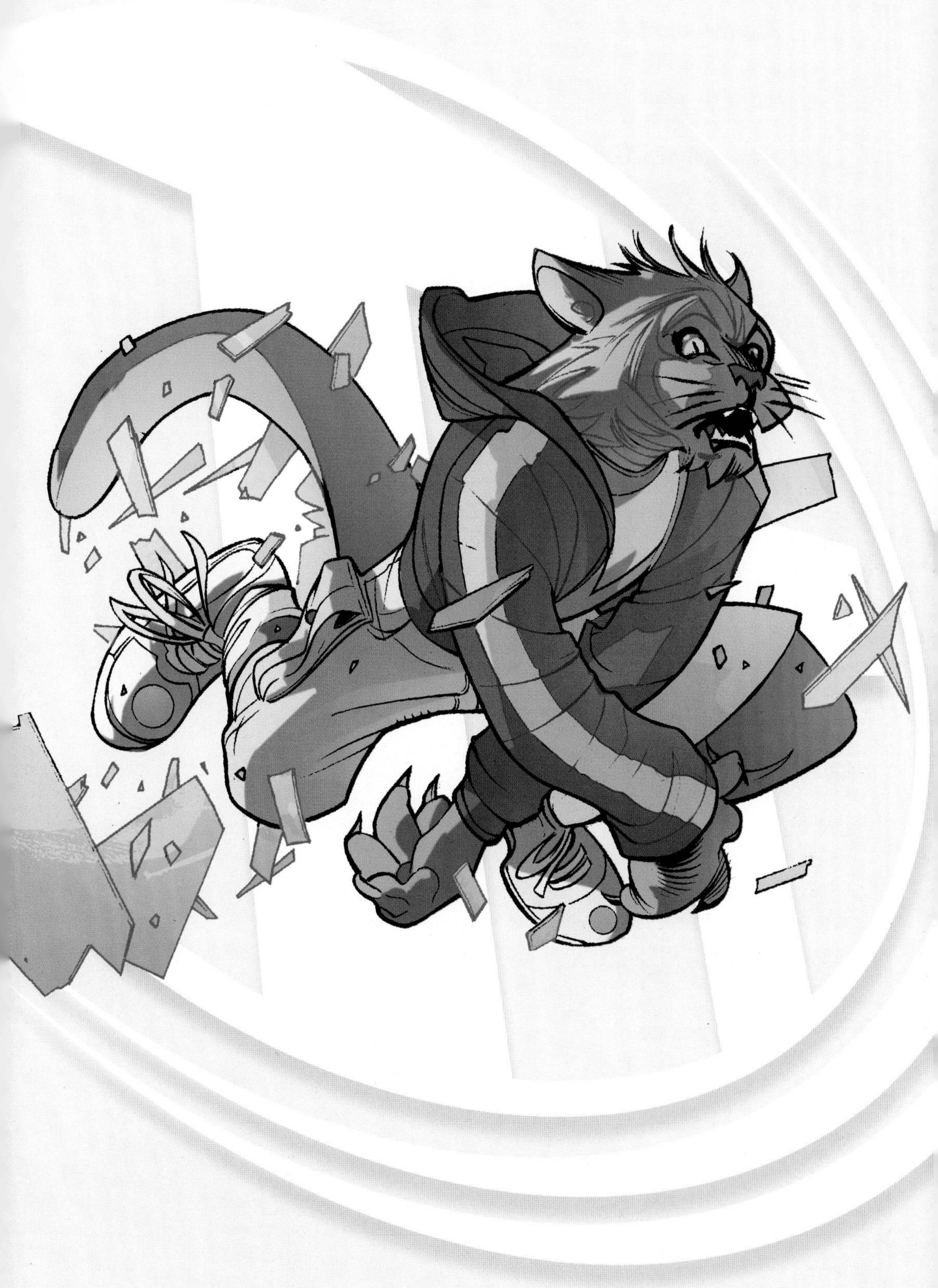

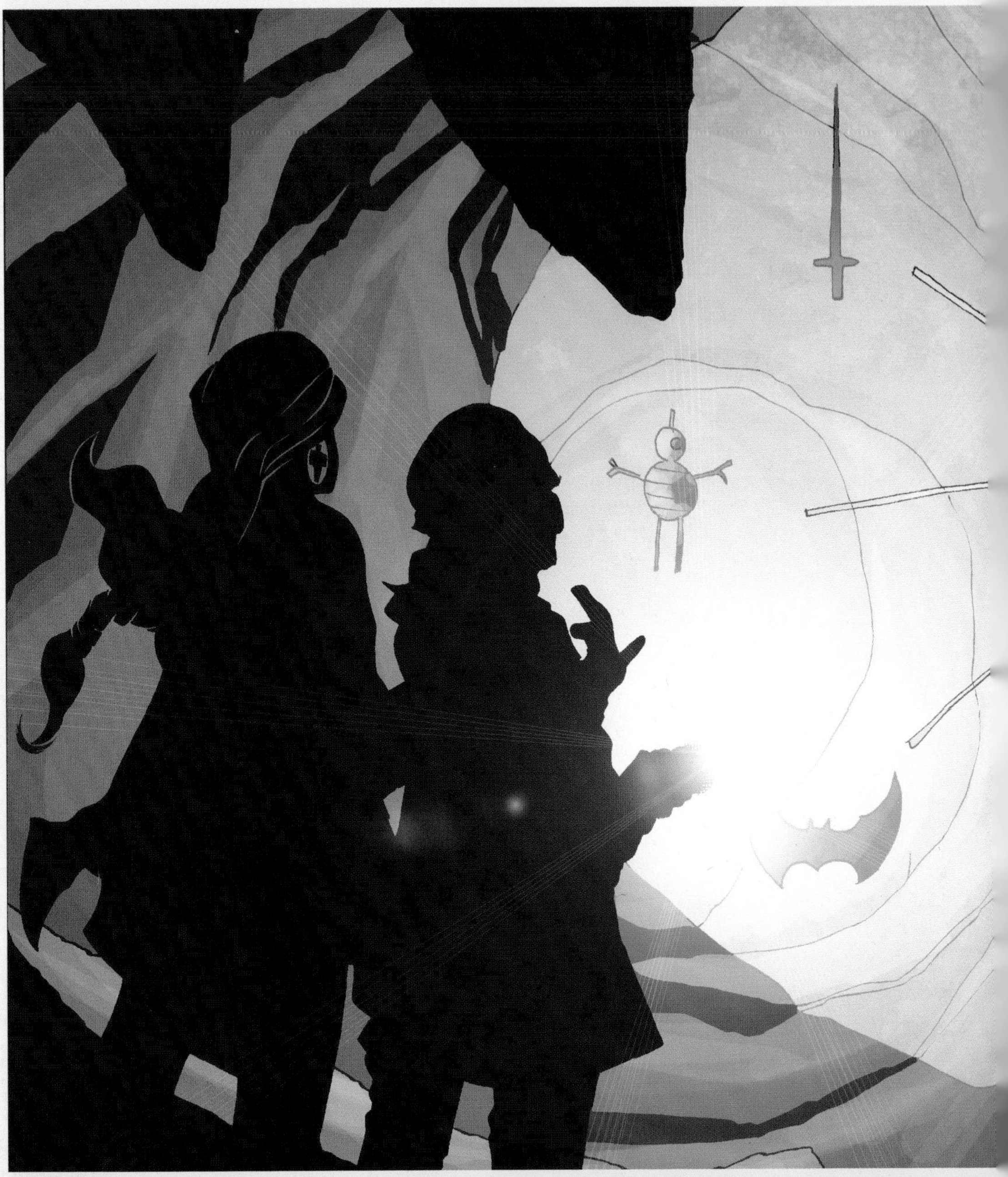

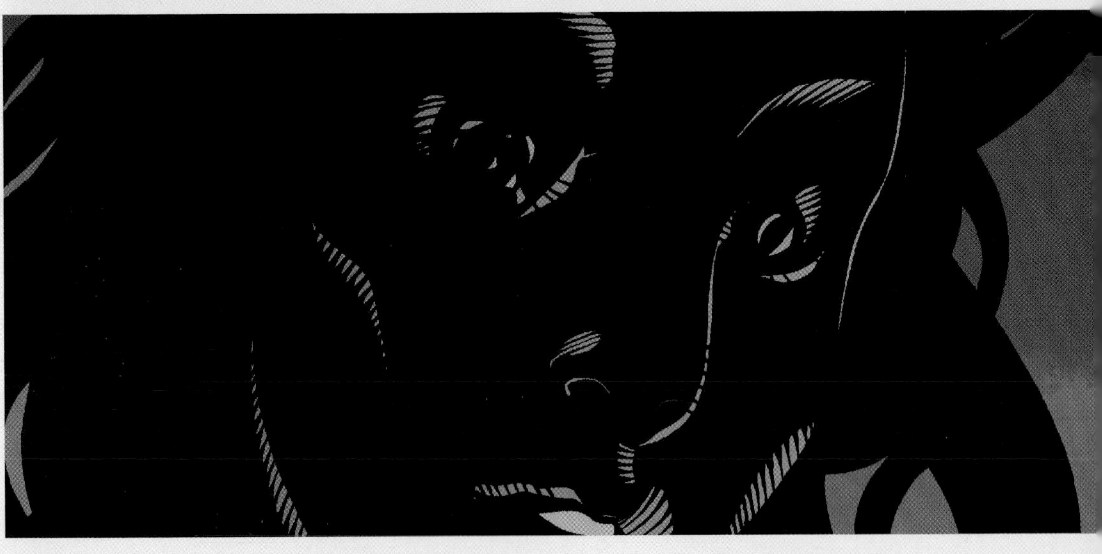

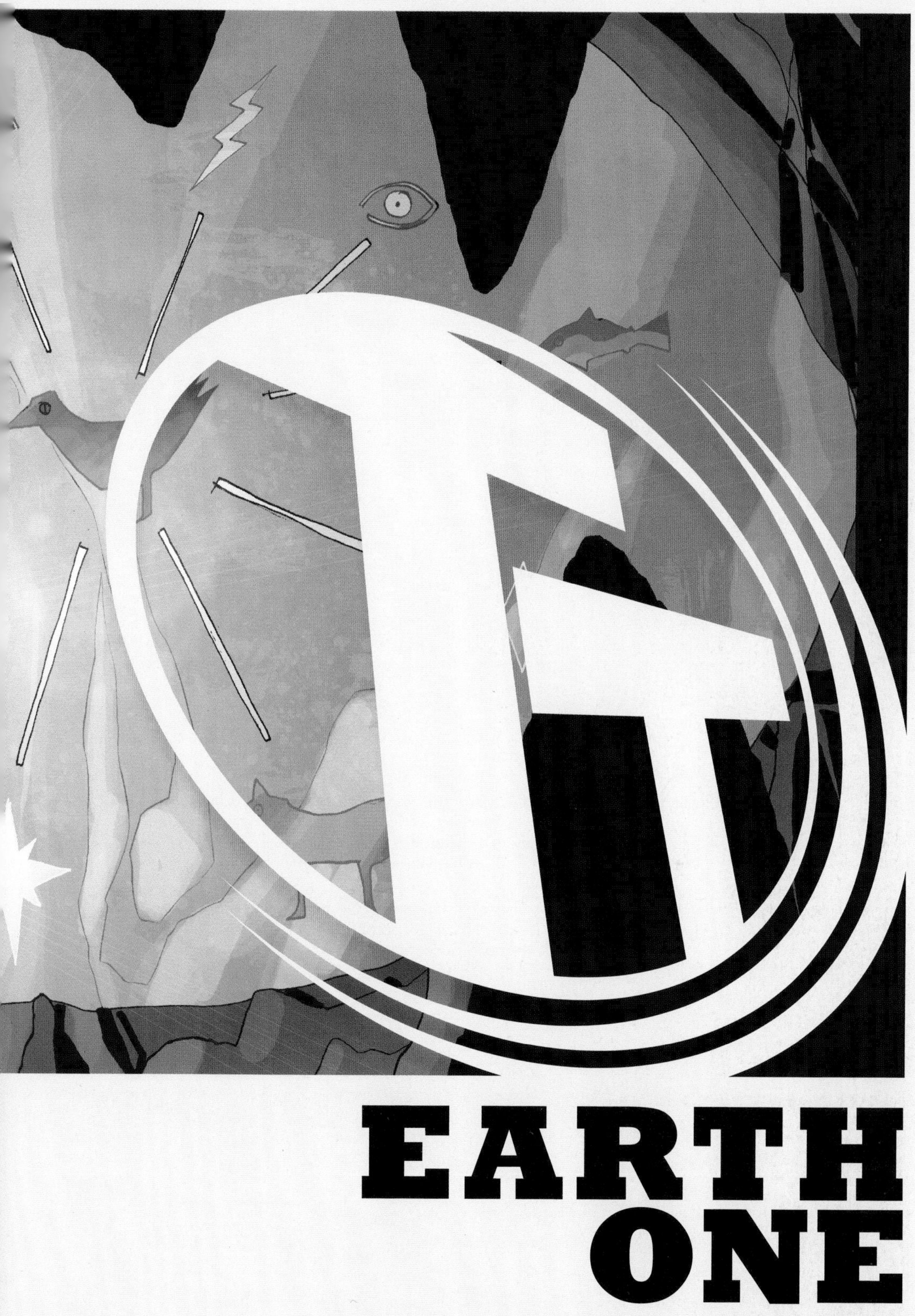

EARTH ONE

Written by Jeff Lemire Pencils by Terry Dodson

Inks by Rachel Dodson with Cam Smith

Colors by Brad Anderson with Terry Dodson

Lettered by Jared K. Fletcher

Dedicated, with respect and gratitude, to Marv Wolfman and George Pérez
for creating these enduring characters, and for all their work, which made
me fall in love with comics in the first place.
Jeff Lemire

To George Pérez and Marv Wolfman for getting the ball rolling and to the
Editorial and Creative teams for putting it in the net!
Terry and Rachel Dodson

Matt Idelson & **Chris Conroy** Editors
Robbin Brosterman Design Director – Books
Louis Prandi Art Director

Bob Harras Senior VP – Editor-in-Chief, DC Comics

Diane Nelson President
Dan DiDio and **Jim Lee** Co-Publishers
Geoff Johns Chief Creative Officer
Amit Desai Senior VP – Marketing & Franchise Management
Amy Genkins Senior VP – Business & Legal Affairs
Nairi Gardiner Senior VP – Finance
Jeff Boison VP – Publishing Planning
Mark Chiarello VP – Art Direction & Design
John Cunningham VP – Marketing
Terri Cunningham VP – Editorial Administration
Larry Ganem VP – Talent Relations & Services
Alison Gill Senior VP – Manufacturing & Operations
Hank Kanalz Senior VP – Vertigo & Integrated Publishing
Jay Kogan VP – Business & Legal Affairs, Publishing
Jack Mahan VP – Business Affairs, Talent
Nick Napolitano VP – Manufacturing Administration
Sue Pohja VP – Book Sales
Fred Ruiz VP – Manufacturing Operations
Courtney Simmons Senior VP – Publicity
Bob Wayne Senior VP – Sales

 TEEN TITANS: EARTH ONE VOLUME ONE

Published by DC Comics, 1700 Broadway, New York, NY 10019. Copyrig
© 2014 by DC Comics. All Rights Reserved. All characters featured in th
publication, the distinctive likenesses thereof and related elements a:
trademarks of DC Comics. Printed by RR Donnelley, Salem, VA, USA. 1/2/
First Printing. DC Comics, a Warner Bros. Entertainment Company.
HC ISBN: 978-1-4012-4556-6

Library of Congress Cataloging-in-Publication Data is Available.

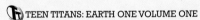

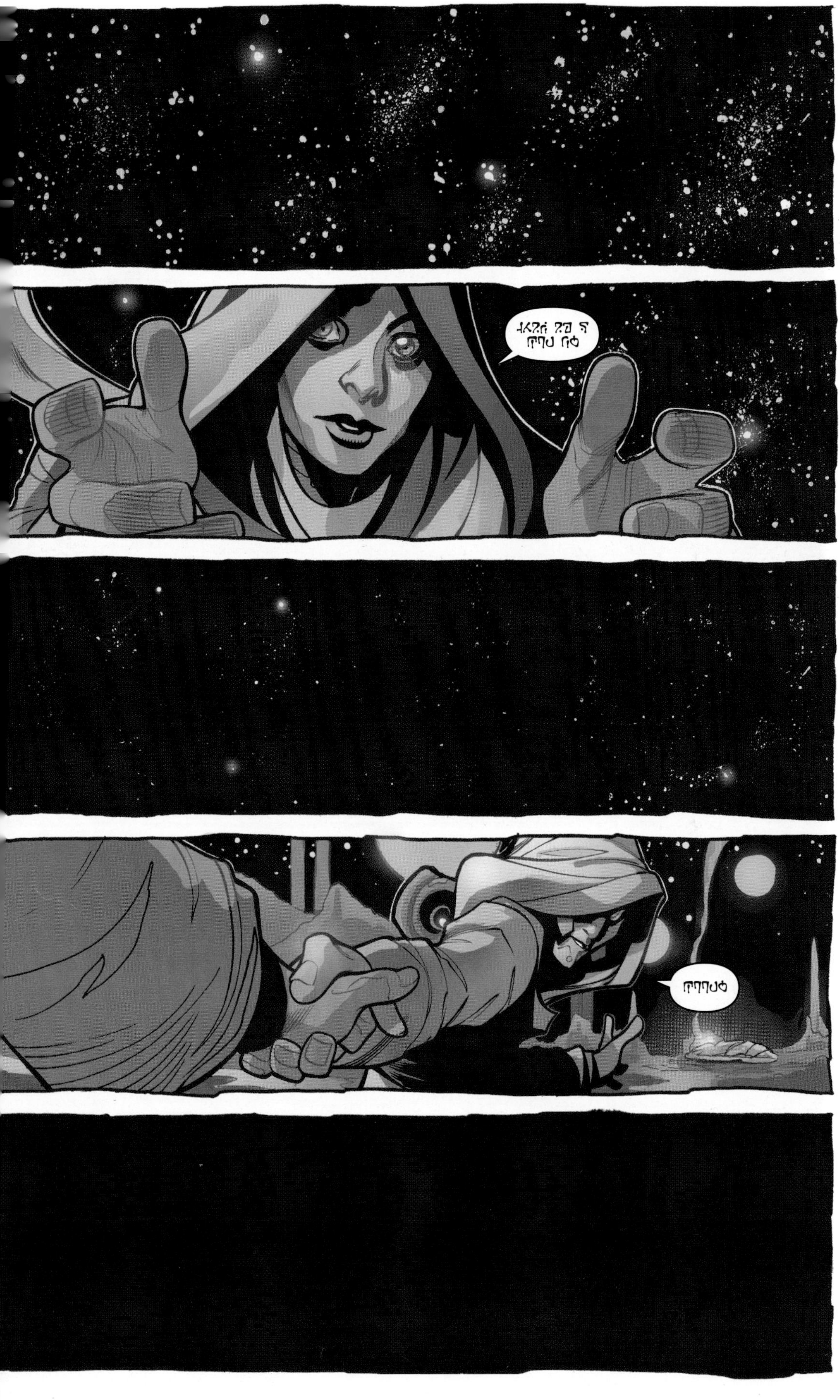

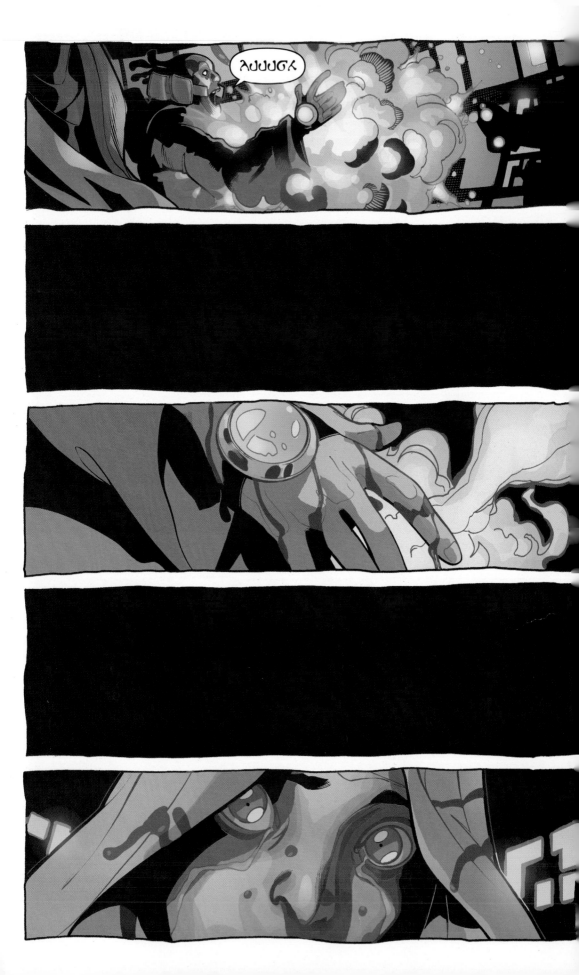

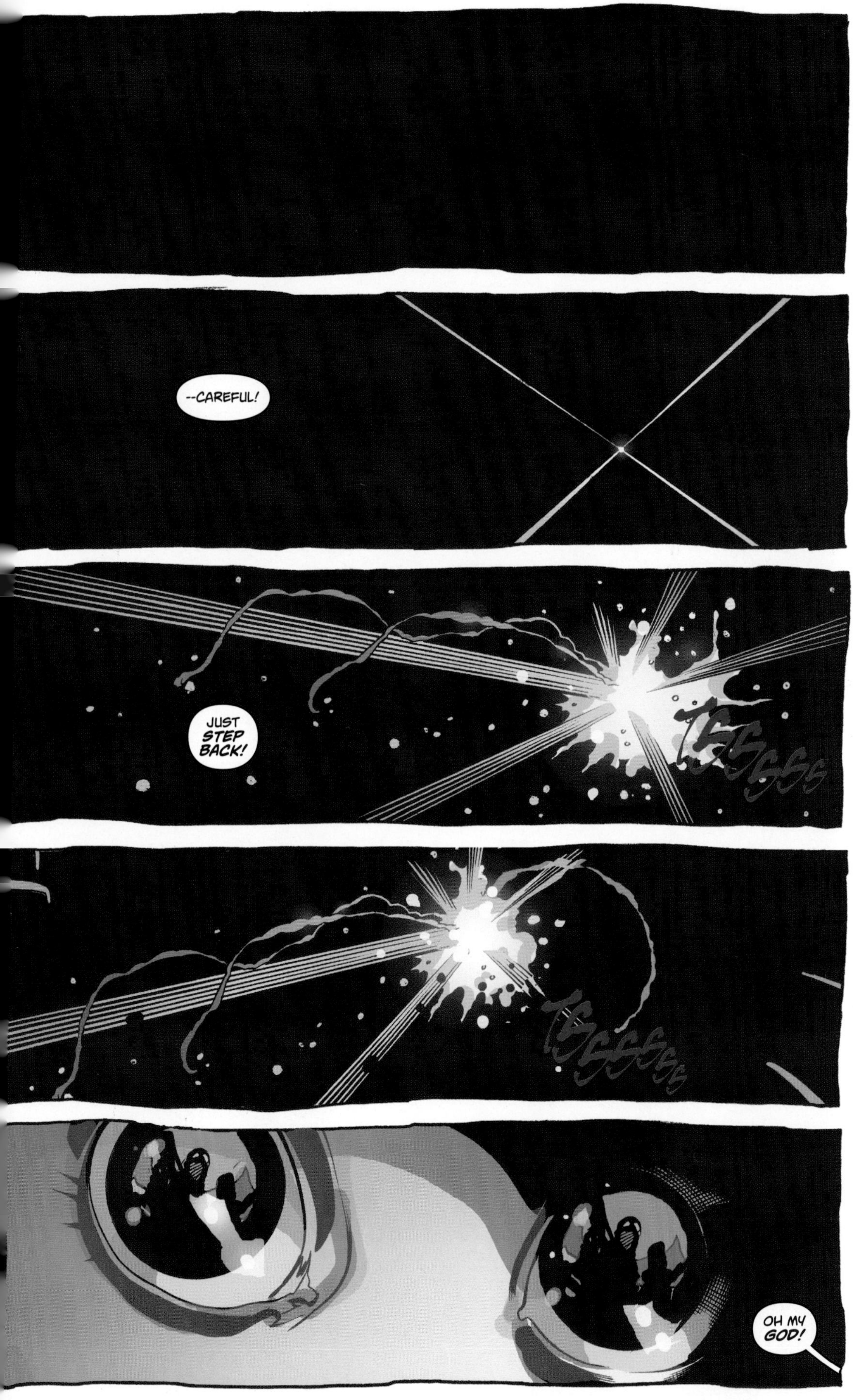
--CAREFUL!
JUST STEP BACK!
TSSSSSS
TSSSSSS
OH MY GOD!

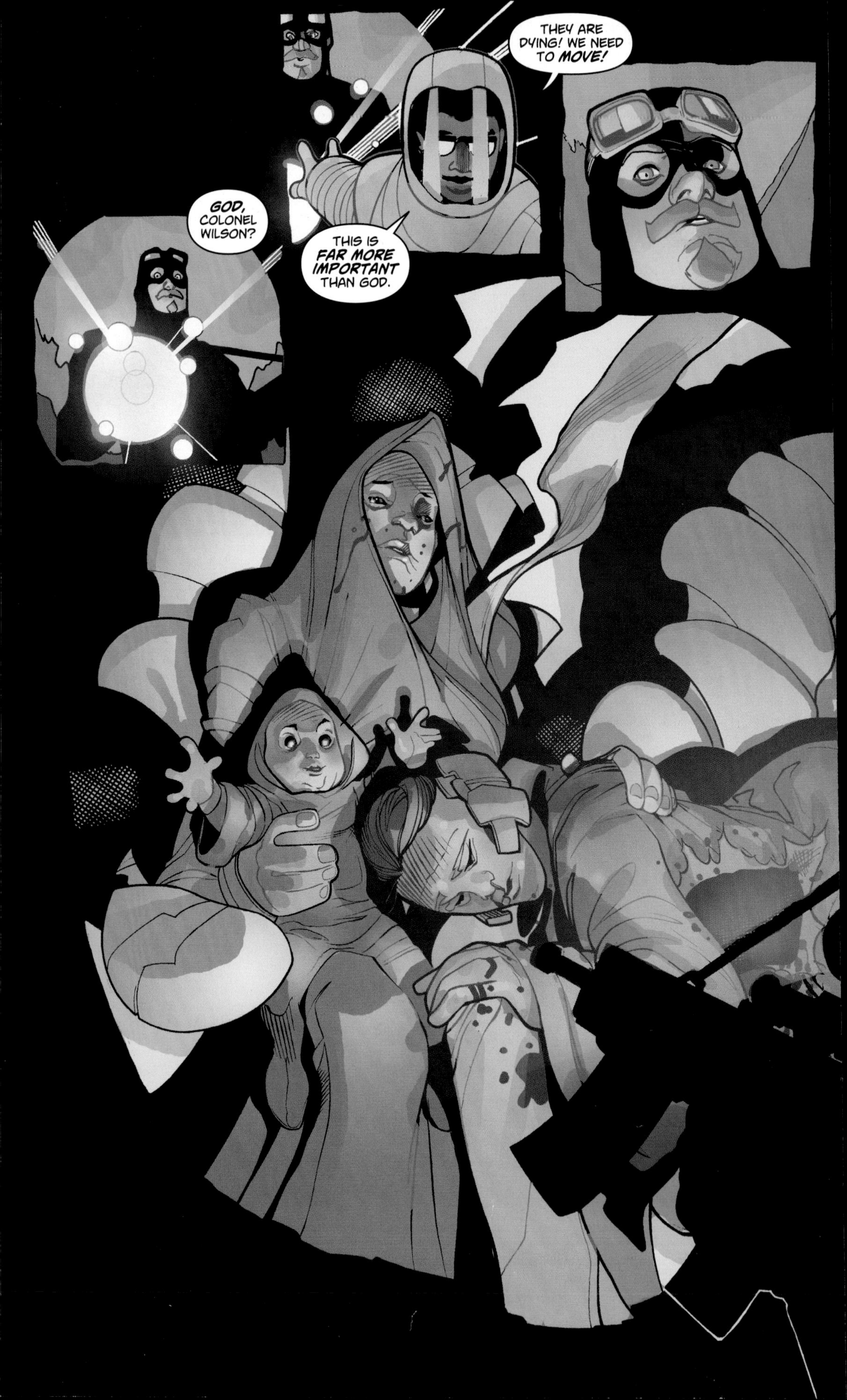
THEY ARE DYING! WE NEED TO **MOVE!**
GOD, COLONEL WILSON?
THIS IS **FAR MORE IMPORTANT** THAN GOD.

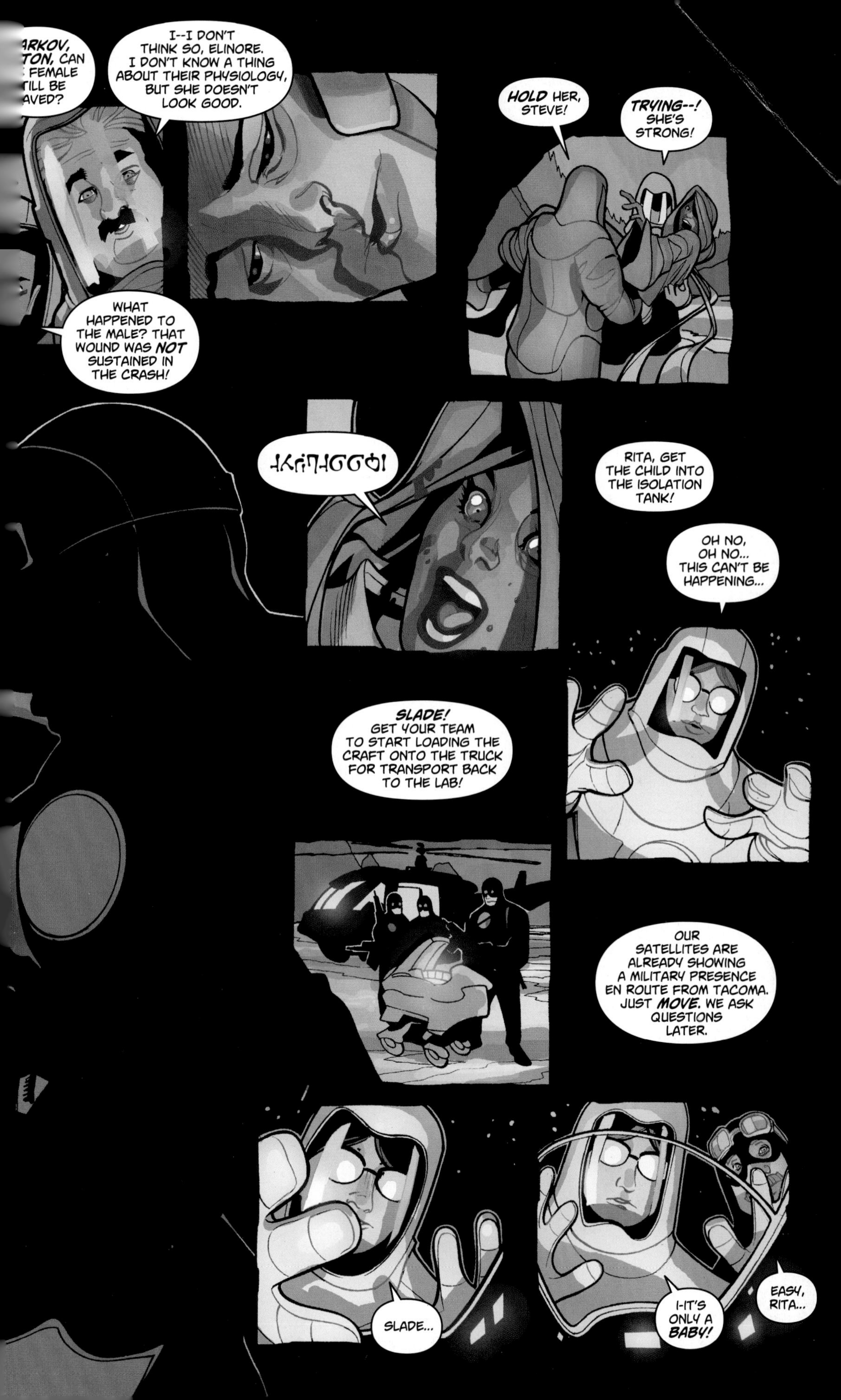
ARKOV, TON, CAN FEMALE TILL BE AVED?
I--I DON'T THINK SO, ELINORE. I DON'T KNOW A THING ABOUT THEIR PHYSIOLOGY, BUT SHE DOESN'T LOOK GOOD.
WHAT HAPPENED TO THE MALE? THAT WOUND WAS **NOT** SUSTAINED IN THE CRASH!
HOLD HER, STEVE!
TRYING--! SHE'S STRONG!
RITA, GET THE CHILD INTO THE ISOLATION TANK!
OH NO, OH NO... THIS CAN'T BE HAPPENING...
SLADE! GET YOUR TEAM TO START LOADING THE CRAFT ONTO THE TRUCK FOR TRANSPORT BACK TO THE LAB!
OUR SATELLITES ARE ALREADY SHOWING A MILITARY PRESENCE EN ROUTE FROM TACOMA. JUST **MOVE**. WE ASK QUESTIONS LATER.
SLADE...
I-IT'S ONLY A **BABY!**
EASY, RITA...

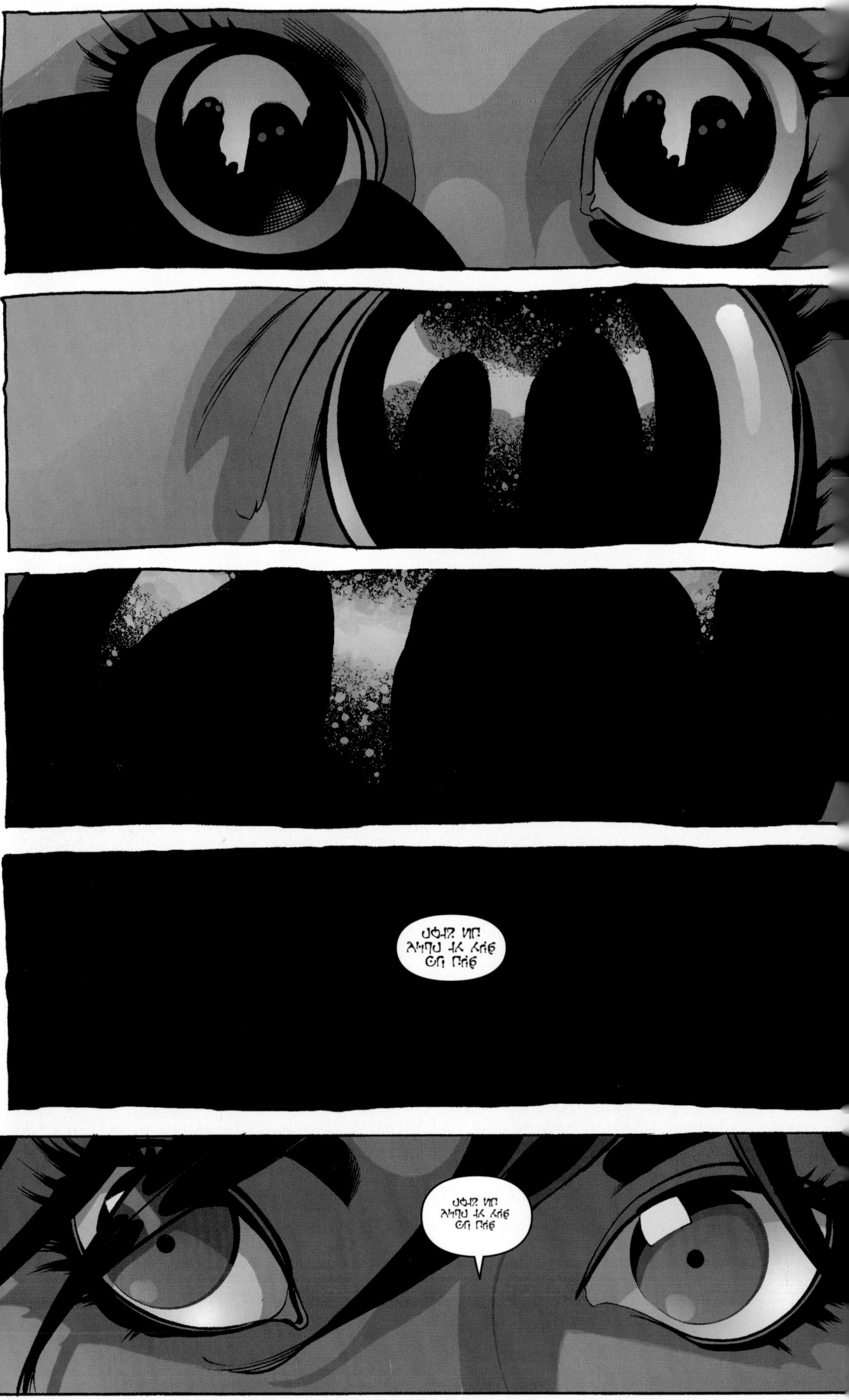

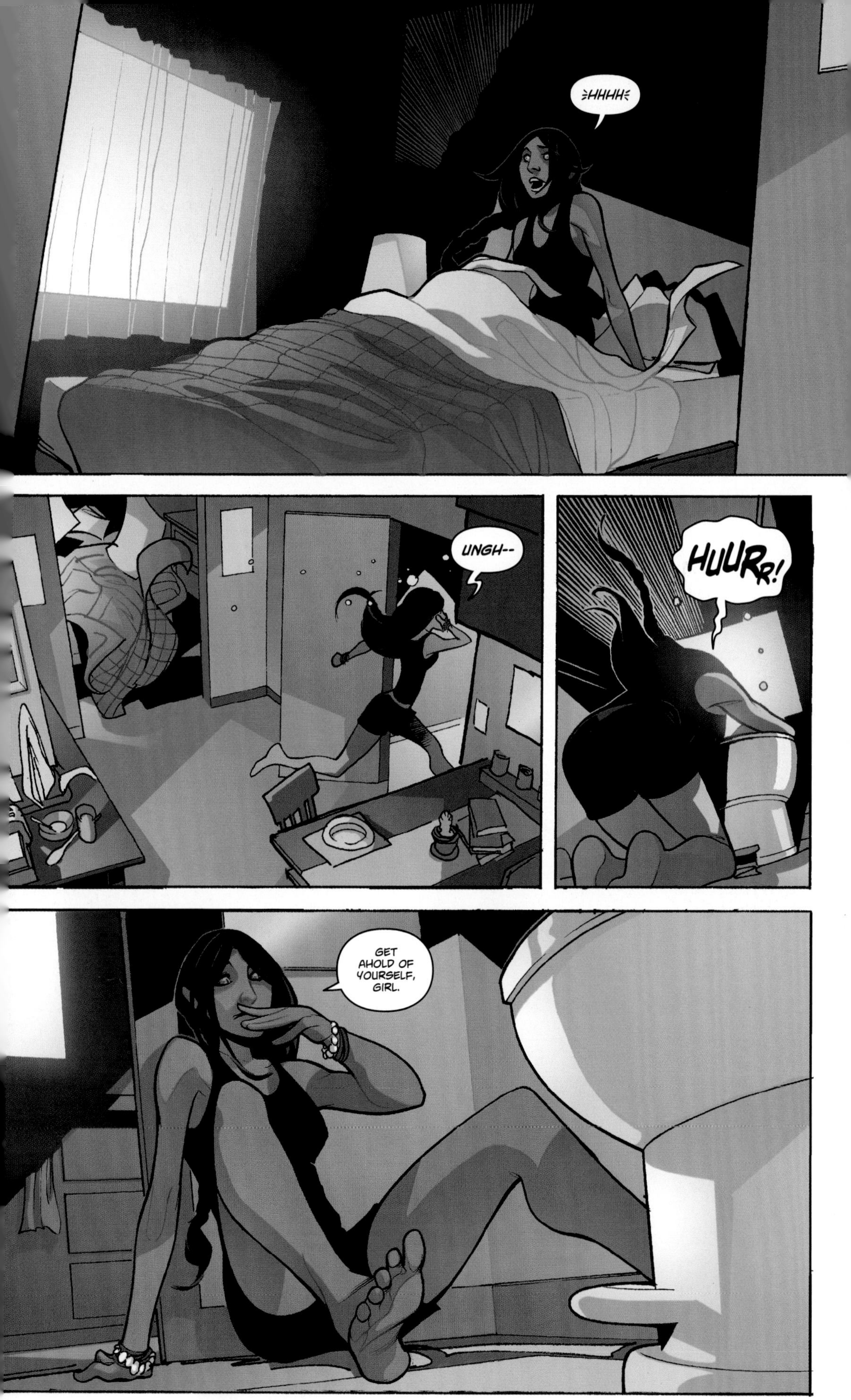
HHHH
UNGH--
HUURR!
GET AHOLD OF YOURSELF, GIRL.

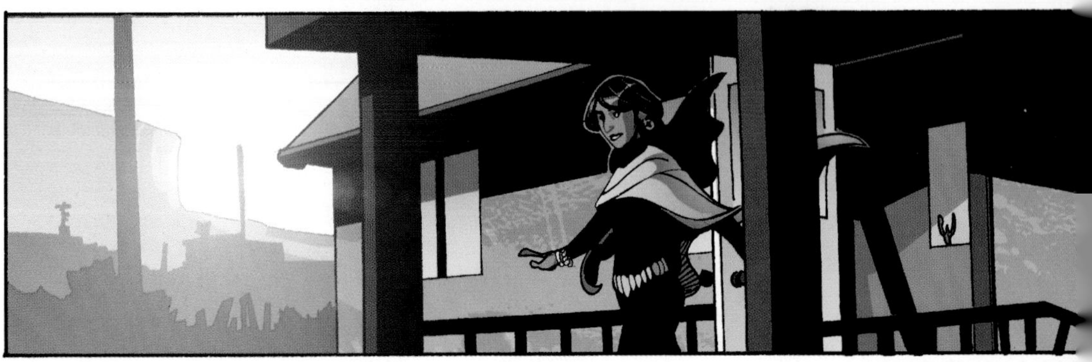

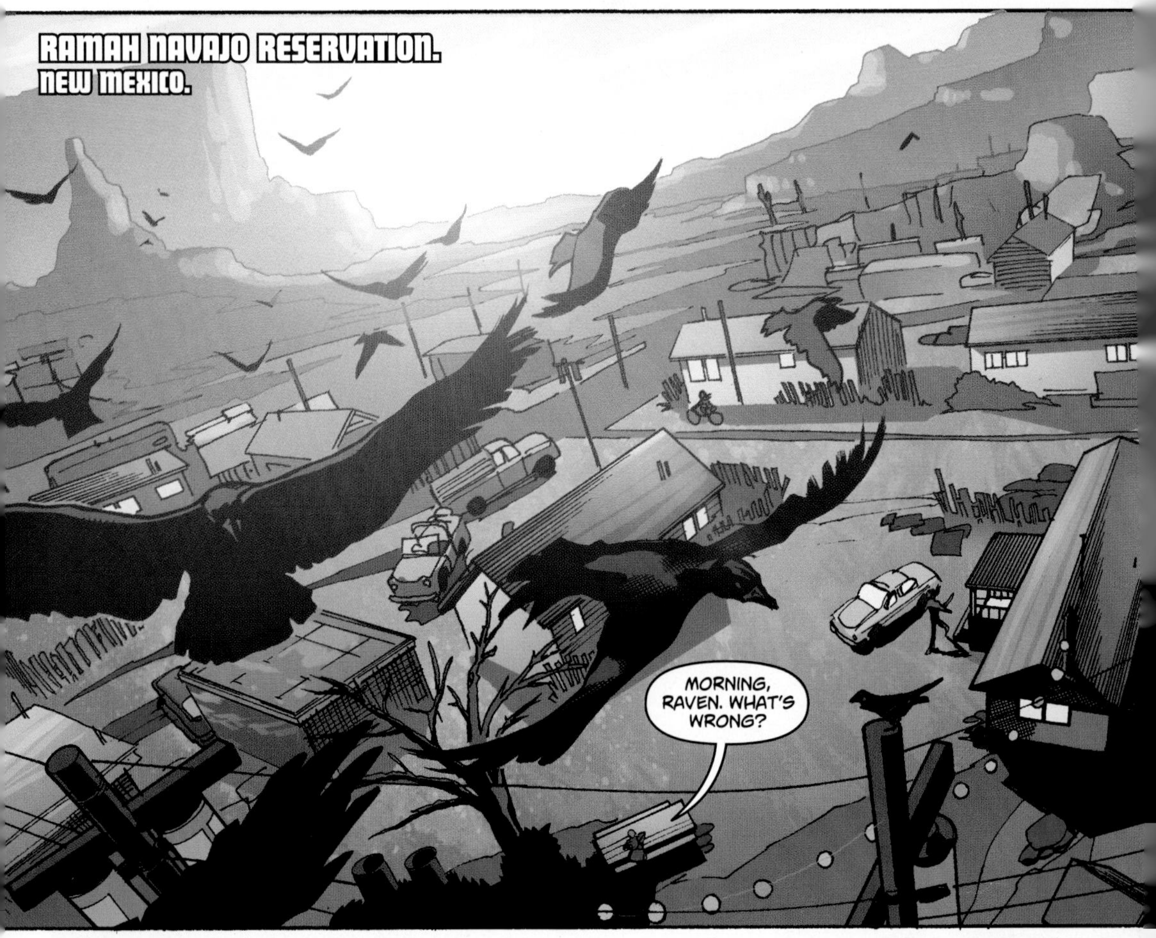
RAMAH NAVAJO RESERVATION.
NEW MEXICO.
MORNING, RAVEN. WHAT'S WRONG?

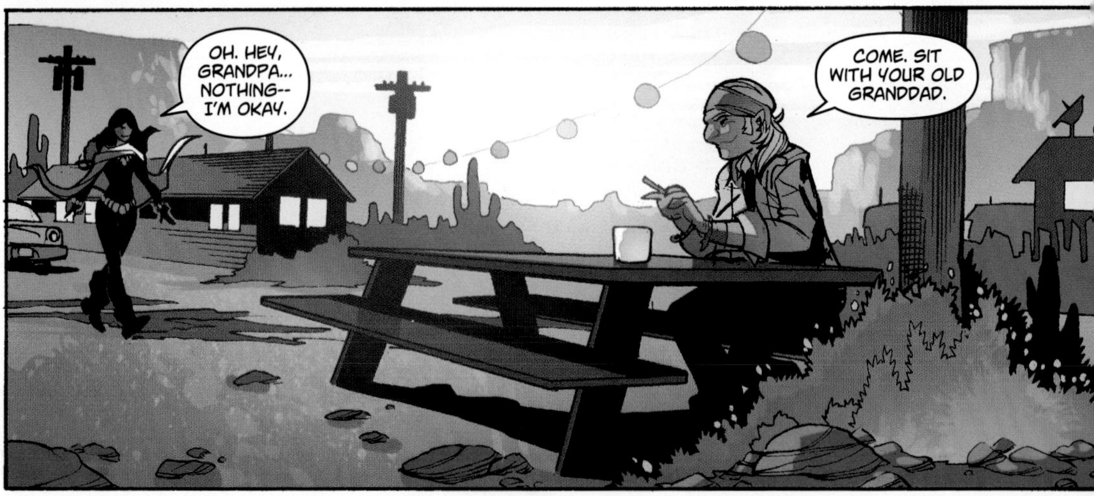
OH. HEY, GRANDPA... NOTHING-- I'M OKAY.
COME. SIT WITH YOUR OLD GRANDDAD.

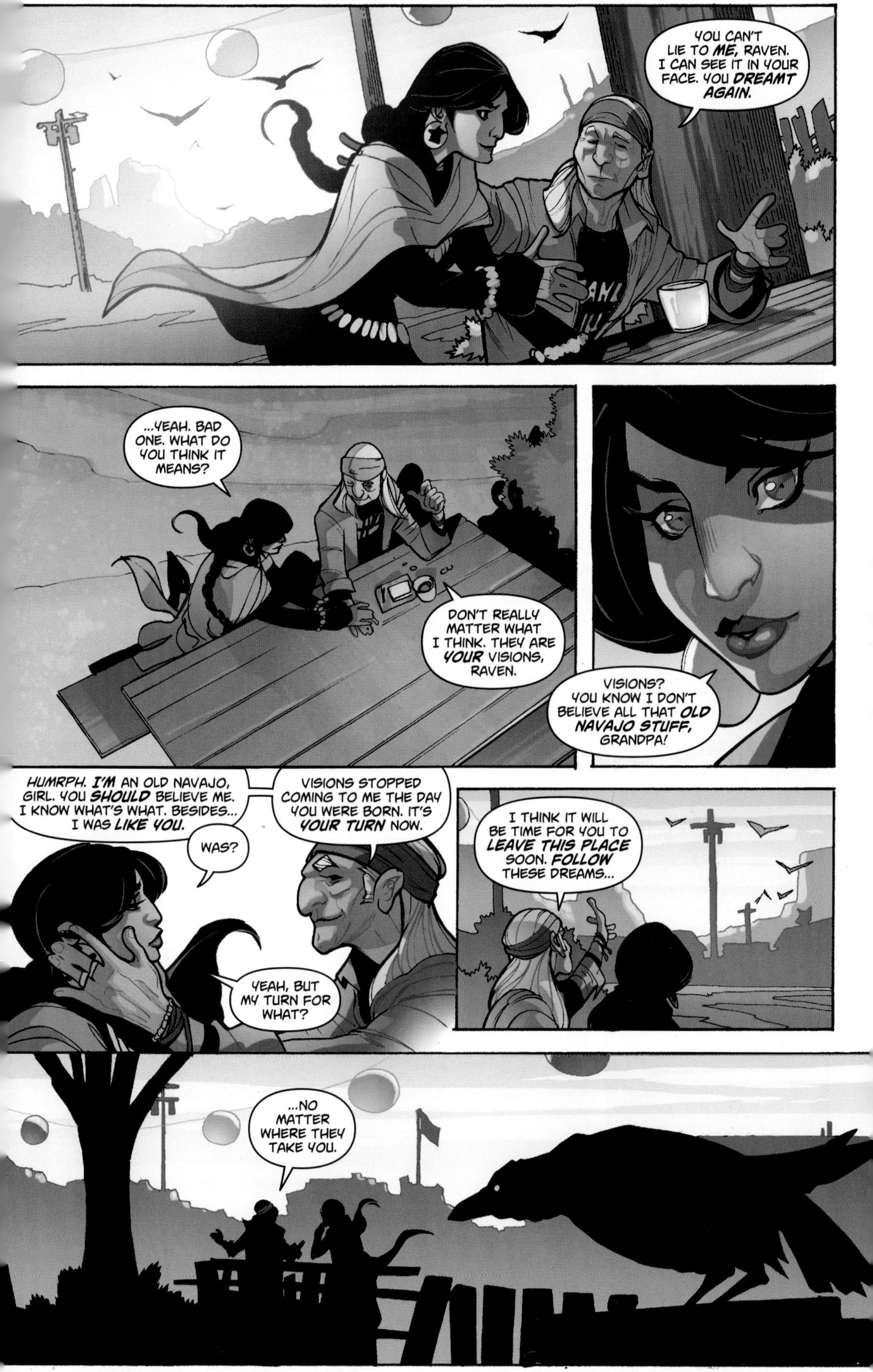
YOU CAN'T LIE TO ME, RAVEN. I CAN SEE IT IN YOUR FACE. YOU DREAMT AGAIN.
...YEAH. BAD ONE. WHAT DO YOU THINK IT MEANS?
DON'T REALLY MATTER WHAT I THINK. THEY ARE YOUR VISIONS, RAVEN.
VISIONS? YOU KNOW I DON'T BELIEVE ALL THAT OLD NAVAJO STUFF, GRANDPA!
HUMRPH. I'M AN OLD NAVAJO, GIRL. YOU SHOULD BELIEVE ME. I KNOW WHAT'S WHAT. BESIDES... I WAS LIKE YOU.
WAS?
VISIONS STOPPED COMING TO ME THE DAY YOU WERE BORN. IT'S YOUR TURN NOW.
YEAH, BUT MY TURN FOR WHAT?
I THINK IT WILL BE TIME FOR YOU TO LEAVE THIS PLACE SOON. FOLLOW THESE DREAMS...
...NO MATTER WHERE THEY TAKE YOU.

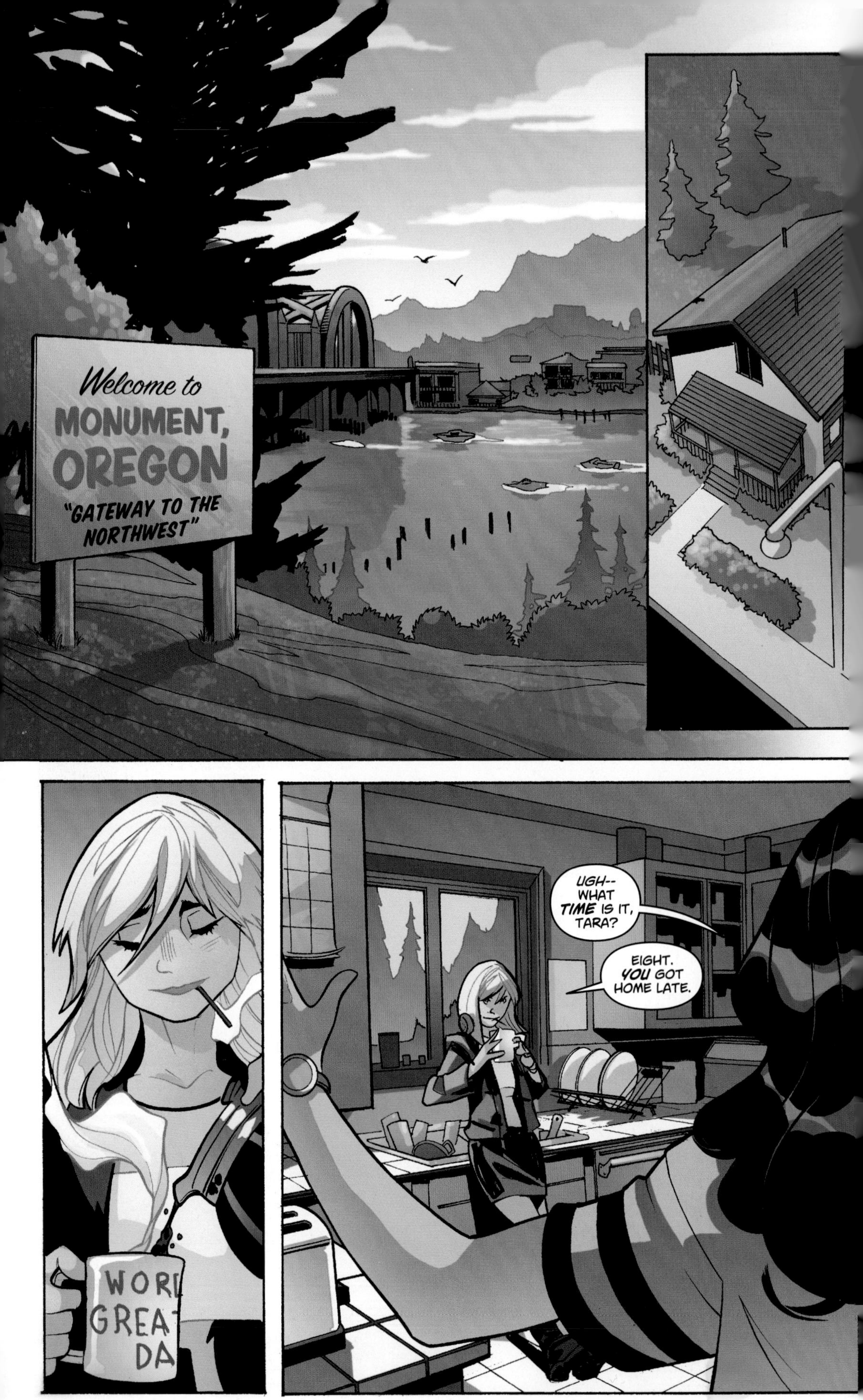
Welcome to
MONUMENT, OREGON
"GATEWAY TO THE NORTHWEST"
UGH-- WHAT TIME IS IT, TARA?
EIGHT. YOU GOT HOME LATE.
WORL
GREA
DA

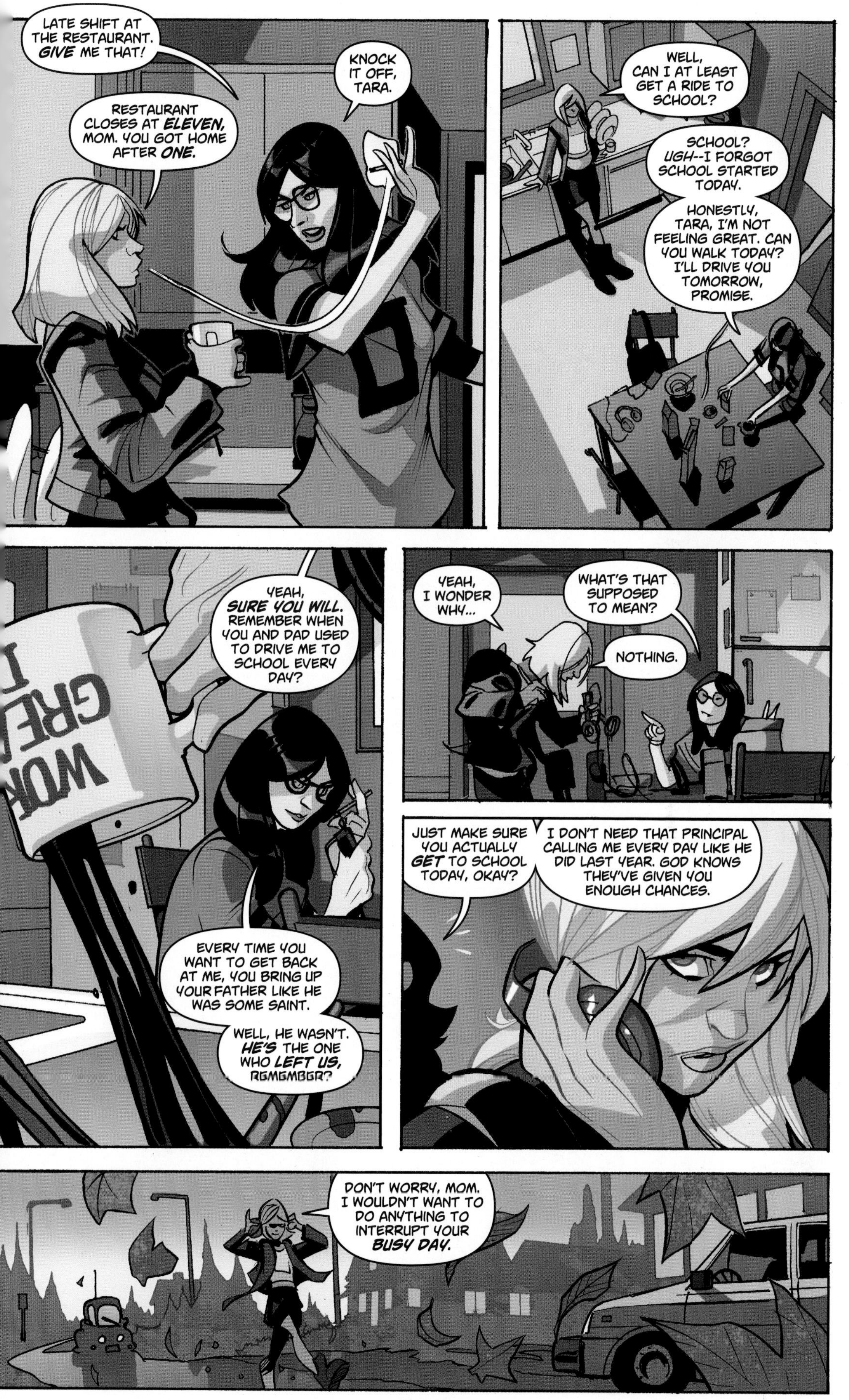
LATE SHIFT AT THE RESTAURANT. *GIVE* ME THAT!
RESTAURANT CLOSES AT *ELEVEN*, MOM. YOU GOT HOME AFTER *ONE*.
KNOCK IT OFF, TARA.
WELL, CAN I AT LEAST GET A RIDE TO SCHOOL?
SCHOOL? *UGH*--I FORGOT SCHOOL STARTED TODAY.
HONESTLY, TARA, I'M NOT FEELING GREAT. CAN YOU WALK TODAY? I'LL DRIVE YOU TOMORROW, PROMISE.
YEAH, *SURE YOU WILL.* REMEMBER WHEN YOU AND DAD USED TO DRIVE ME TO SCHOOL EVERY DAY?
EVERY TIME YOU WANT TO GET BACK AT ME, YOU BRING UP YOUR FATHER LIKE HE WAS SOME SAINT.
WELL, HE WASN'T. *HE'S* THE ONE WHO *LEFT US,* REMEMBER?
YEAH, I WONDER WHY...
WHAT'S THAT SUPPOSED TO MEAN?
NOTHING.
JUST MAKE SURE YOU ACTUALLY *GET* TO SCHOOL TODAY, OKAY?
I DON'T NEED THAT PRINCIPAL CALLING ME EVERY DAY LIKE HE DID LAST YEAR. GOD KNOWS THEY'VE GIVEN YOU ENOUGH CHANCES.
DON'T WORRY, MOM. I WOULDN'T WANT TO DO ANYTHING TO INTERRUPT YOUR *BUSY DAY*.

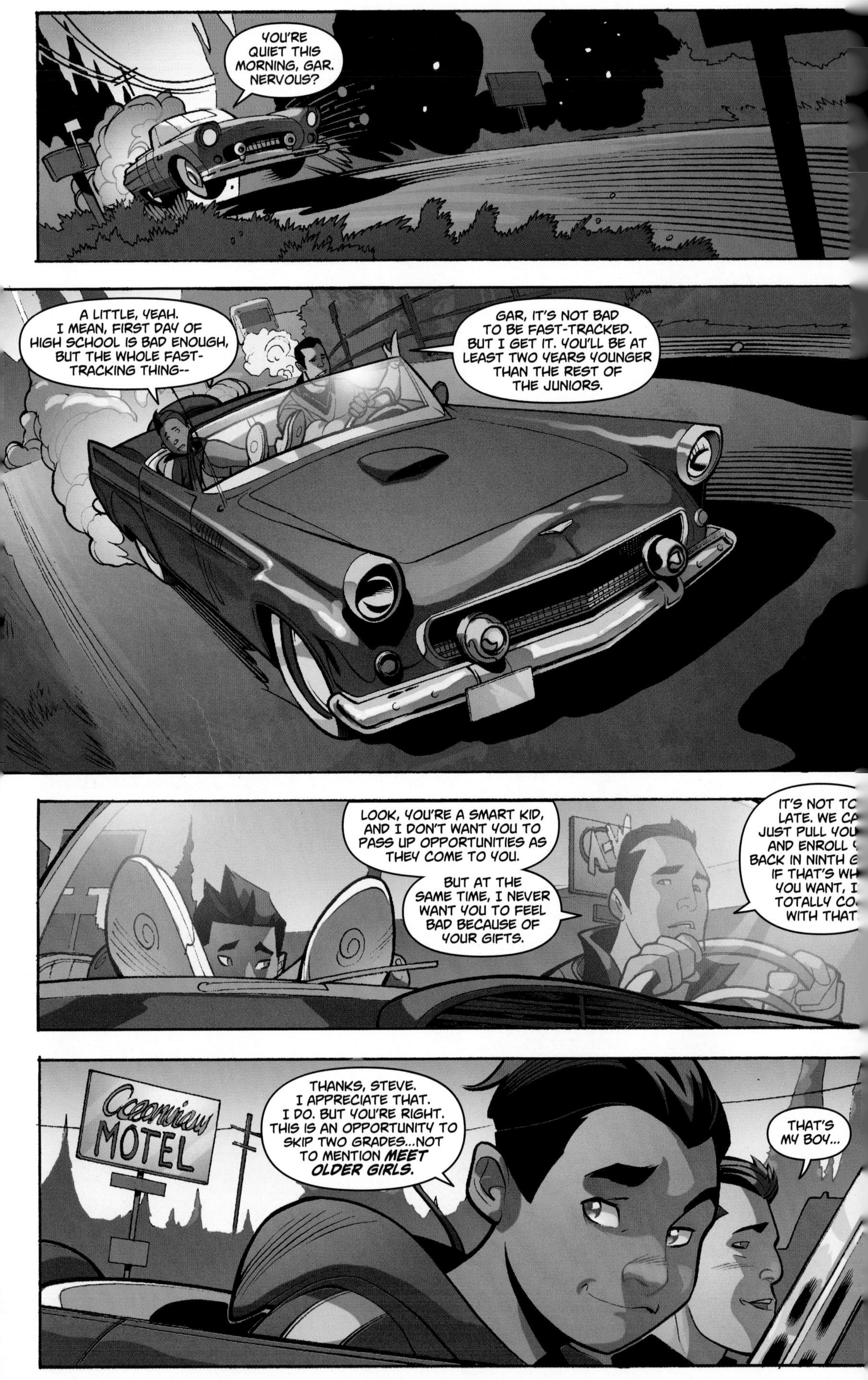
YOU'RE QUIET THIS MORNING, GAR. NERVOUS?
A LITTLE, YEAH. I MEAN, FIRST DAY OF HIGH SCHOOL IS BAD ENOUGH, BUT THE WHOLE FAST-TRACKING THING--
GAR, IT'S NOT BAD TO BE FAST-TRACKED. BUT I GET IT. YOU'LL BE AT LEAST TWO YEARS YOUNGER THAN THE REST OF THE JUNIORS.
LOOK, YOU'RE A SMART KID, AND I DON'T WANT YOU TO PASS UP OPPORTUNITIES AS THEY COME TO YOU.
BUT AT THE SAME TIME, I NEVER WANT YOU TO FEEL BAD BECAUSE OF YOUR GIFTS.
IT'S NOT TO LATE. WE CA JUST PULL YOU AND ENROLL BACK IN NINTH G IF THAT'S WH YOU WANT, I TOTALLY CO WITH THAT.
Oceanview MOTEL
THANKS, STEVE. I APPRECIATE THAT. I DO. BUT YOU'RE RIGHT. THIS IS AN OPPORTUNITY TO SKIP TWO GRADES...NOT TO MENTION MEET OLDER GIRLS.
THAT'S MY BOY...

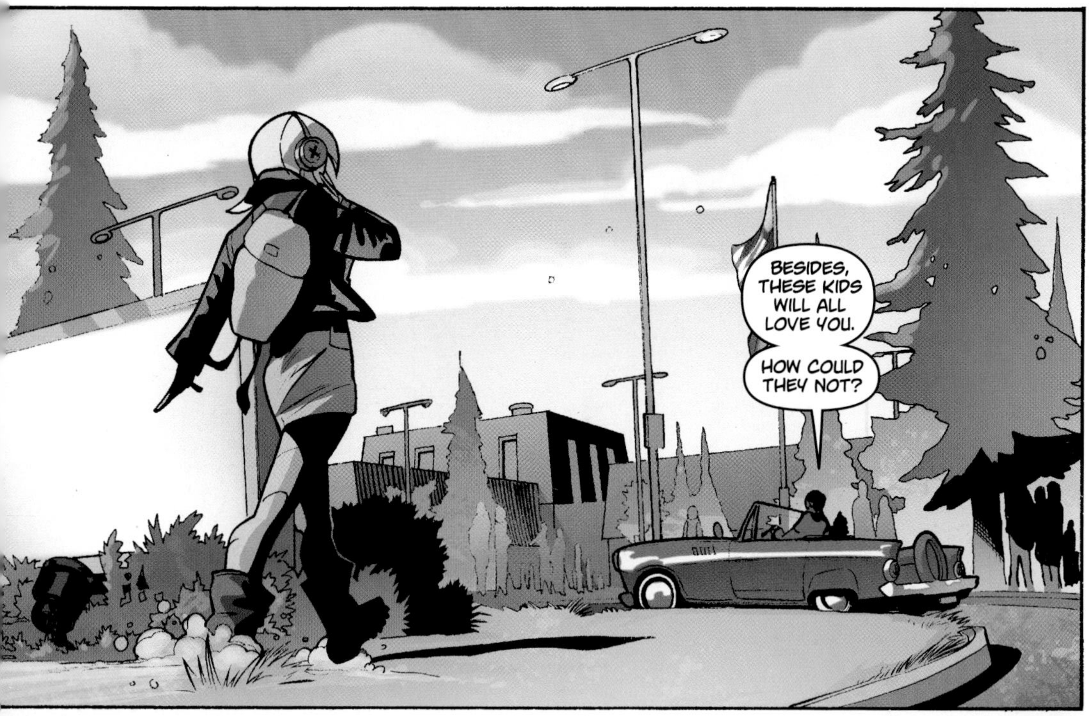
BESIDES, THESE KIDS WILL ALL LOVE YOU.
HOW COULD THEY NOT?

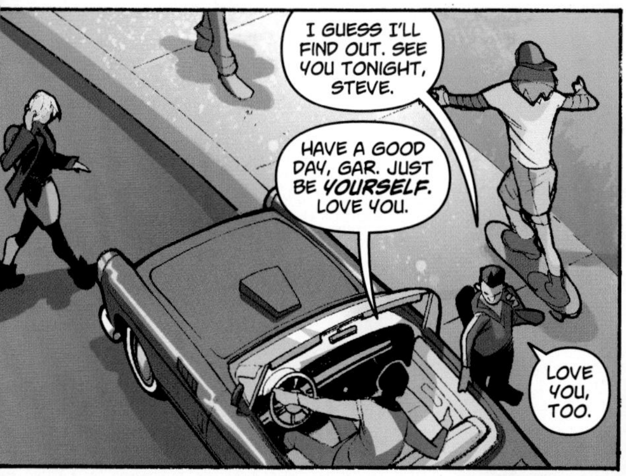
I GUESS I'LL FIND OUT. SEE YOU TONIGHT, STEVE.
HAVE A GOOD DAY, GAR. JUST BE *YOURSELF.* LOVE YOU.
LOVE YOU, TOO.

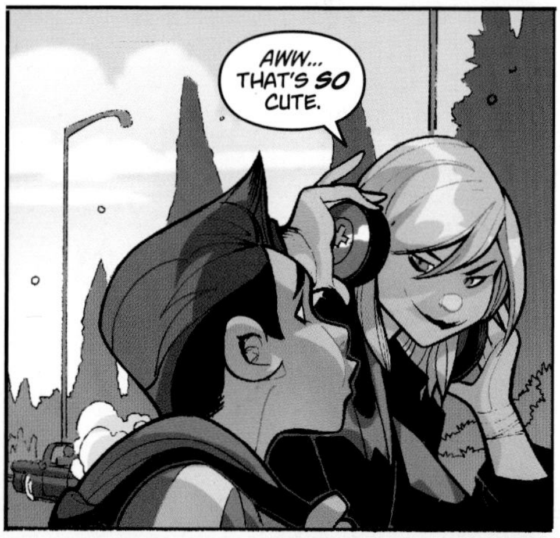
AWW... THAT'S ***SO*** CUTE.

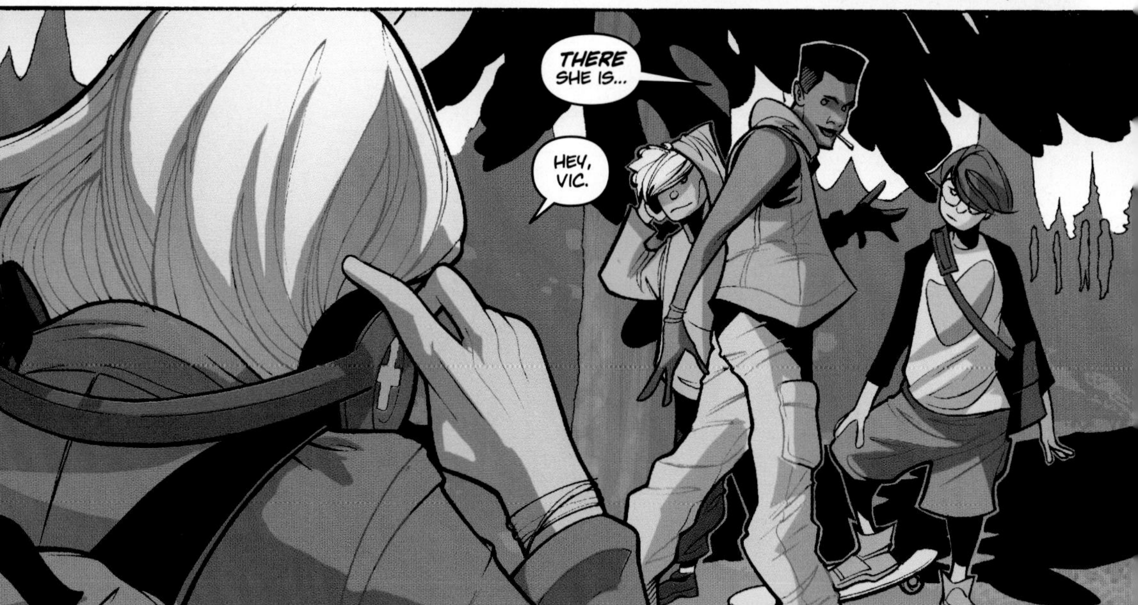
THERE SHE IS...
HEY, VIC.

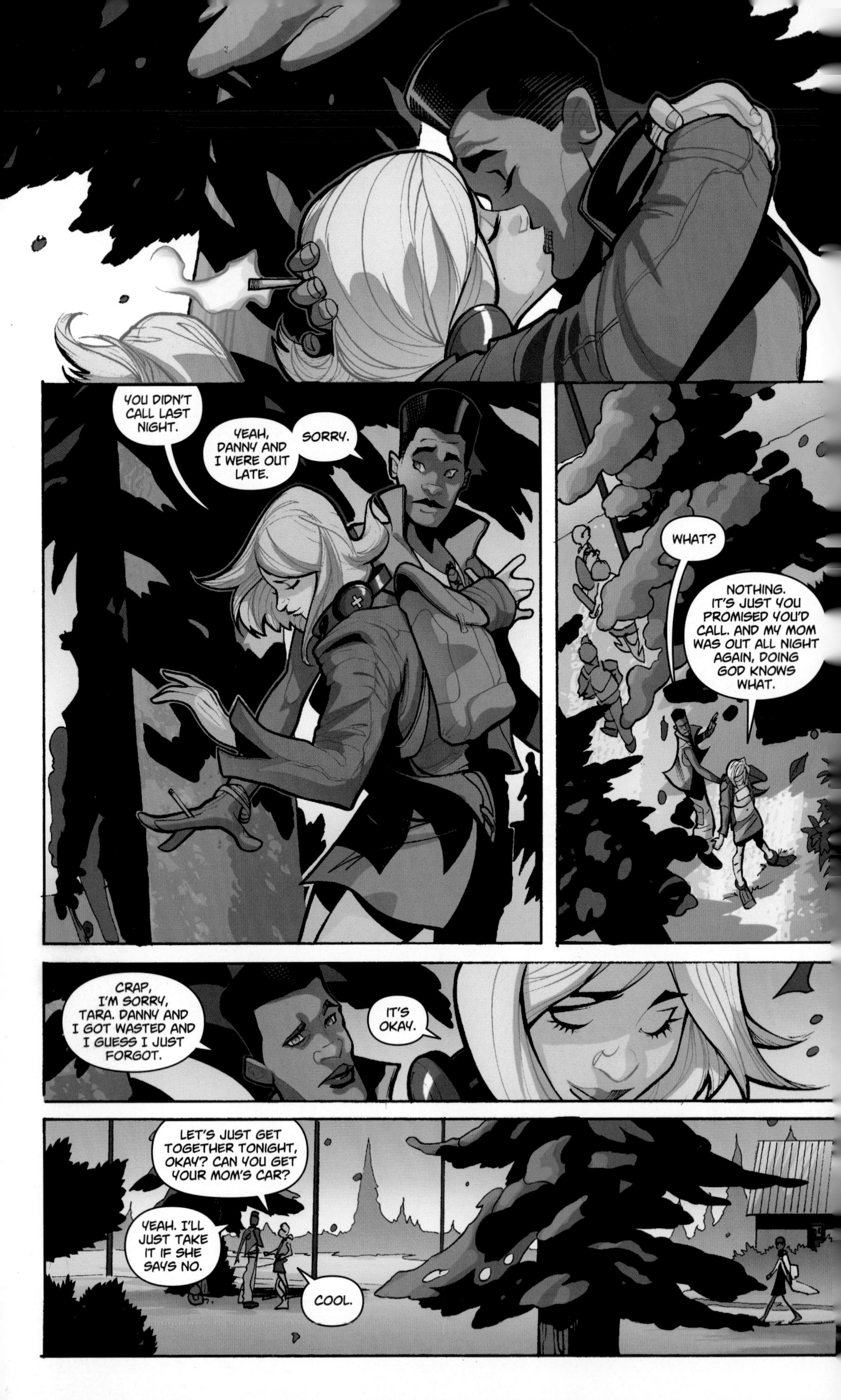
YOU DIDN'T CALL LAST NIGHT.
YEAH, DANNY AND I WERE OUT LATE.
SORRY.
WHAT?
NOTHING. IT'S JUST YOU PROMISED YOU'D CALL. AND MY MOM WAS OUT ALL NIGHT AGAIN, DOING GOD KNOWS WHAT.
CRAP, I'M SORRY, TARA. DANNY AND I GOT WASTED AND I GUESS I JUST FORGOT.
IT'S OKAY.
LET'S JUST GET TOGETHER TONIGHT, OKAY? CAN YOU GET YOUR MOM'S CAR?
YEAH. I'LL JUST TAKE IT IF SHE SAYS NO.
COOL.

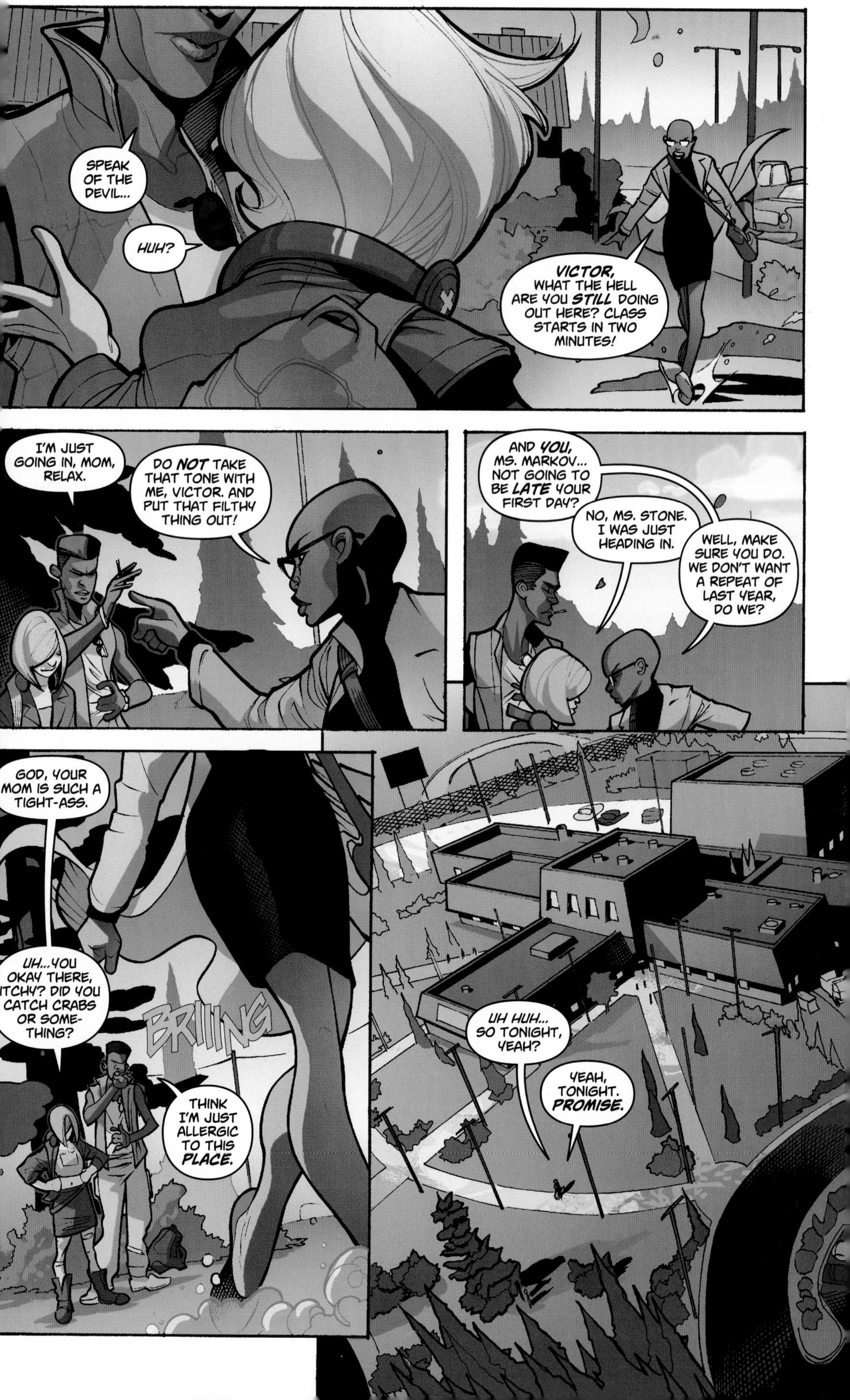
SPEAK OF THE DEVIL...
HUH?
VICTOR, WHAT THE HELL ARE YOU STILL DOING OUT HERE? CLASS STARTS IN TWO MINUTES!
I'M JUST GOING IN, MOM, RELAX.
DO NOT TAKE THAT TONE WITH ME, VICTOR. AND PUT THAT FILTHY THING OUT!
AND YOU, MS. MARKOV... NOT GOING TO BE LATE YOUR FIRST DAY?
NO, MS. STONE. I WAS JUST HEADING IN.
WELL, MAKE SURE YOU DO. WE DON'T WANT A REPEAT OF LAST YEAR, DO WE?
GOD, YOUR MOM IS SUCH A TIGHT-ASS.
UH...YOU OKAY THERE, ITCHY? DID YOU CATCH CRABS OR SOME-THING?
BRIIING
THINK I'M JUST ALLERGIC TO THIS PLACE.
UH HUH... SO TONIGHT, YEAH?
YEAH, TONIGHT. PROMISE.

TARA MARKOV?
MS. MARKOV?
HUH? OH, SORRY. I'M HERE.
≷SIGH≶
AND NOW OUR NEW ARRIVALS...
GARFIELD LOGAN?

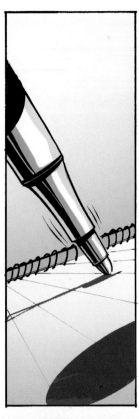

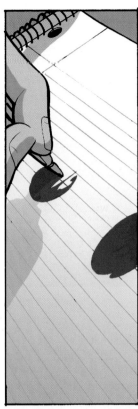

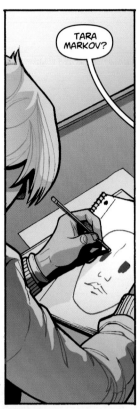

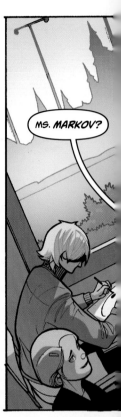

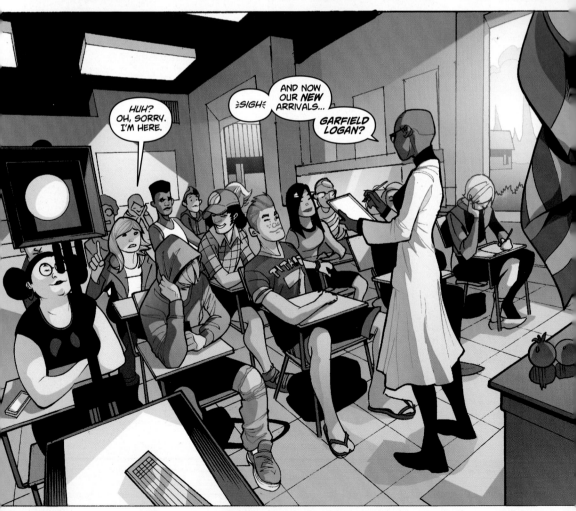

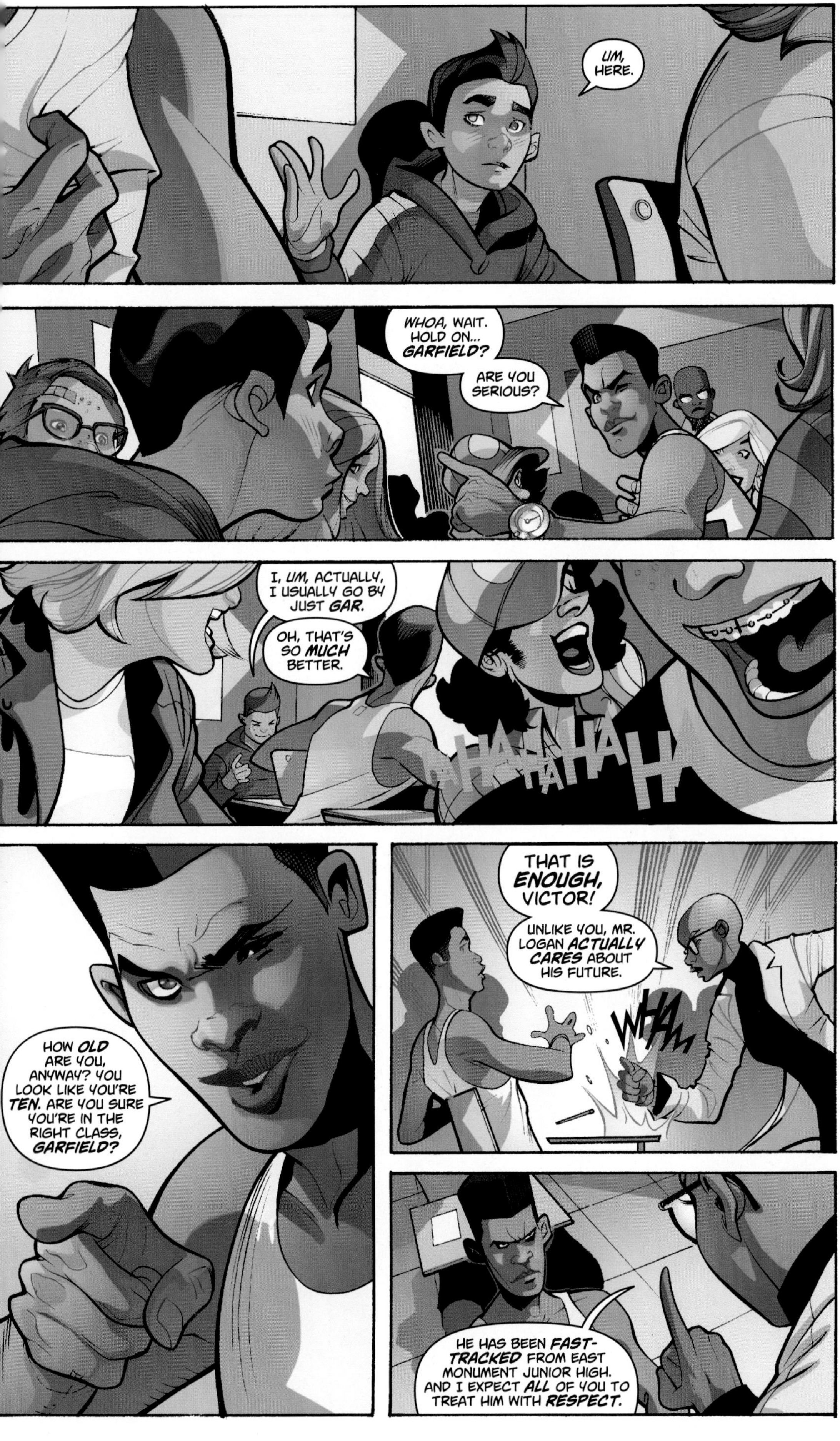
UM, HERE.
WHOA, WAIT. HOLD ON... GARFIELD?
ARE YOU SERIOUS?
I, UM, ACTUALLY, I USUALLY GO BY JUST GAR.
OH, THAT'S SO MUCH BETTER.
HAHAHAHAHAHA
HOW OLD ARE YOU, ANYWAY? YOU LOOK LIKE YOU'RE TEN. ARE YOU SURE YOU'RE IN THE RIGHT CLASS, GARFIELD?
THAT IS ENOUGH, VICTOR!
UNLIKE YOU, MR. LOGAN ACTUALLY CARES ABOUT HIS FUTURE.
WHAM
HE HAS BEEN FAST-TRACKED FROM EAST MONUMENT JUNIOR HIGH. AND I EXPECT ALL OF YOU TO TREAT HIM WITH RESPECT.

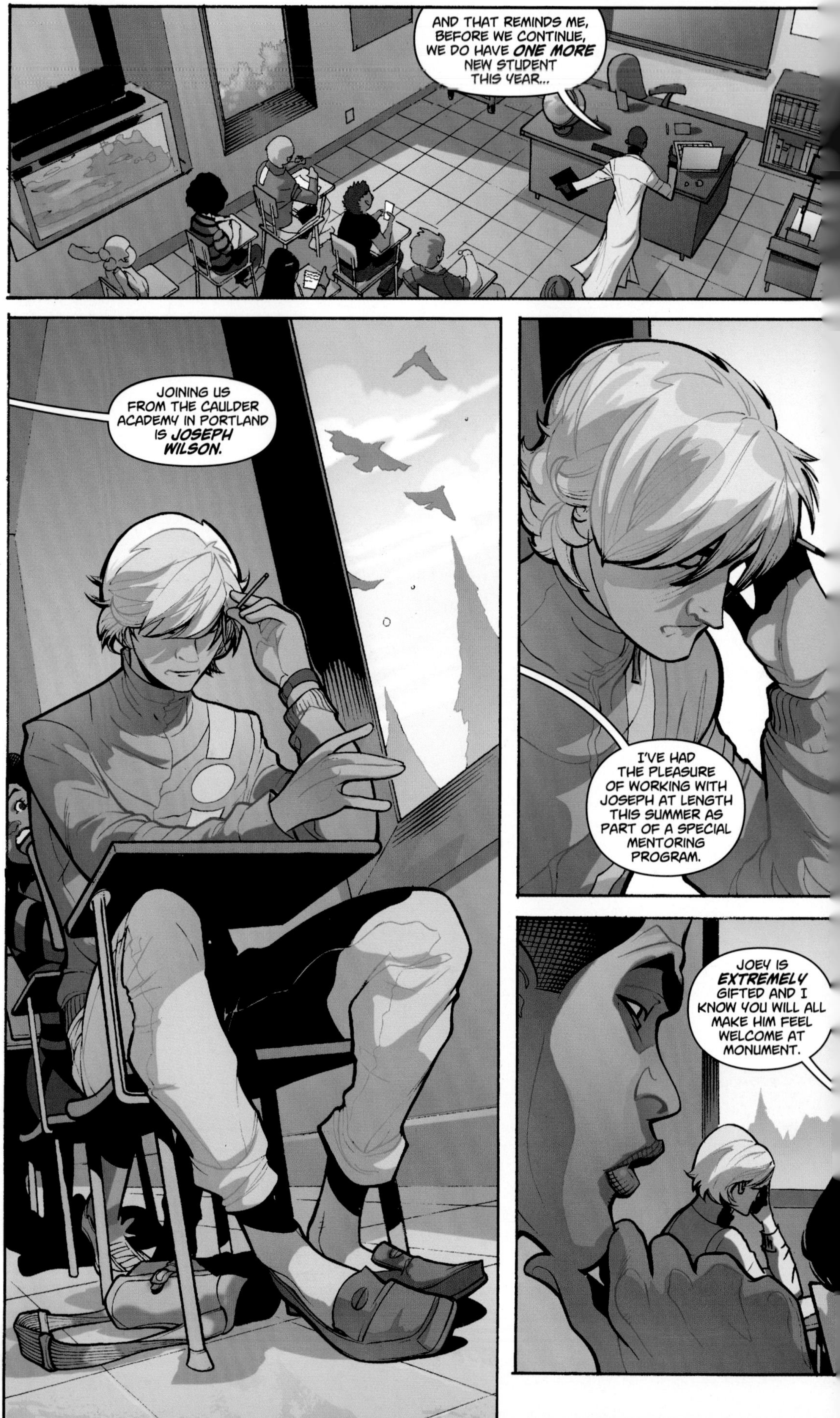
AND THAT REMINDS ME, BEFORE WE CONTINUE, WE DO HAVE ONE MORE NEW STUDENT THIS YEAR...
JOINING US FROM THE CAULDER ACADEMY IN PORTLAND IS JOSEPH WILSON.
I'VE HAD THE PLEASURE OF WORKING WITH JOSEPH AT LENGTH THIS SUMMER AS PART OF A SPECIAL MENTORING PROGRAM.
JOEY IS EXTREMELY GIFTED AND I KNOW YOU WILL ALL MAKE HIM FEEL WELCOME AT MONUMENT.

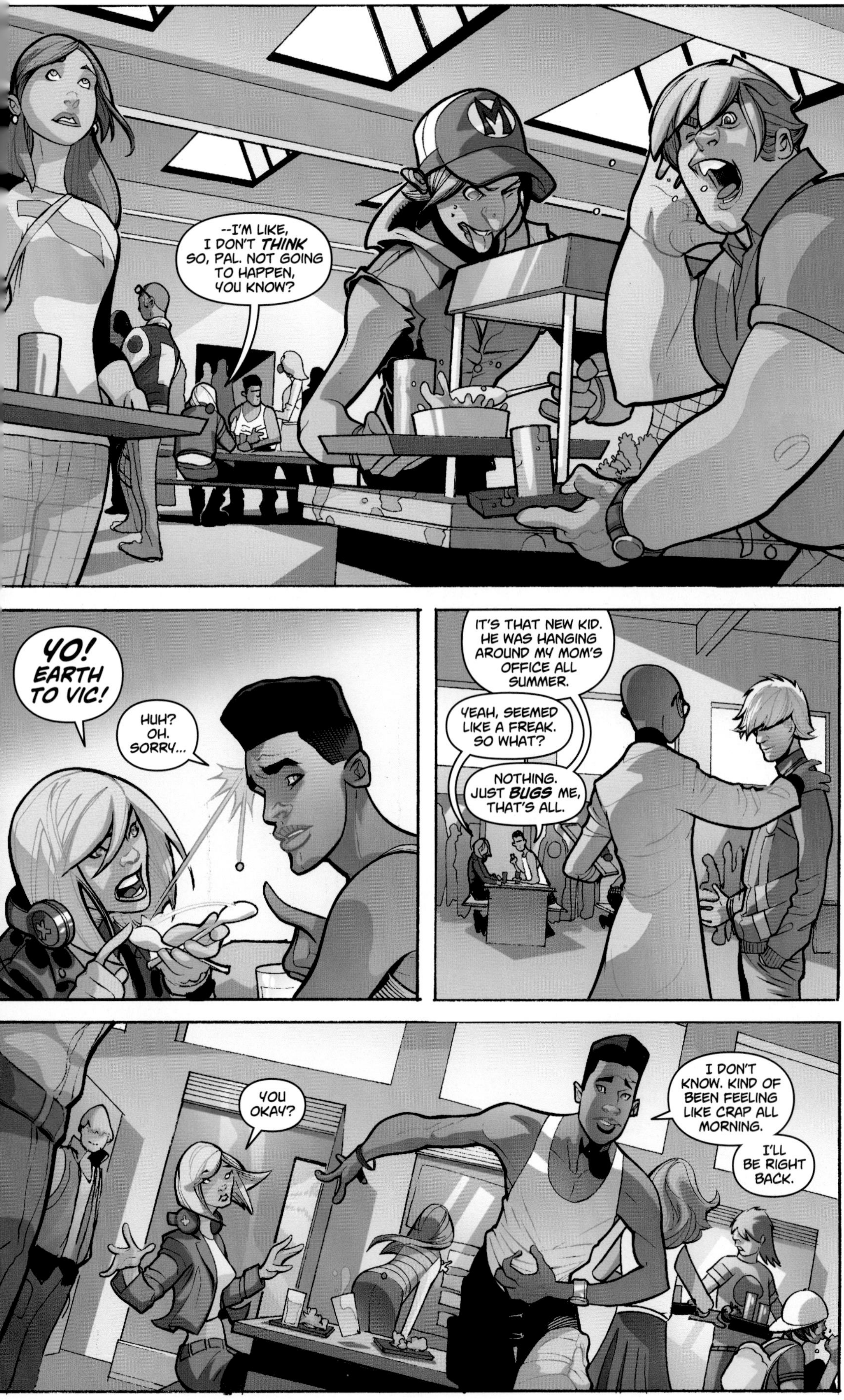
--I'M LIKE, I DON'T THINK SO, PAL. NOT GOING TO HAPPEN, YOU KNOW?
YO! EARTH TO VIC!
HUH? OH. SORRY...
IT'S THAT NEW KID. HE WAS HANGING AROUND MY MOM'S OFFICE ALL SUMMER.
YEAH, SEEMED LIKE A FREAK. SO WHAT?
NOTHING. JUST BUGS ME, THAT'S ALL.
YOU OKAY?
I DON'T KNOW. KIND OF BEEN FEELING LIKE CRAP ALL MORNING.
I'LL BE RIGHT BACK.

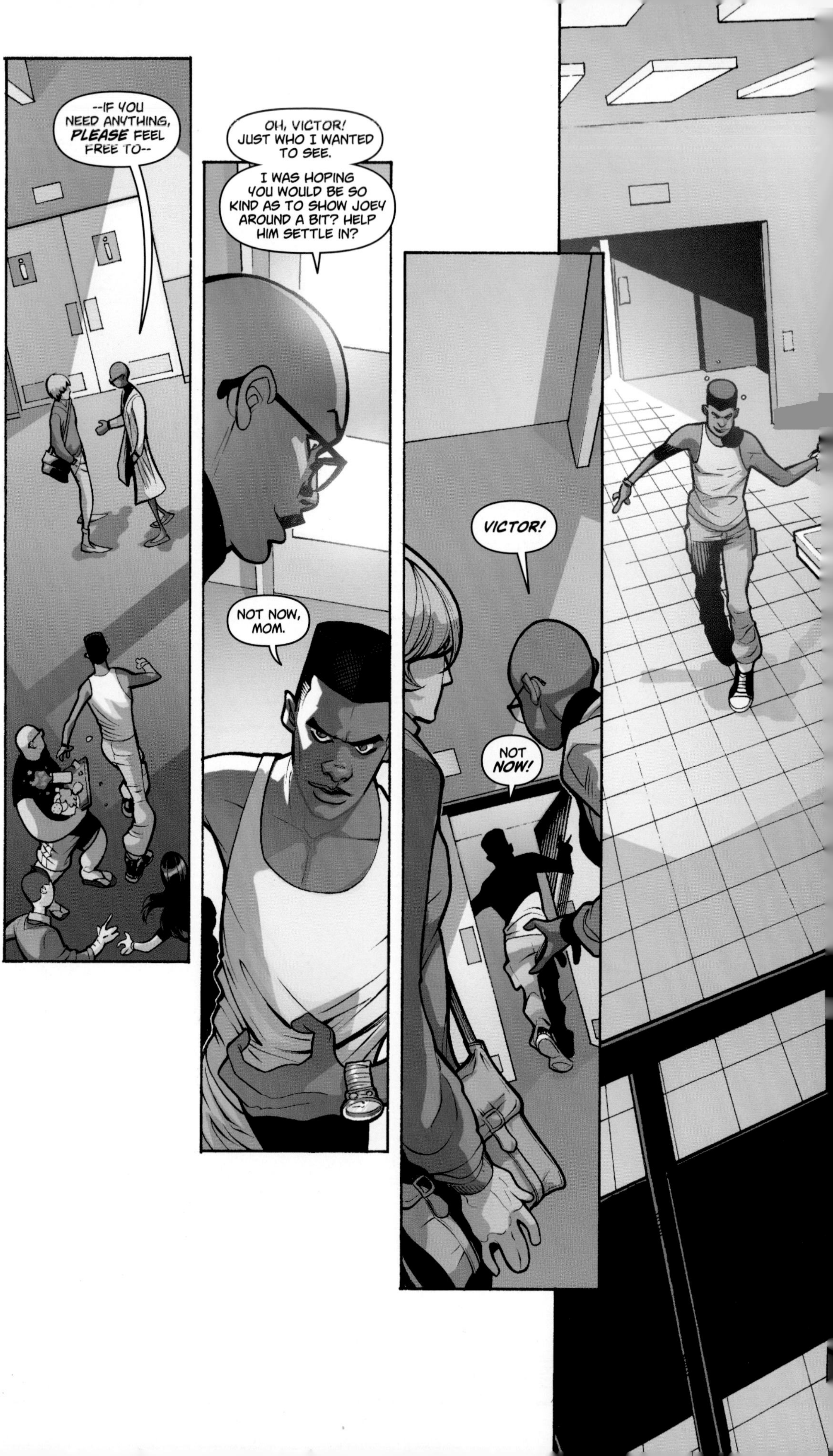
--IF YOU NEED ANYTHING, **PLEASE** FEEL FREE TO--
OH, VICTOR! JUST WHO I WANTED TO SEE.
I WAS HOPING YOU WOULD BE SO KIND AS TO SHOW JOEY AROUND A BIT? HELP HIM SETTLE IN?
NOT NOW, MOM.
VICTOR!
NOT *NOW!*

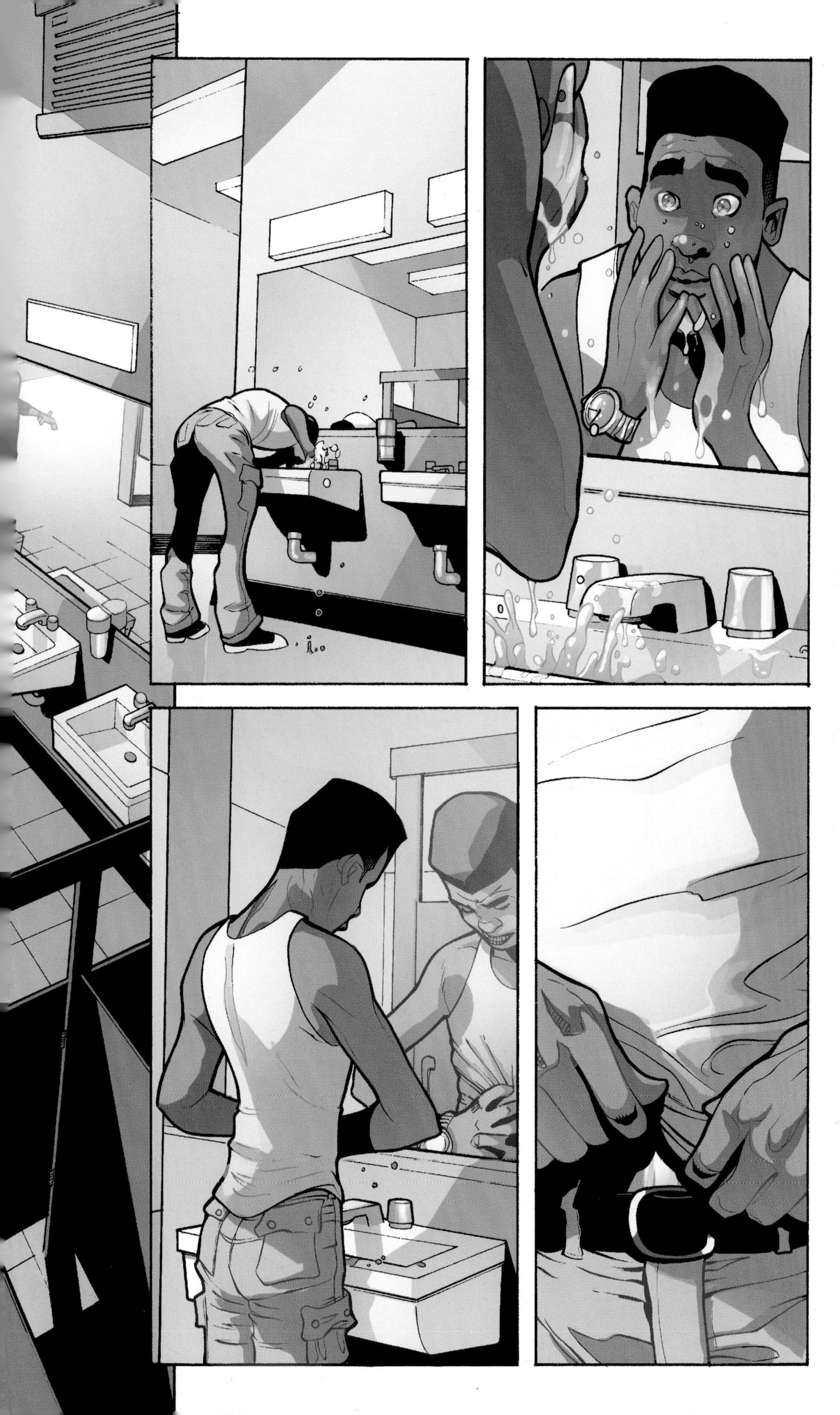

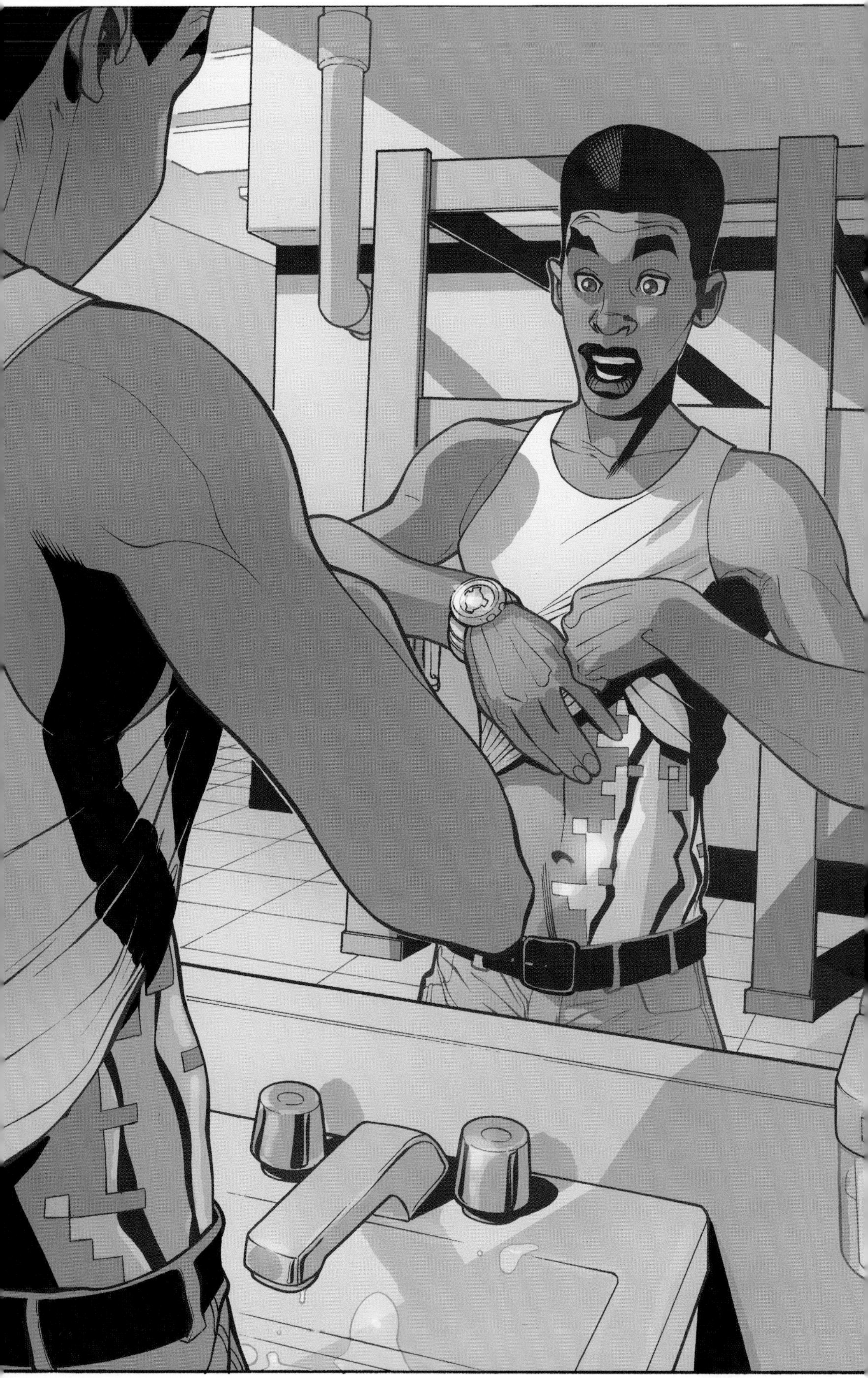

≷GASP≷

YIU UH SW RTTC RY HELP.

GAAAAH!

SQUIT

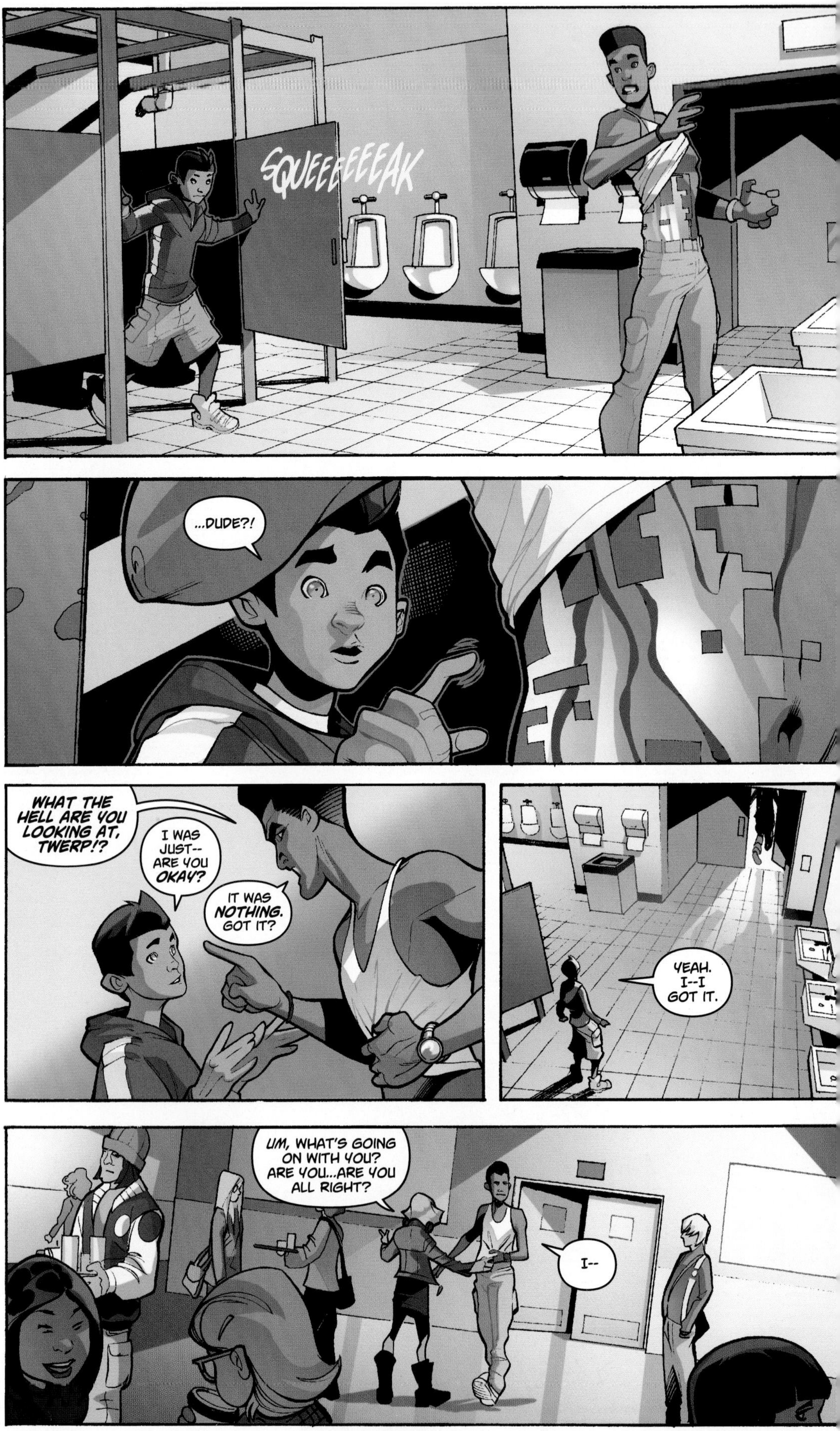
SQUEEEEEEAK
...DUDE?!
WHAT THE HELL ARE YOU LOOKING AT, TWERP!?
I WAS JUST-- ARE YOU OKAY?
IT WAS NOTHING. GOT IT?
YEAH. I--I GOT IT.
UM, WHAT'S GOING ON WITH YOU? ARE YOU...ARE YOU ALL RIGHT?
I--

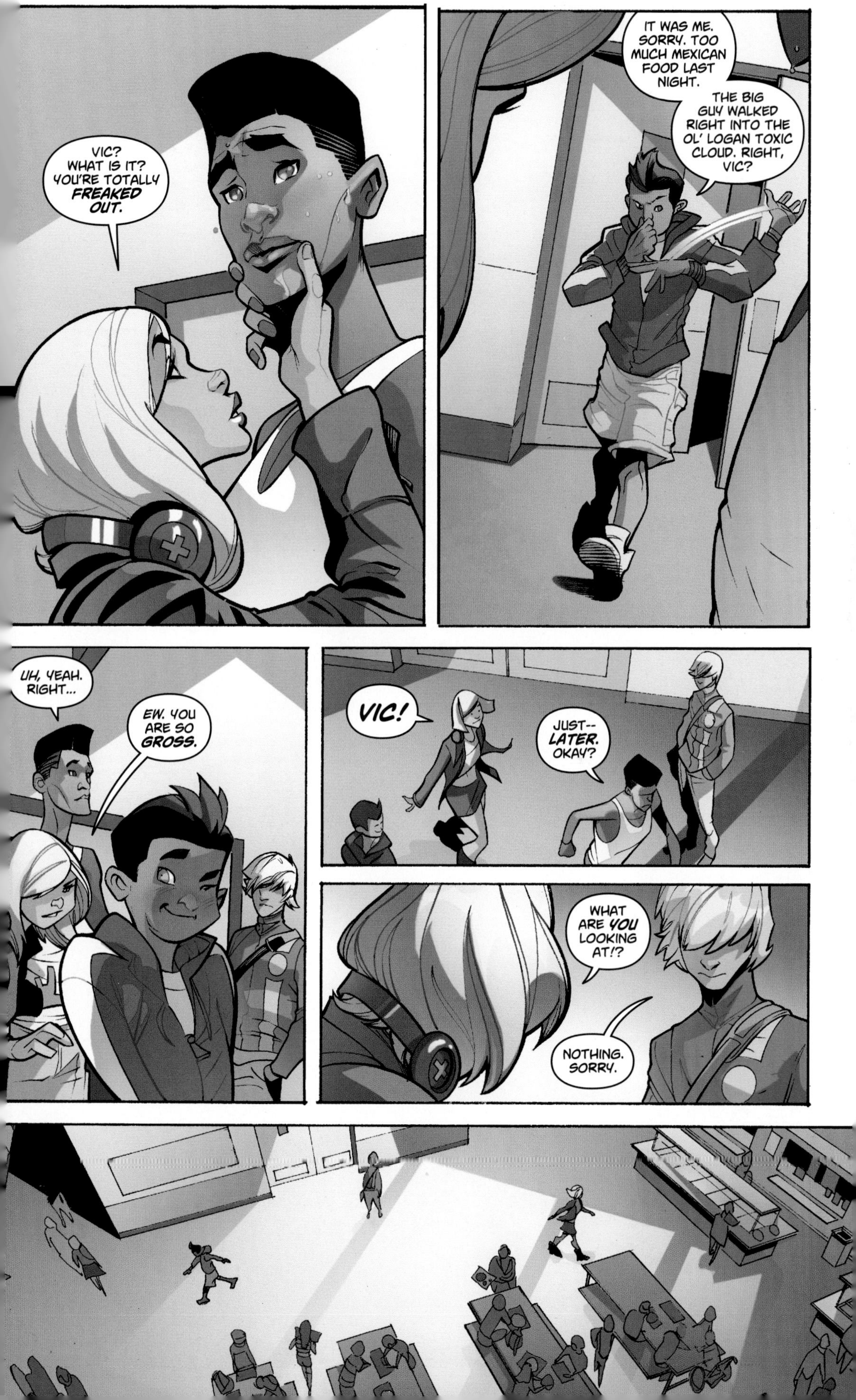
VIC? WHAT IS IT? YOU'RE TOTALLY FREAKED OUT.
IT WAS ME. SORRY. TOO MUCH MEXICAN FOOD LAST NIGHT.
THE BIG GUY WALKED RIGHT INTO THE OL' LOGAN TOXIC CLOUD. RIGHT, VIC?
UH, YEAH. RIGHT...
EW. YOU ARE SO GROSS.
VIC!
JUST-- LATER. OKAY?
WHAT ARE YOU LOOKING AT!?
NOTHING. SORRY.

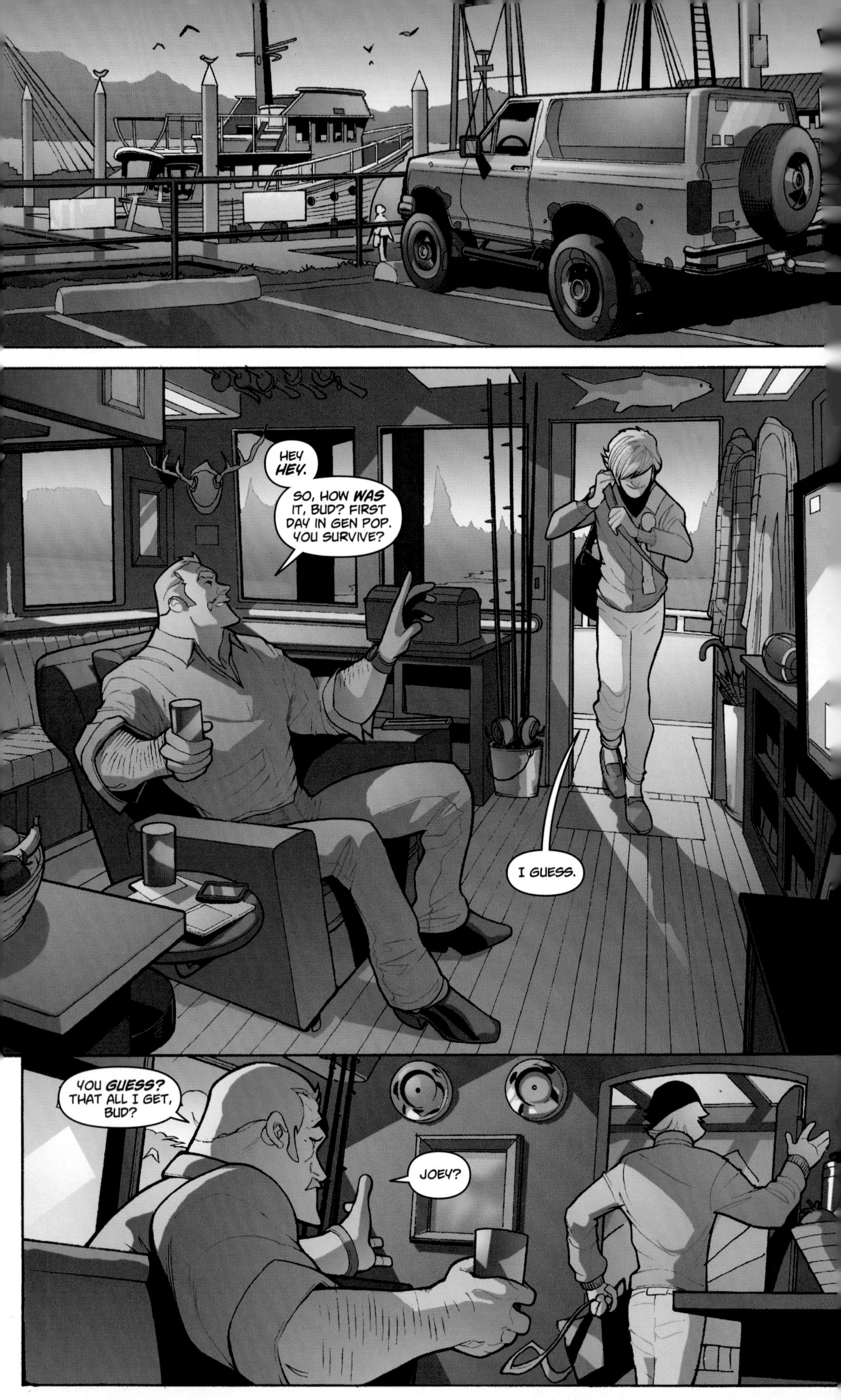
HEY *HEY*.
SO, HOW *WAS* IT, BUD? FIRST DAY IN GEN POP. YOU SURVIVE?
I GUESS.
YOU *GUESS?* THAT ALL I GET, BUD?
JOEY?

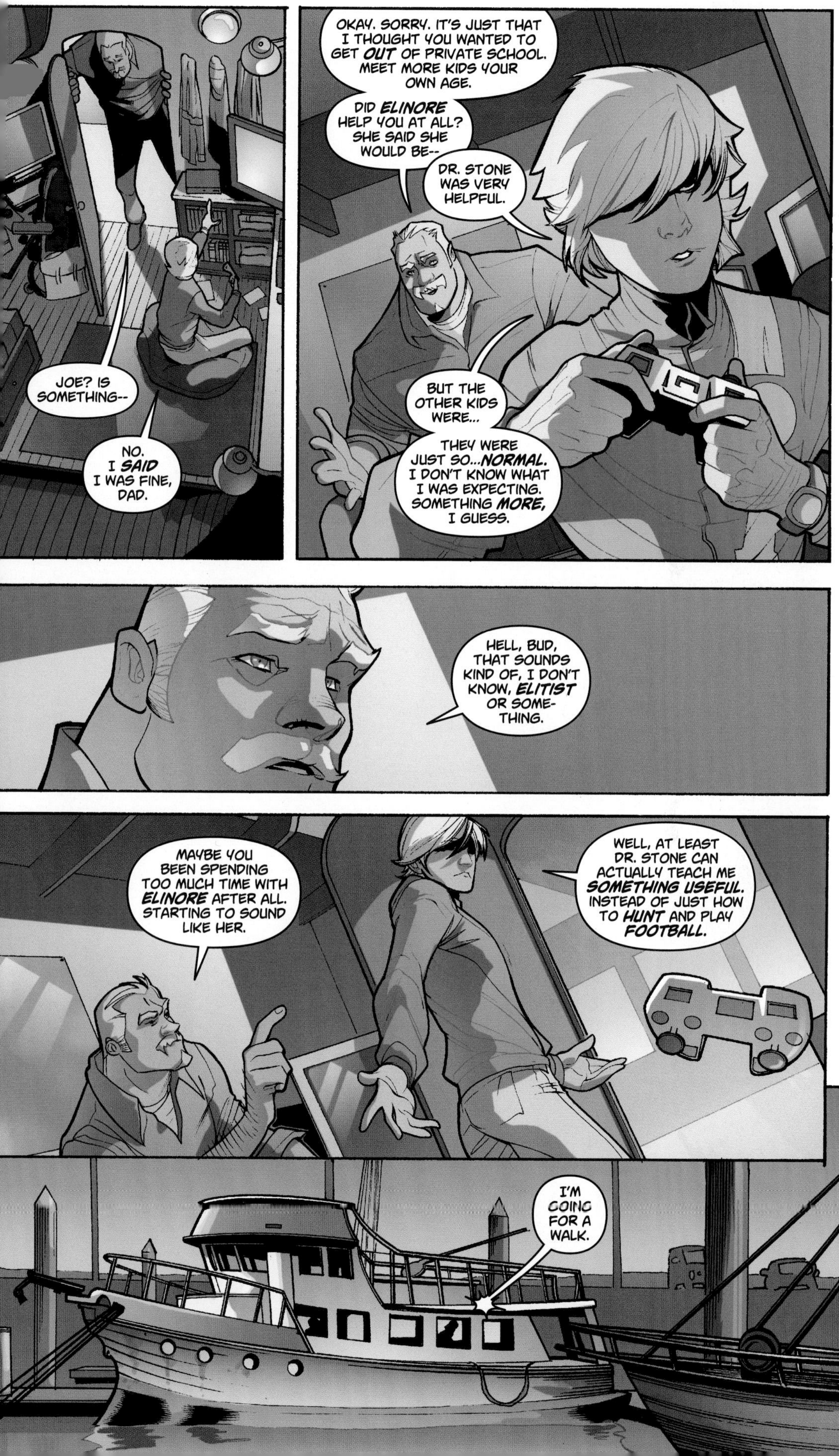
JOE? IS SOMETHING--
NO. I SAID I WAS FINE, DAD.
OKAY. SORRY. IT'S JUST THAT I THOUGHT YOU WANTED TO GET OUT OF PRIVATE SCHOOL. MEET MORE KIDS YOUR OWN AGE.
DID ELINORE HELP YOU AT ALL? SHE SAID SHE WOULD BE--
DR. STONE WAS VERY HELPFUL.
BUT THE OTHER KIDS WERE...
THEY WERE JUST SO...NORMAL. I DON'T KNOW WHAT I WAS EXPECTING. SOMETHING MORE, I GUESS.
HELL, BUD, THAT SOUNDS KIND OF, I DON'T KNOW, ELITIST OR SOME-THING.
MAYBE YOU BEEN SPENDING TOO MUCH TIME WITH ELINORE AFTER ALL. STARTING TO SOUND LIKE HER.
WELL, AT LEAST DR. STONE CAN ACTUALLY TEACH ME SOMETHING USEFUL. INSTEAD OF JUST HOW TO HUNT AND PLAY FOOTBALL.
I'M GOING FOR A WALK.

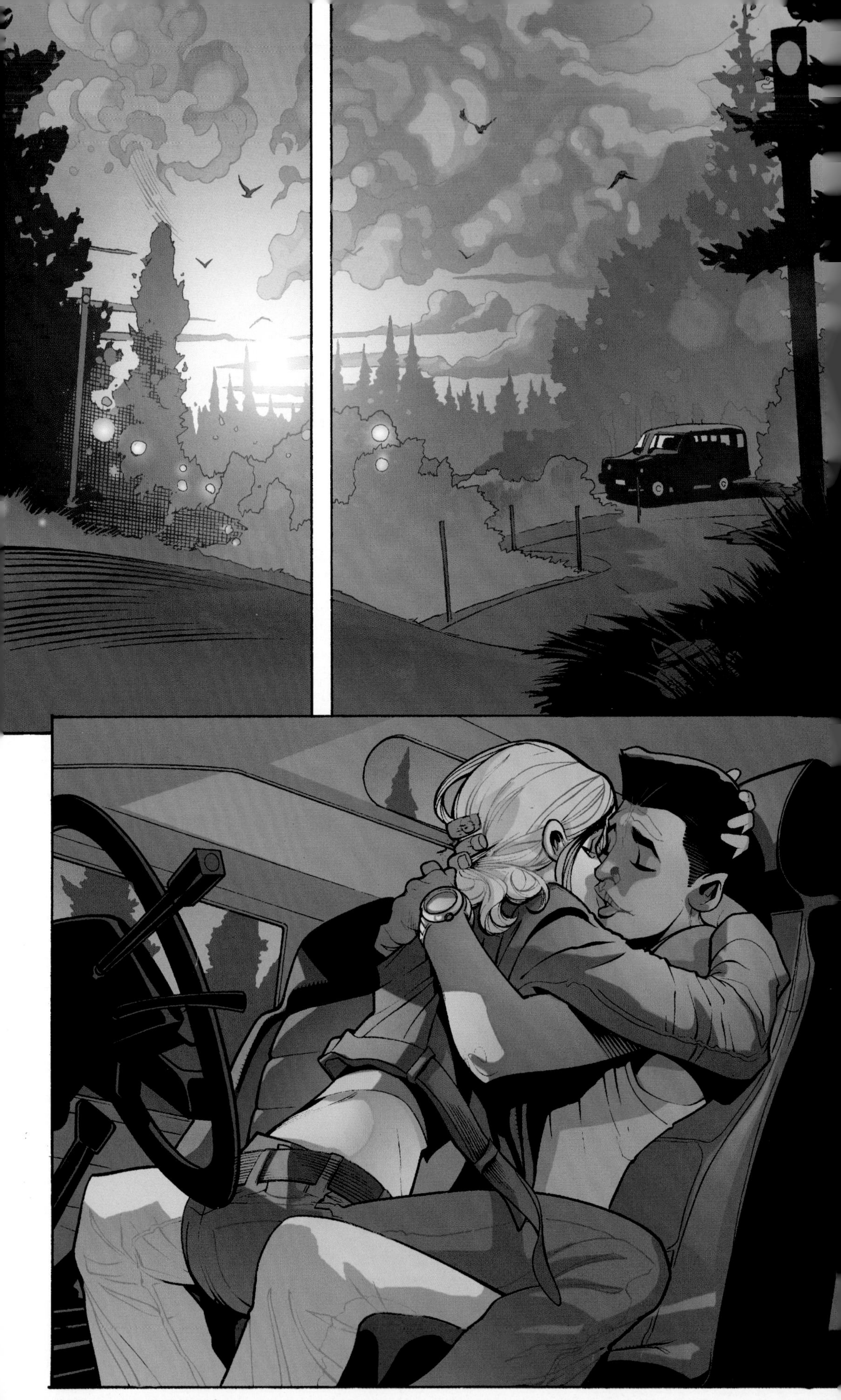

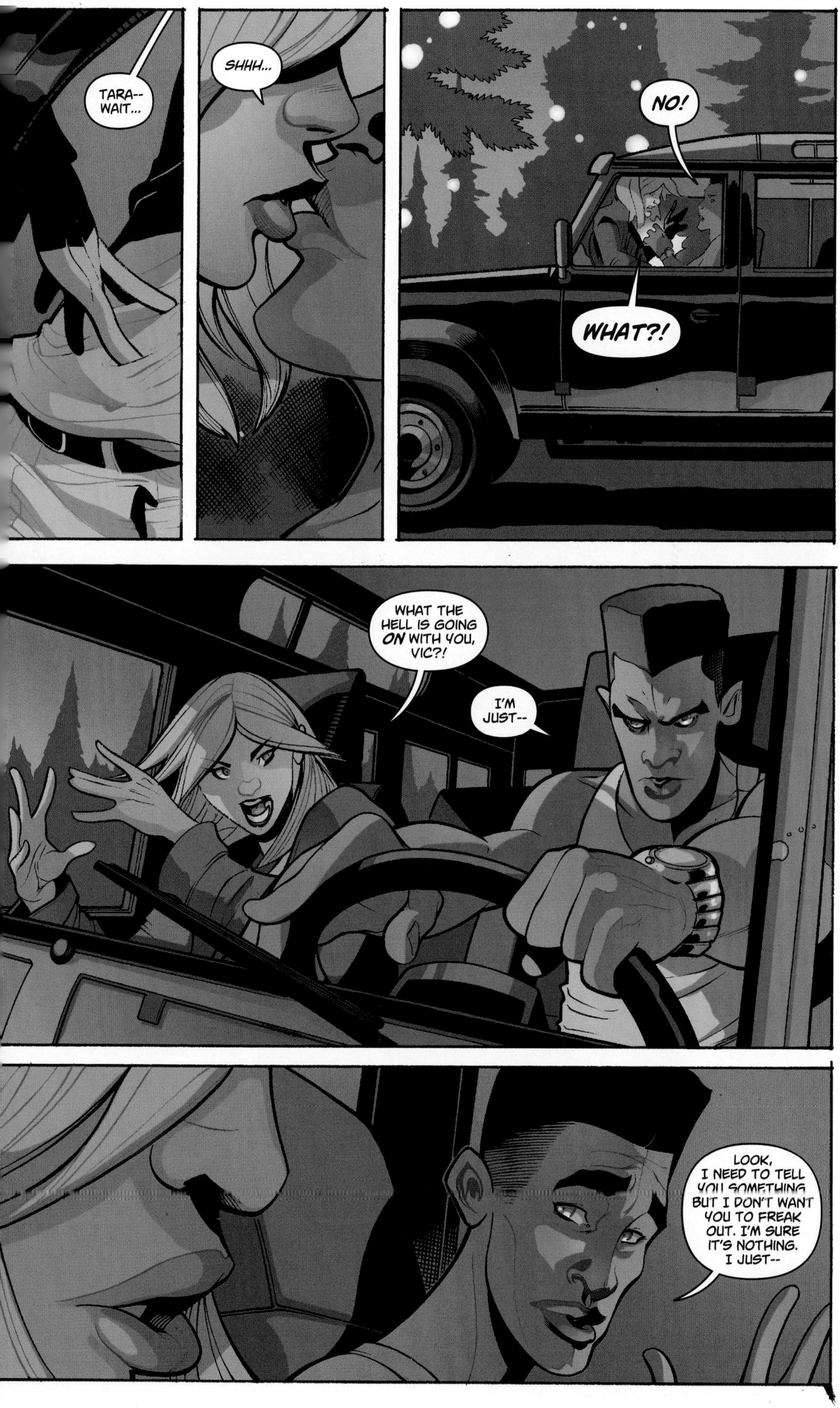
TARA--
WAIT...
SHHH...
NO!
WHAT?!
WHAT THE HELL IS GOING ON WITH YOU, VIC?!
I'M JUST--
LOOK, I NEED TO TELL YOU SOMETHING BUT I DON'T WANT YOU TO FREAK OUT. I'M SURE IT'S NOTHING. I JUST--

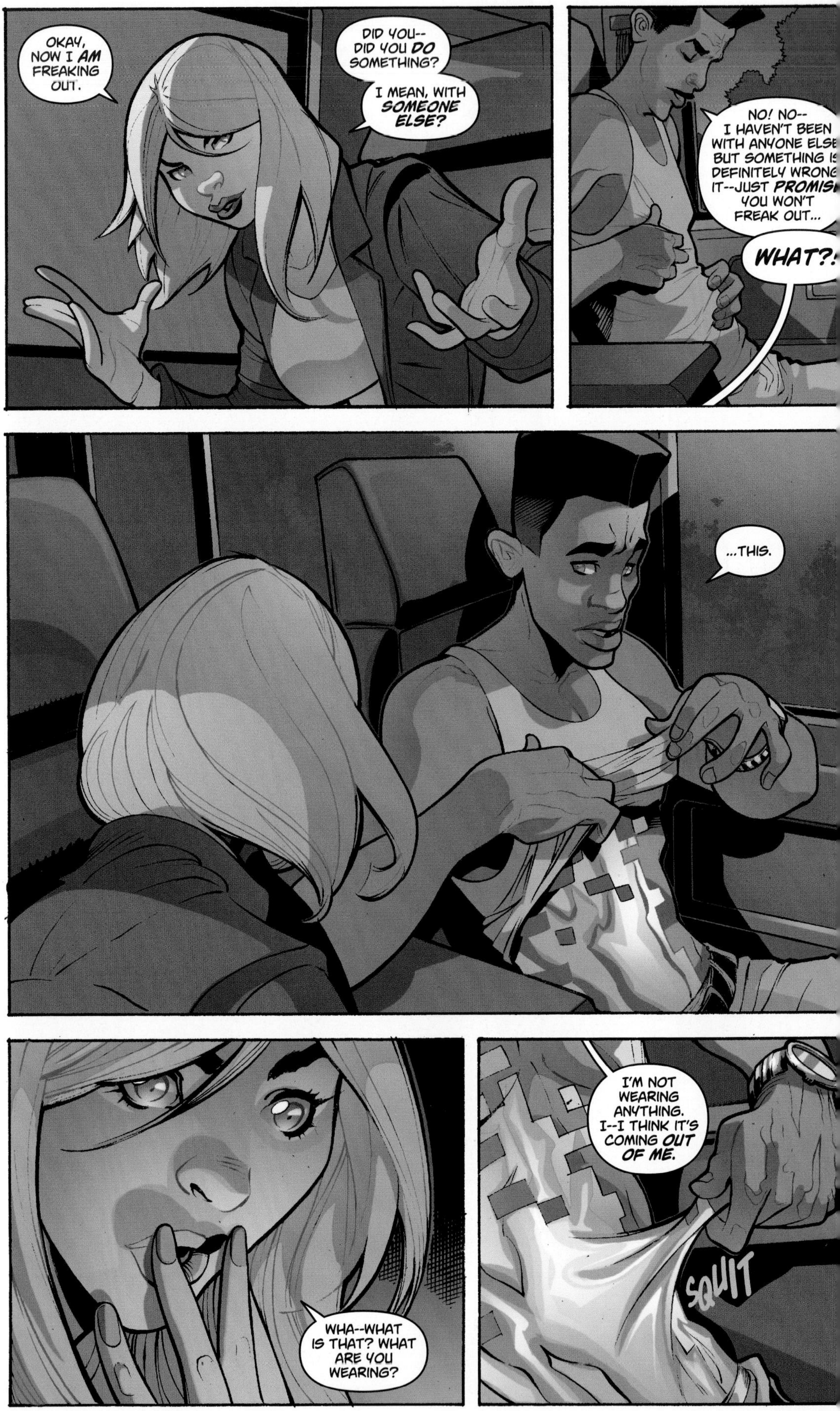
OKAY, NOW I AM FREAKING OUT.
DID YOU-- DID YOU DO SOMETHING?
I MEAN, WITH SOMEONE ELSE?
NO! NO-- I HAVEN'T BEEN WITH ANYONE ELS BUT SOMETHING I DEFINITELY WRON IT--JUST PROMIS YOU WON'T FREAK OUT...
WHAT?!
...THIS.
WHA--WHAT IS THAT? WHAT ARE YOU WEARING?
I'M NOT WEARING ANYTHING. I--I THINK IT'S COMING OUT OF ME.
SQUIT

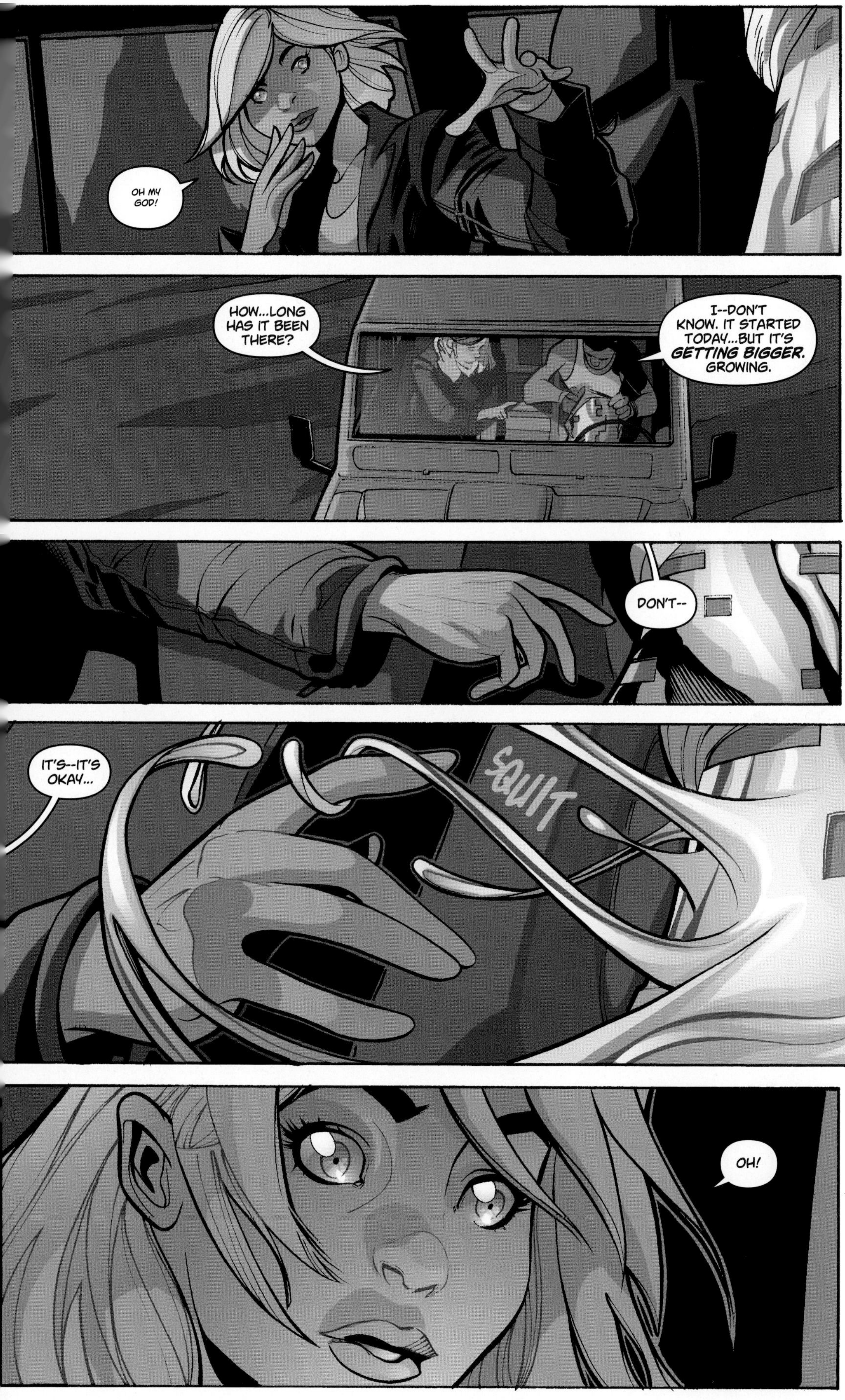
OH MY GOD!
HOW...LONG HAS IT BEEN THERE?
I--DON'T KNOW. IT STARTED TODAY...BUT IT'S GETTING BIGGER. GROWING.
DON'T--
IT'S--IT'S OKAY...
SQUIT
OH!

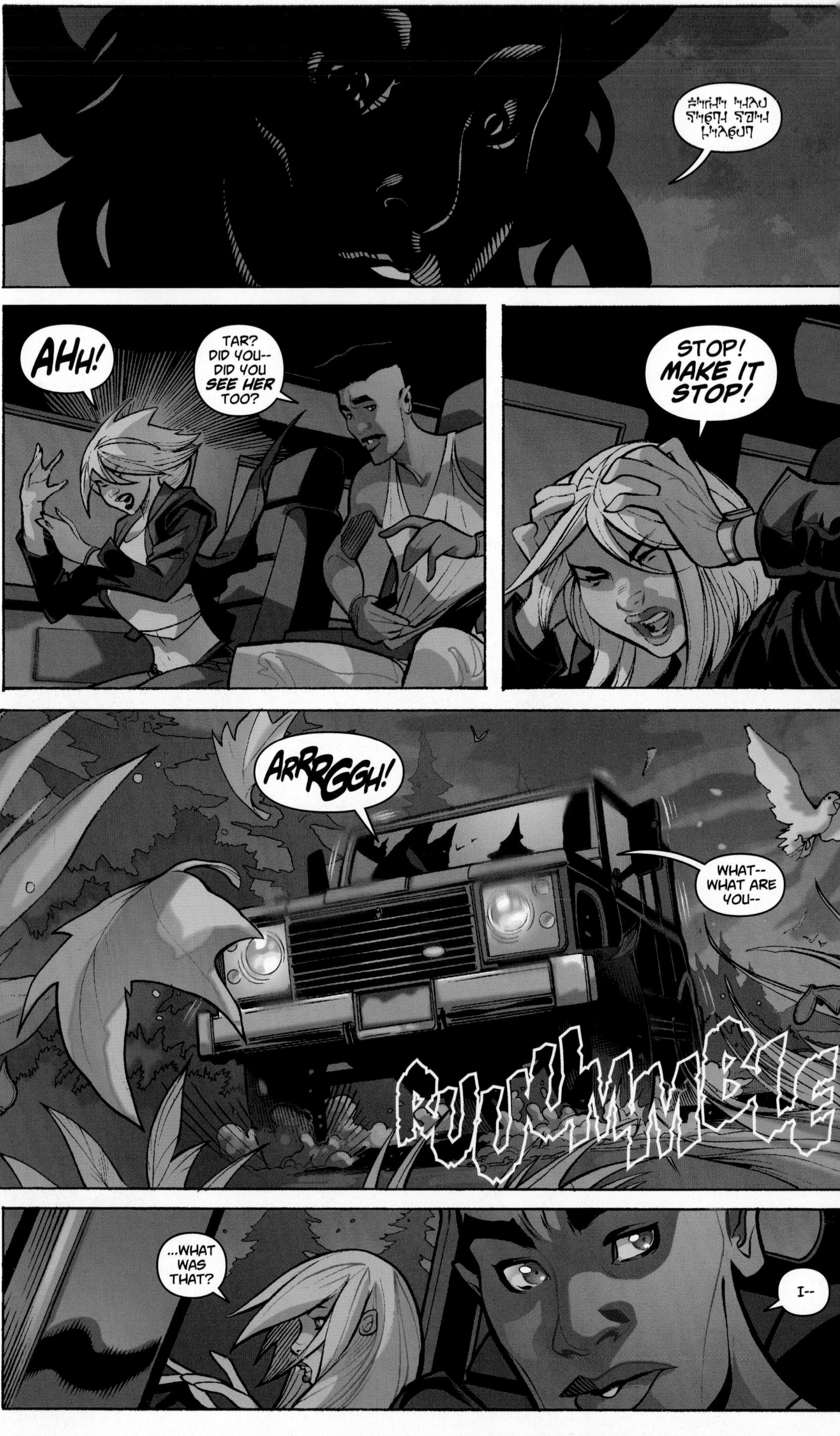
AHH!
TAR? DID YOU-- DID YOU SEE HER TOO?
STOP! MAKE IT STOP!
ARRRGGH!
WHAT-- WHAT ARE YOU--
RUUUMMBLE
...WHAT WAS THAT?
I--

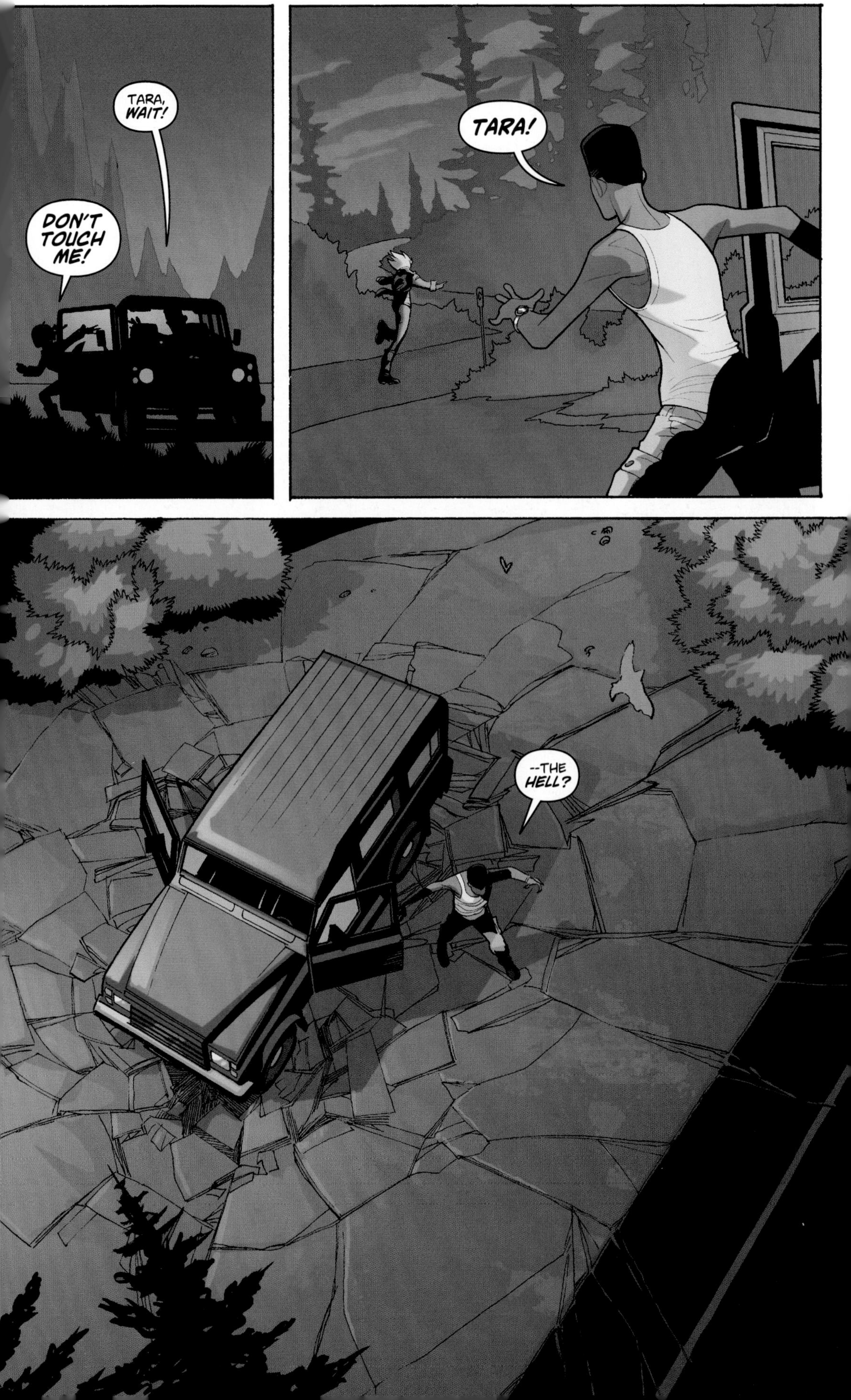
TARA, WAIT!
DON'T TOUCH ME!
TARA!
--THE HELL?

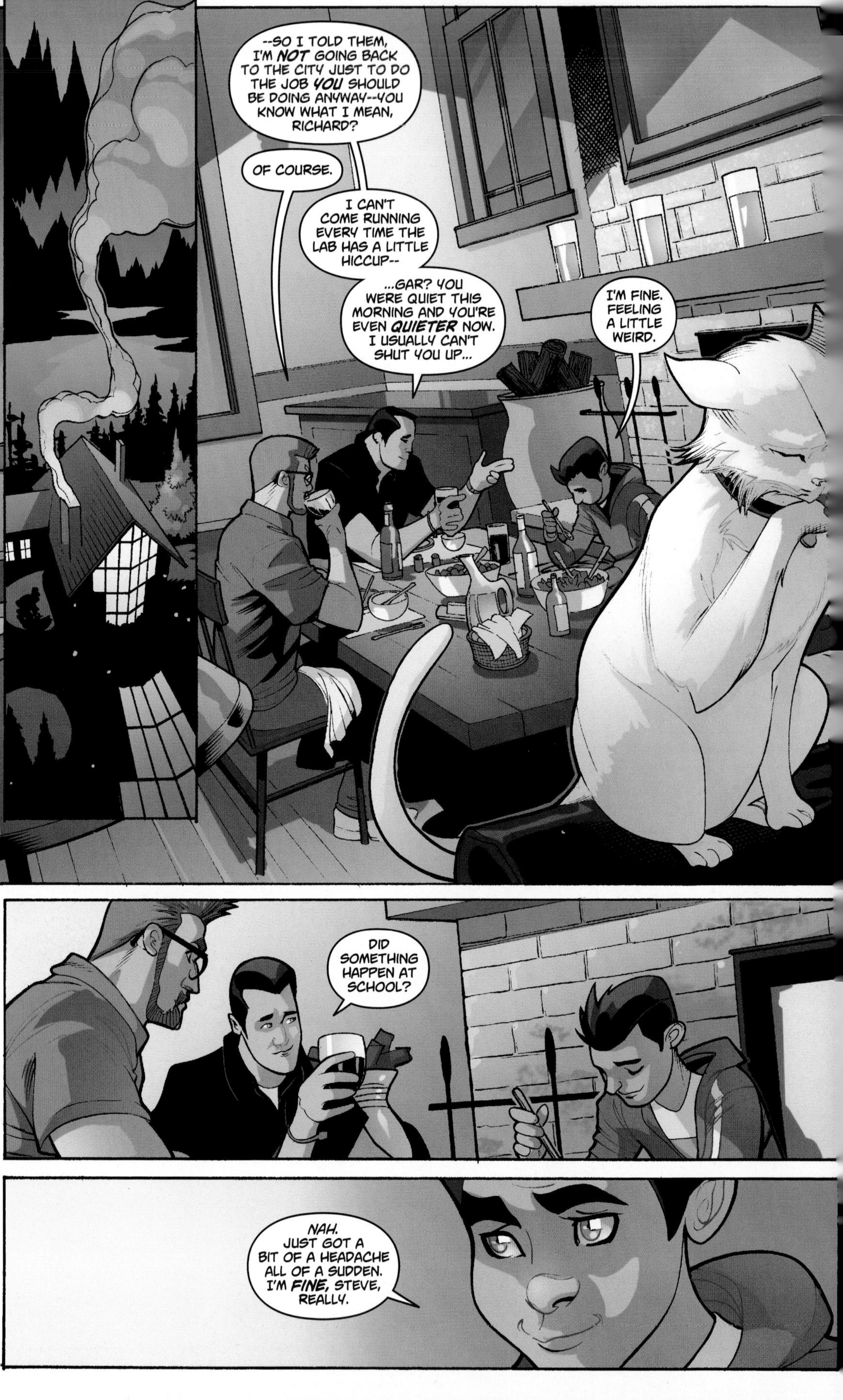
--SO I TOLD THEM, I'M NOT GOING BACK TO THE CITY JUST TO DO THE JOB YOU SHOULD BE DOING ANYWAY--YOU KNOW WHAT I MEAN, RICHARD?
OF COURSE.
I CAN'T COME RUNNING EVERY TIME THE LAB HAS A LITTLE HICCUP--
...GAR? YOU WERE QUIET THIS MORNING AND YOU'RE EVEN QUIETER NOW. I USUALLY CAN'T SHUT YOU UP...
I'M FINE. FEELING A LITTLE WEIRD.
DID SOMETHING HAPPEN AT SCHOOL?
NAH. JUST GOT A BIT OF A HEADACHE ALL OF A SUDDEN. I'M FINE, STEVE, REALLY.

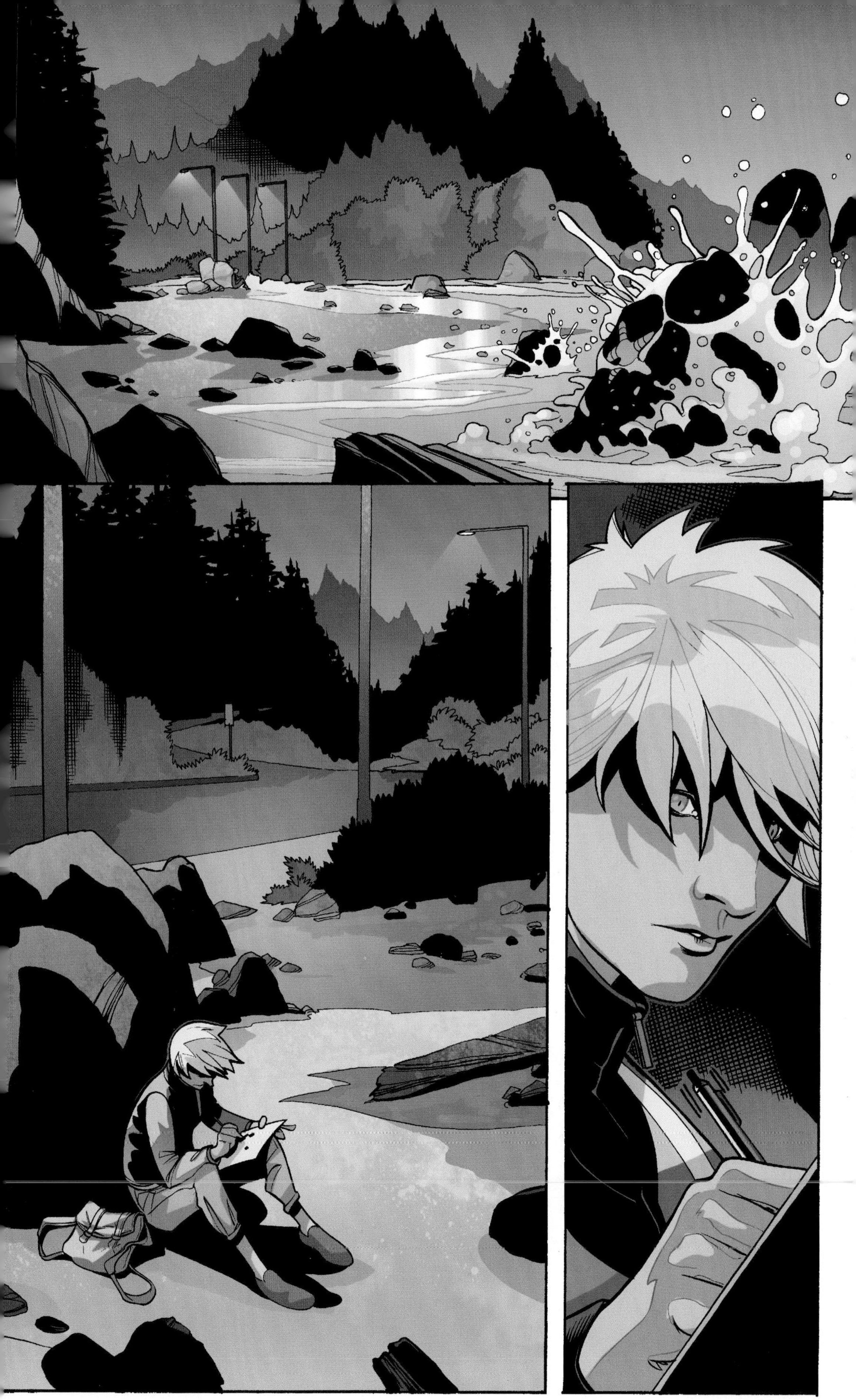

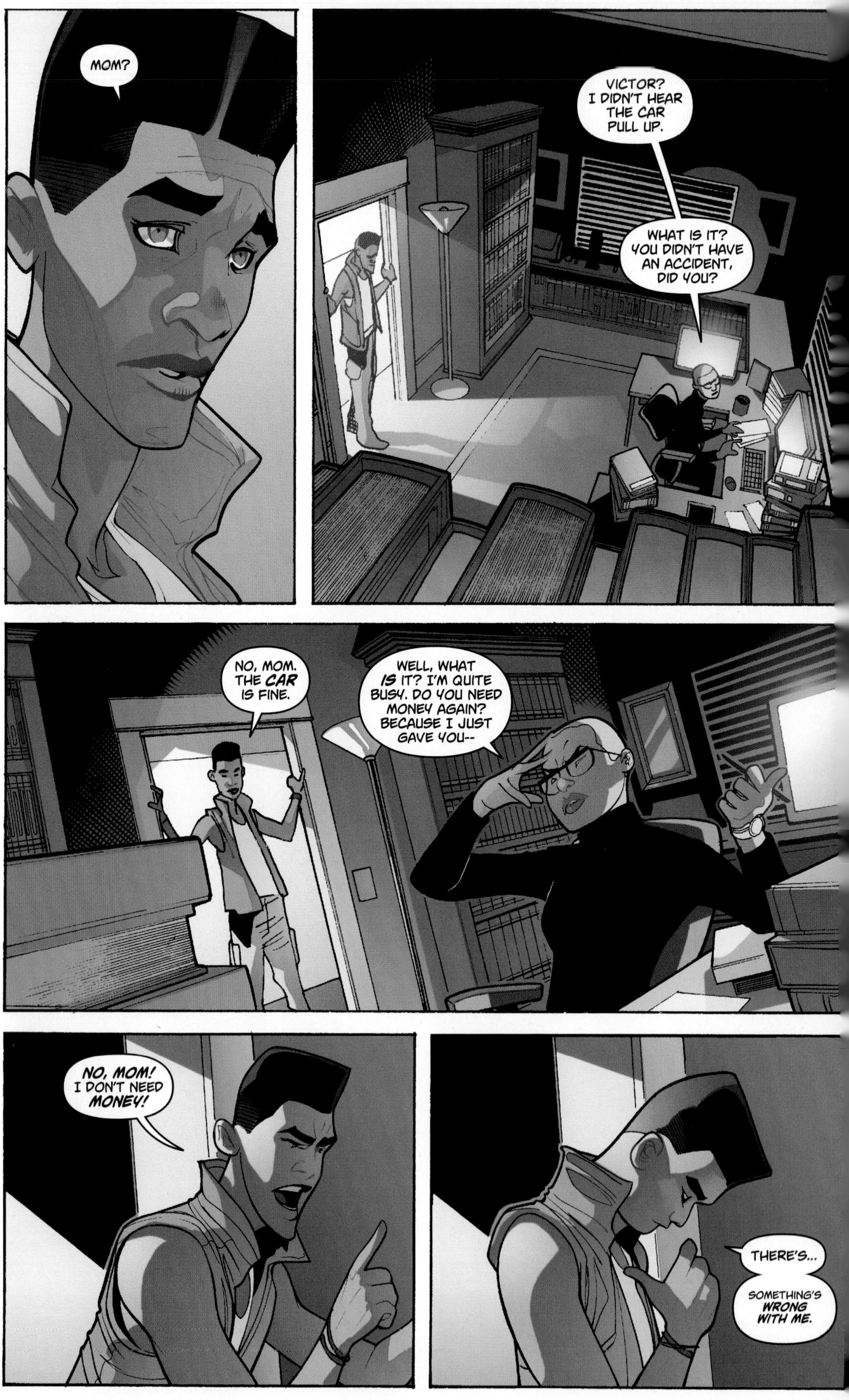
MOM?
VICTOR? I DIDN'T HEAR THE CAR PULL UP.
WHAT IS IT? YOU DIDN'T HAVE AN ACCIDENT, DID YOU?
NO, MOM. THE CAR IS FINE.
WELL, WHAT IS IT? I'M QUITE BUSY. DO YOU NEED MONEY AGAIN? BECAUSE I JUST GAVE YOU--
NO, MOM! I DON'T NEED MONEY!
THERE'S...
SOMETHING'S WRONG WITH ME.

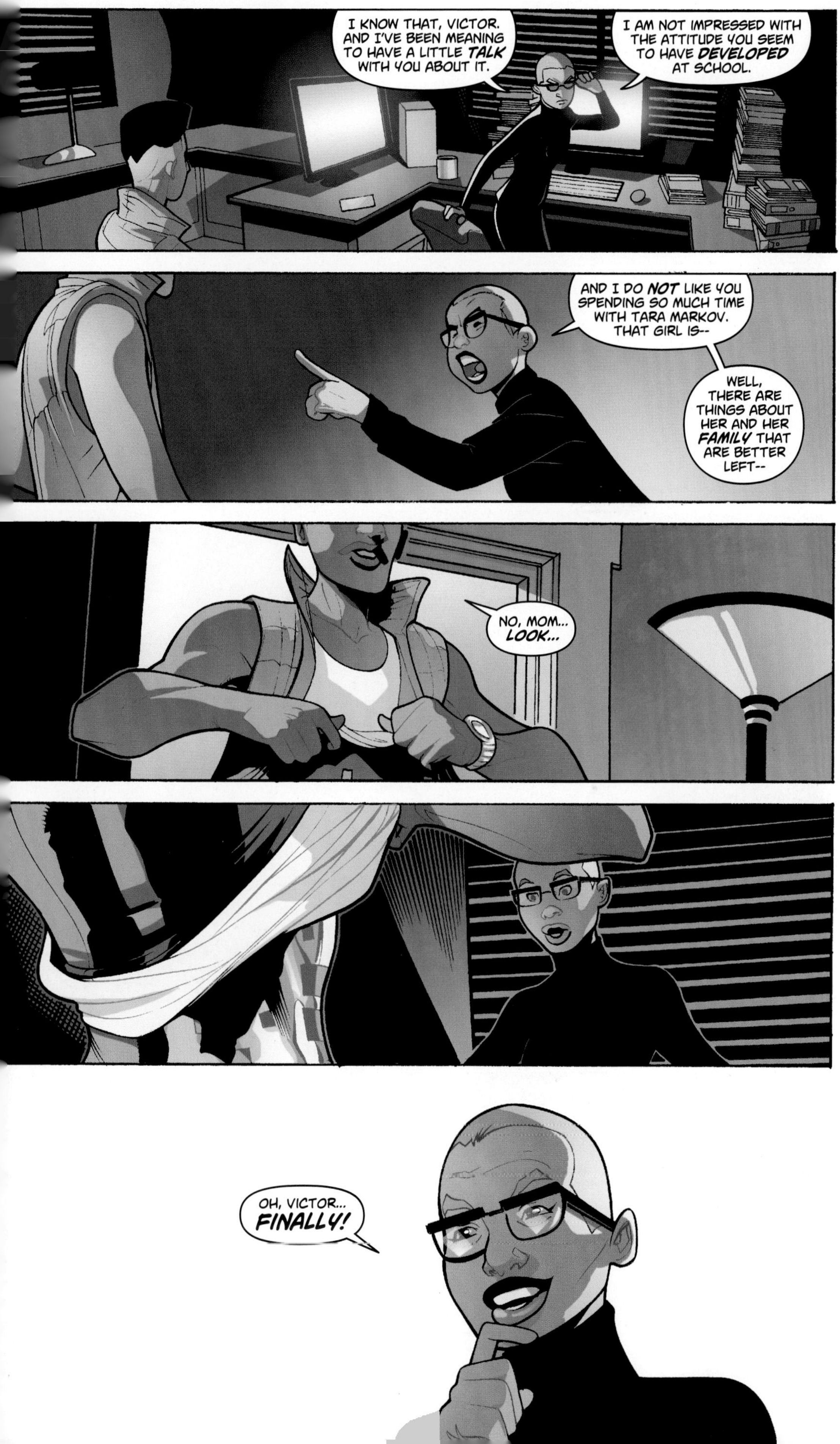

I KNOW THAT, VICTOR. AND I'VE BEEN MEANING TO HAVE A LITTLE TALK WITH YOU ABOUT IT.
I AM NOT IMPRESSED WITH THE ATTITUDE YOU SEEM TO HAVE DEVELOPED AT SCHOOL.
AND I DO NOT LIKE YOU SPENDING SO MUCH TIME WITH TARA MARKOV. THAT GIRL IS--
WELL, THERE ARE THINGS ABOUT HER AND HER FAMILY THAT ARE BETTER LEFT--
NO, MOM... LOOK...
OH, VICTOR... FINALLY!

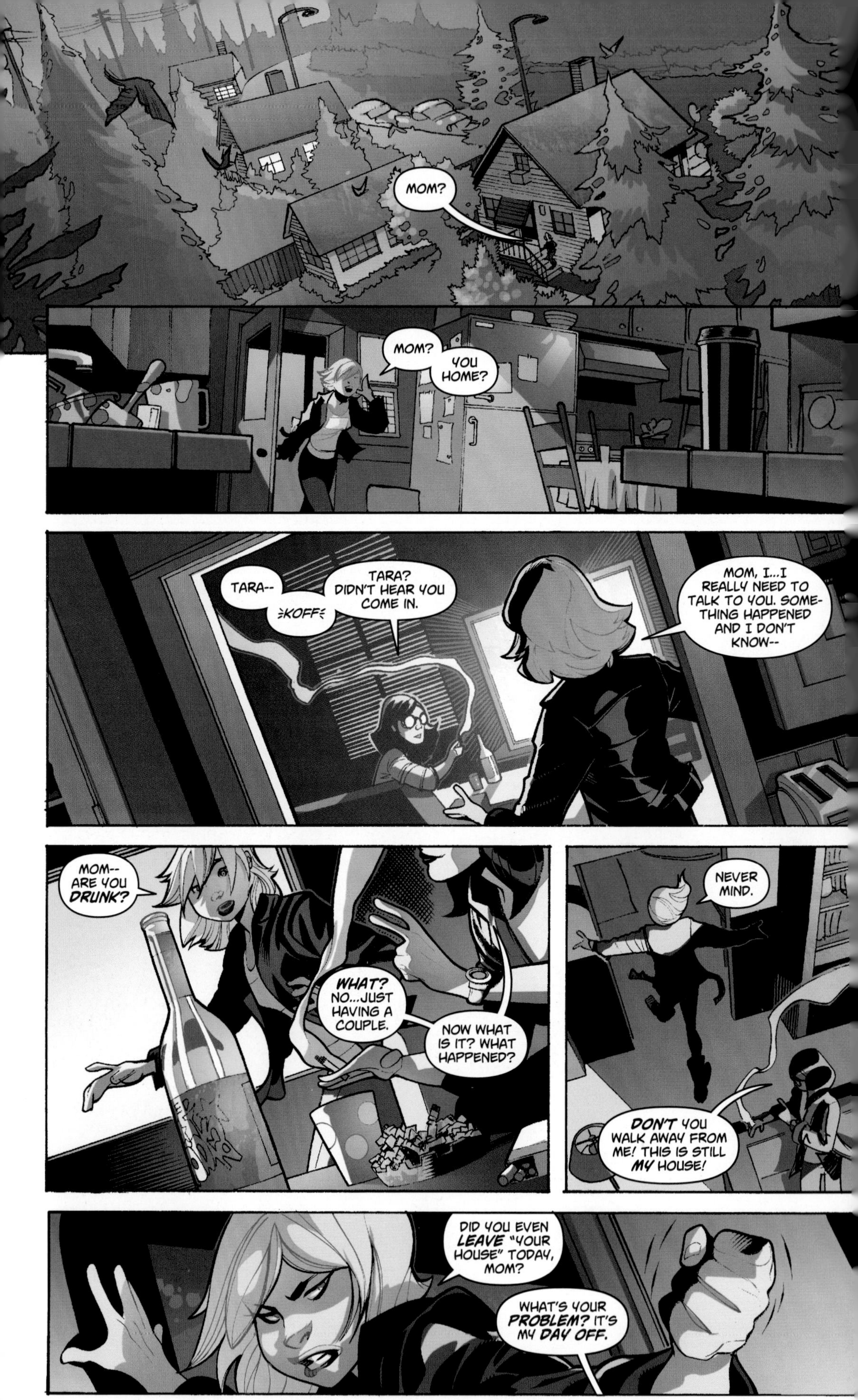

MOM?
MOM?
YOU HOME?
TARA--
KOFF
TARA? DIDN'T HEAR YOU COME IN.
MOM, I...I REALLY NEED TO TALK TO YOU. SOMETHING HAPPENED AND I DON'T KNOW--
MOM-- ARE YOU DRUNK?
WHAT? NO...JUST HAVING A COUPLE.
NOW WHAT IS IT? WHAT HAPPENED?
NEVER MIND.
DON'T YOU WALK AWAY FROM ME! THIS IS STILL MY HOUSE!
DID YOU EVEN LEAVE "YOUR HOUSE" TODAY, MOM?
WHAT'S YOUR PROBLEM? IT'S MY DAY OFF.

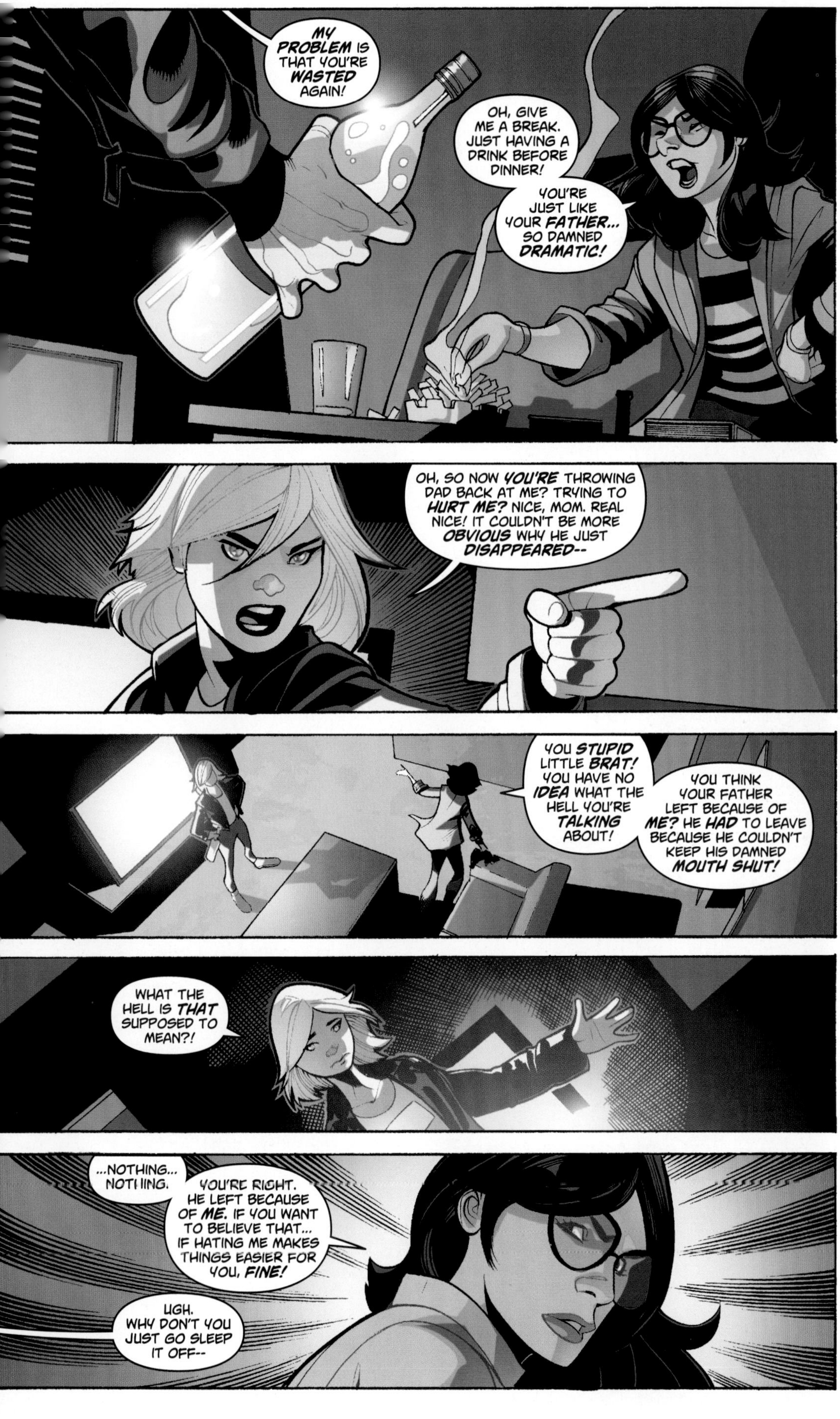
MY PROBLEM IS THAT YOU'RE WASTED AGAIN!
OH, GIVE ME A BREAK. JUST HAVING A DRINK BEFORE DINNER!
YOU'RE JUST LIKE YOUR FATHER... SO DAMNED DRAMATIC!
OH, SO NOW YOU'RE THROWING DAD BACK AT ME? TRYING TO HURT ME? NICE, MOM. REAL NICE! IT COULDN'T BE MORE OBVIOUS WHY HE JUST DISAPPEARED--
YOU STUPID LITTLE BRAT! YOU HAVE NO IDEA WHAT THE HELL YOU'RE TALKING ABOUT!
YOU THINK YOUR FATHER LEFT BECAUSE OF ME? HE HAD TO LEAVE BECAUSE HE COULDN'T KEEP HIS DAMNED MOUTH SHUT!
WHAT THE HELL IS THAT SUPPOSED TO MEAN?!
...NOTHING... NOTHING.
YOU'RE RIGHT. HE LEFT BECAUSE OF ME. IF YOU WANT TO BELIEVE THAT... IF HATING ME MAKES THINGS EASIER FOR YOU, FINE!
UGH. WHY DON'T YOU JUST GO SLEEP IT OFF--

SMACK

UNGH!

YOU THINK ANY OF THIS WAS *MY CHOICE?!* IT WAS *FORCED* ON ME! I NEVER *WANTED* ANY OF THIS.

I NEVER *WANTED* YOU!

TAKE-- TAKE THAT *BACK.*

YOU HAVE NO IDEA WHAT I'M *GOING* THROUGH! YOU HAVE NO IDEA WHAT'S *HAPPENING* TO ME! AND NOW *THIS,* TOO?! YOU LAY *THIS* ON ME?!

RUUUMMM

TARA... STOP IT. I--I'M *SORRY...*

YOU'RE *SORRY?*

YOU'RE *SORRY?!*

RUUUMMMBLE

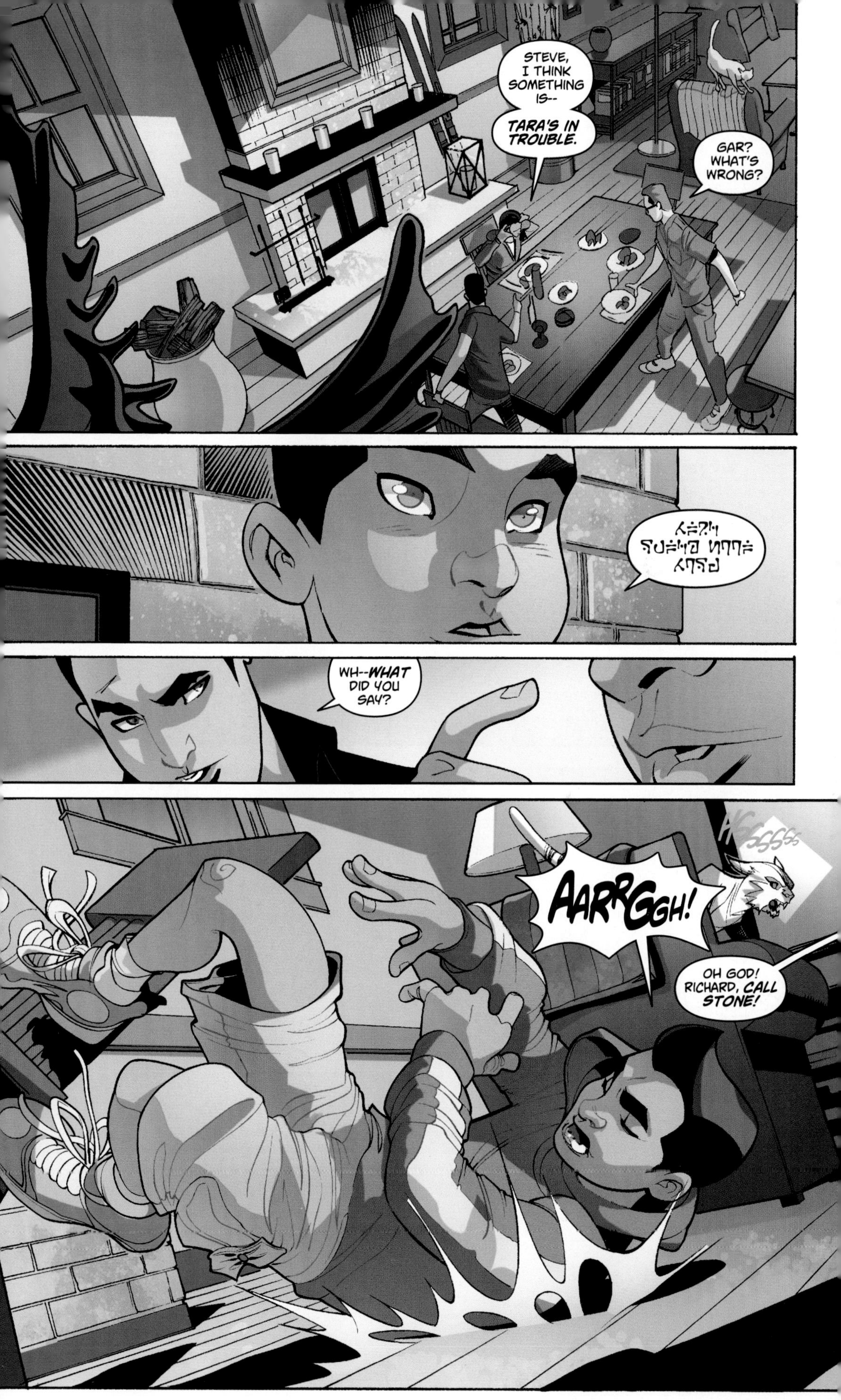
STEVE, I THINK SOMETHING IS--
TARA'S IN TROUBLE.
GAR? WHAT'S WRONG?
WH--WHAT DID YOU SAY?
AARRGGH!
OH GOD! RICHARD, CALL STONE!

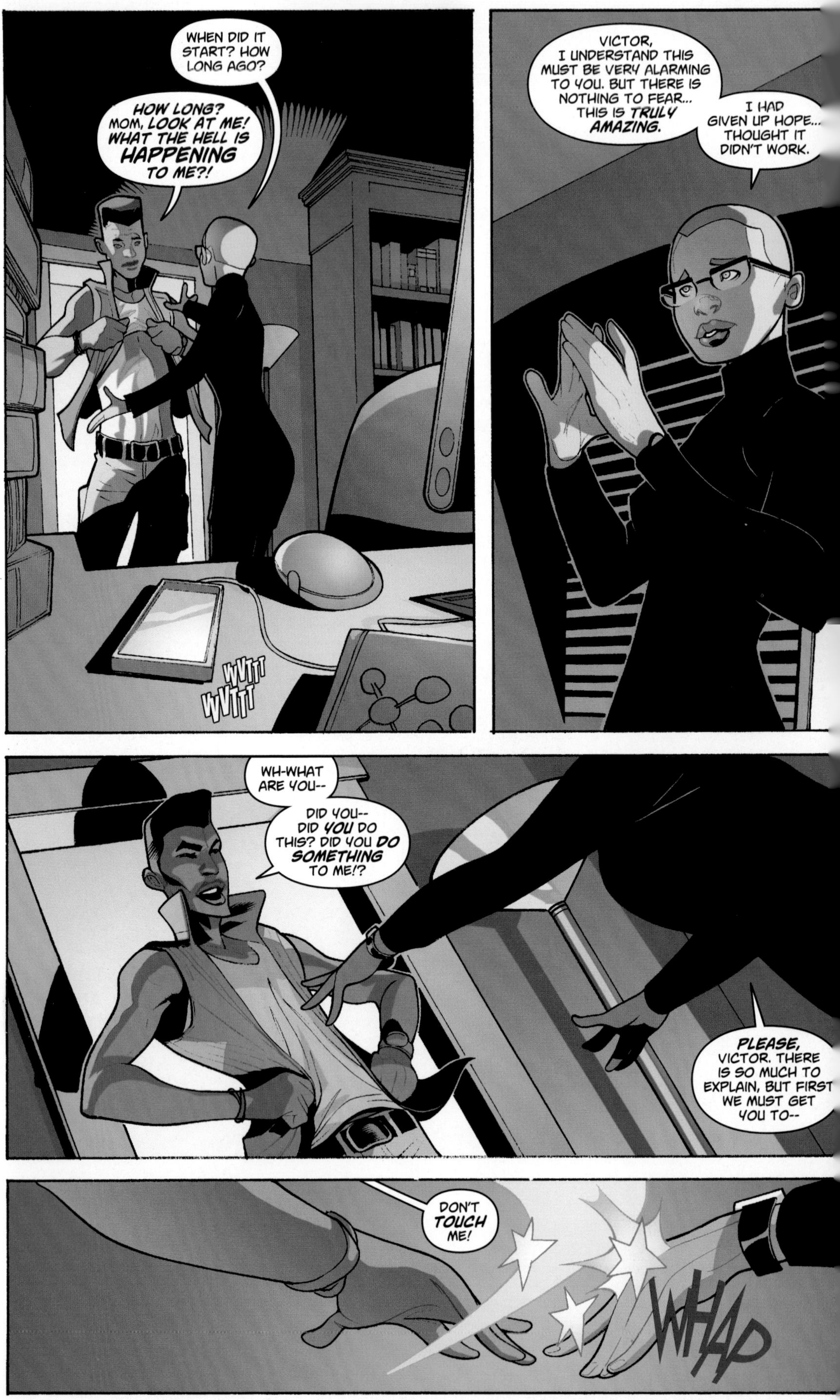
WHEN DID IT START? HOW LONG AGO?
HOW LONG? MOM, LOOK AT ME! WHAT THE HELL IS HAPPENING TO ME?!
VVVTTT VVVTTT
VICTOR, I UNDERSTAND THIS MUST BE VERY ALARMING TO YOU. BUT THERE IS NOTHING TO FEAR... THIS IS TRULY AMAZING.
I HAD GIVEN UP HOPE... THOUGHT IT DIDN'T WORK.
WH-WHAT ARE YOU--
DID YOU-- DID YOU DO THIS? DID YOU DO SOMETHING TO ME!?
PLEASE, VICTOR. THERE IS SO MUCH TO EXPLAIN, BUT FIRST WE MUST GET YOU TO--
DON'T TOUCH ME!
WHAP

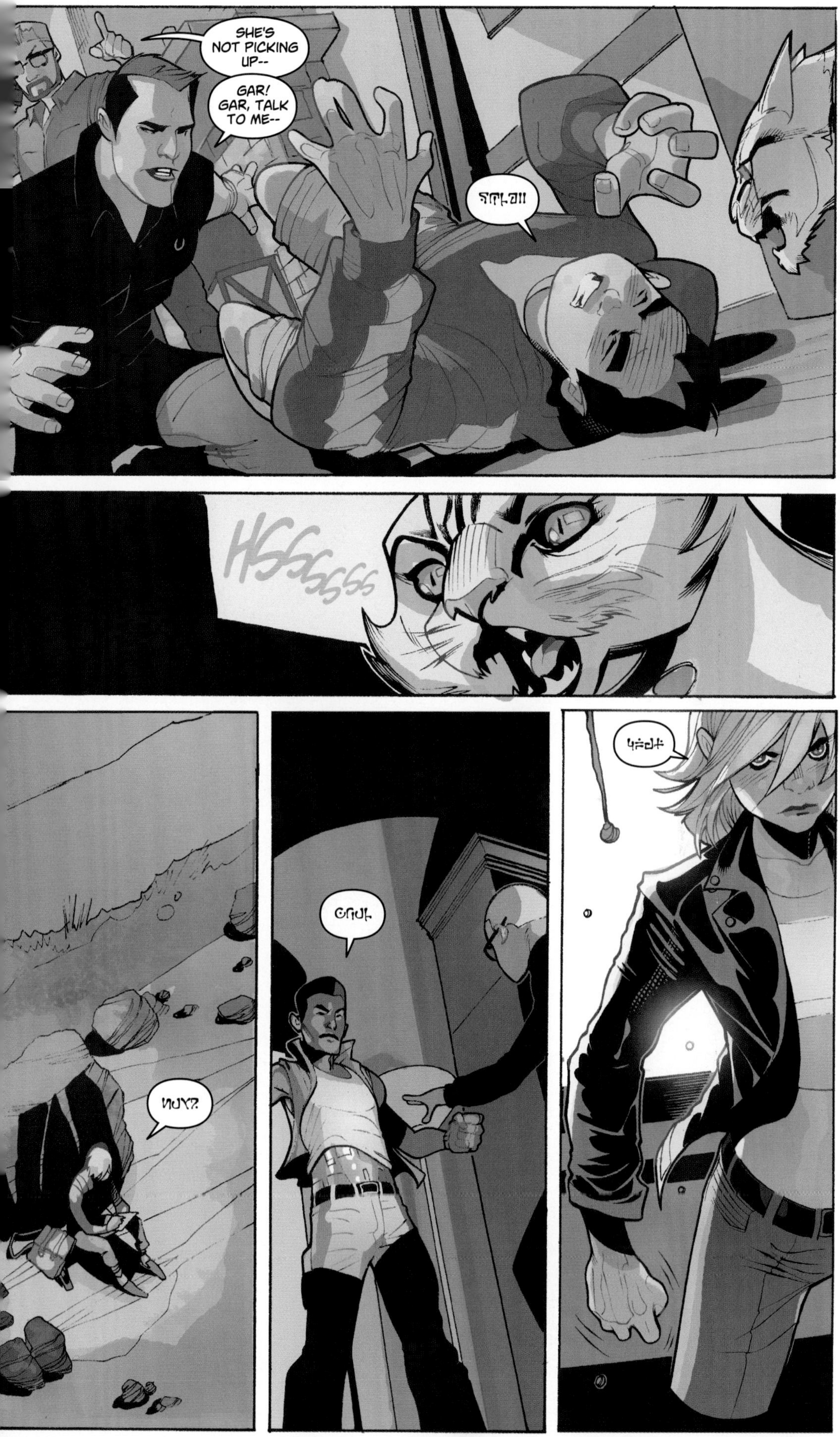
SHE'S NOT PICKING UP--
GAR! GAR, TALK TO ME--
HSSSSSSH

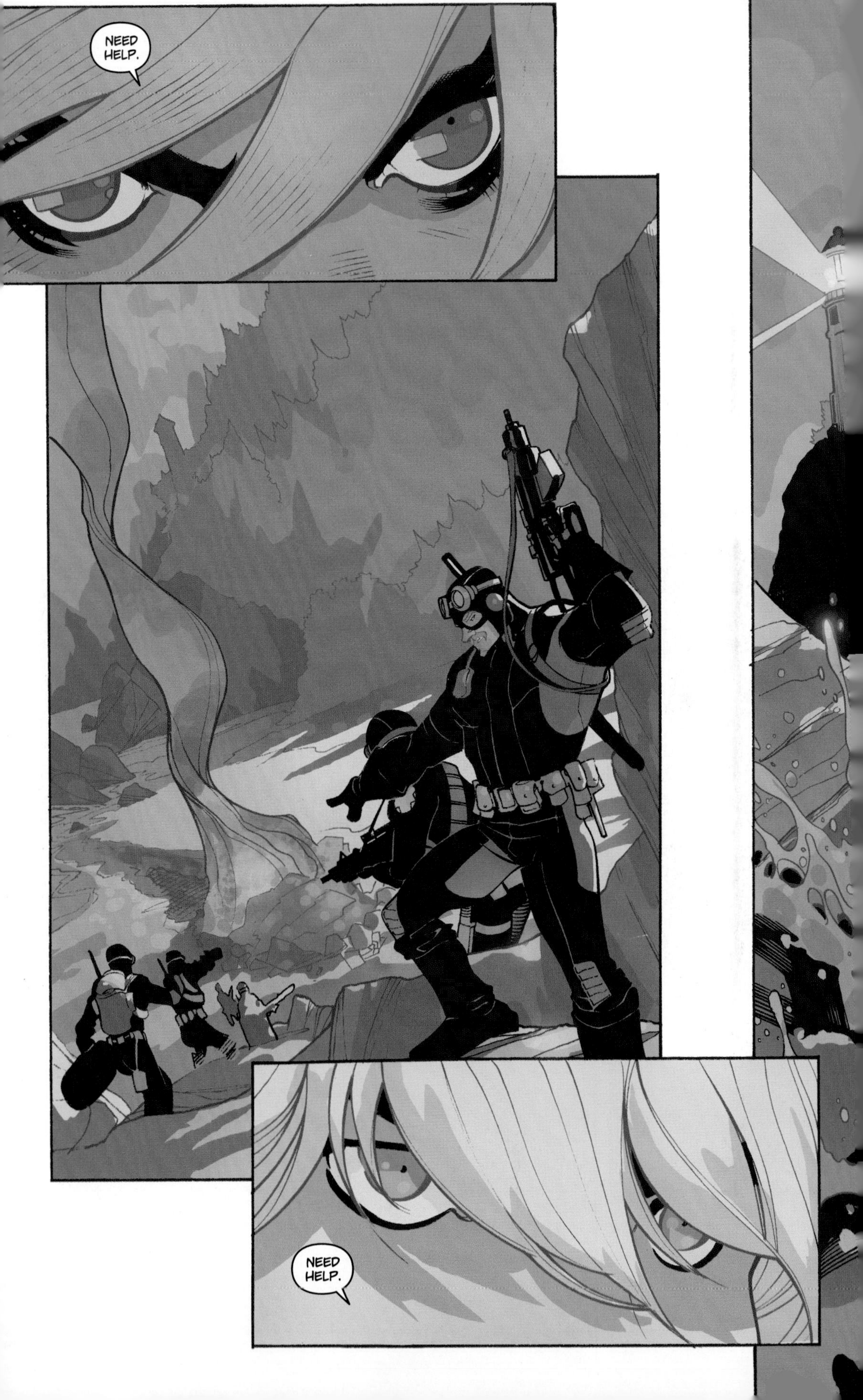

NEED HELP.
NEED HELP.

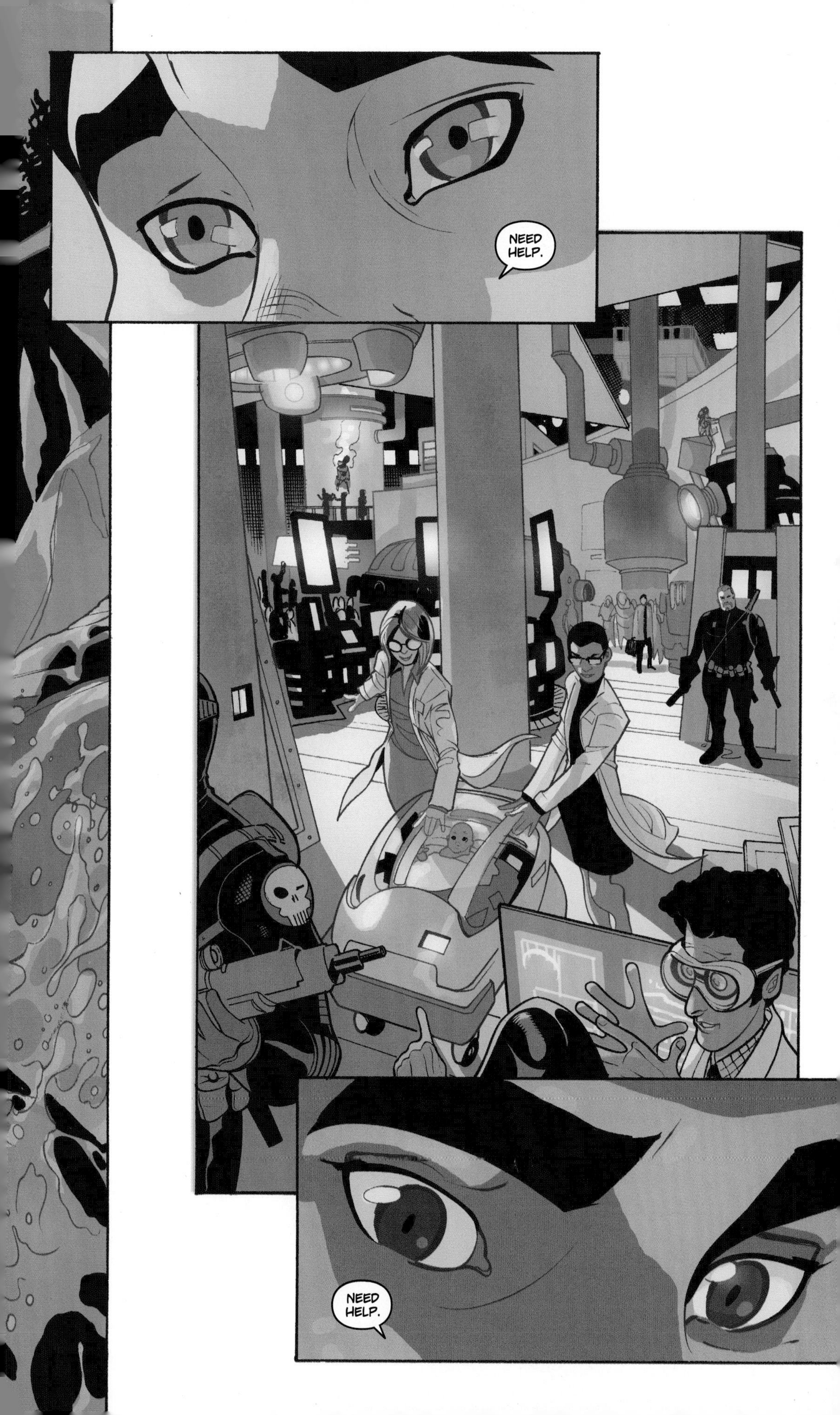
NEED HELP.
NEED HELP.

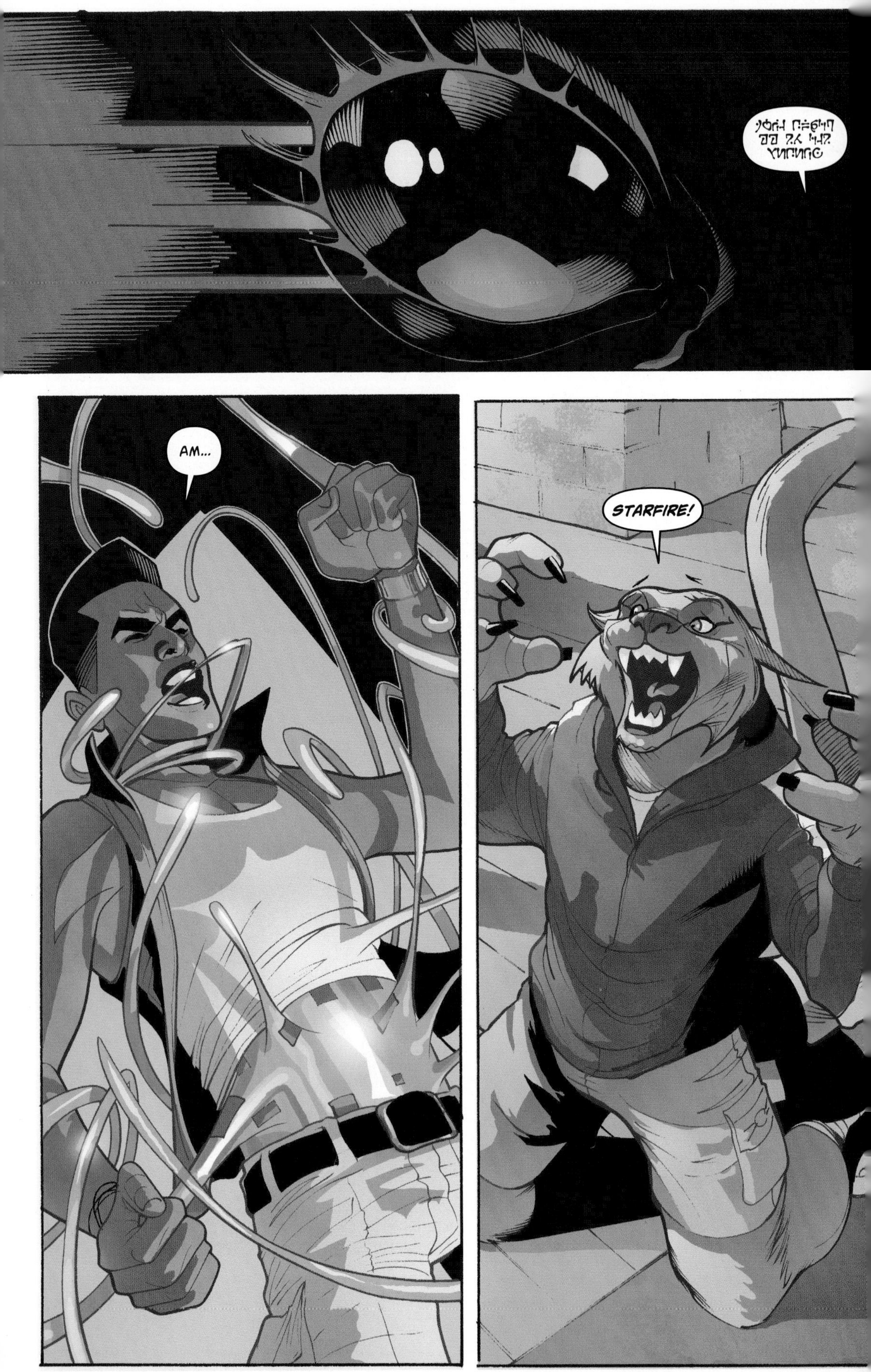
AM...
STARFIRE!

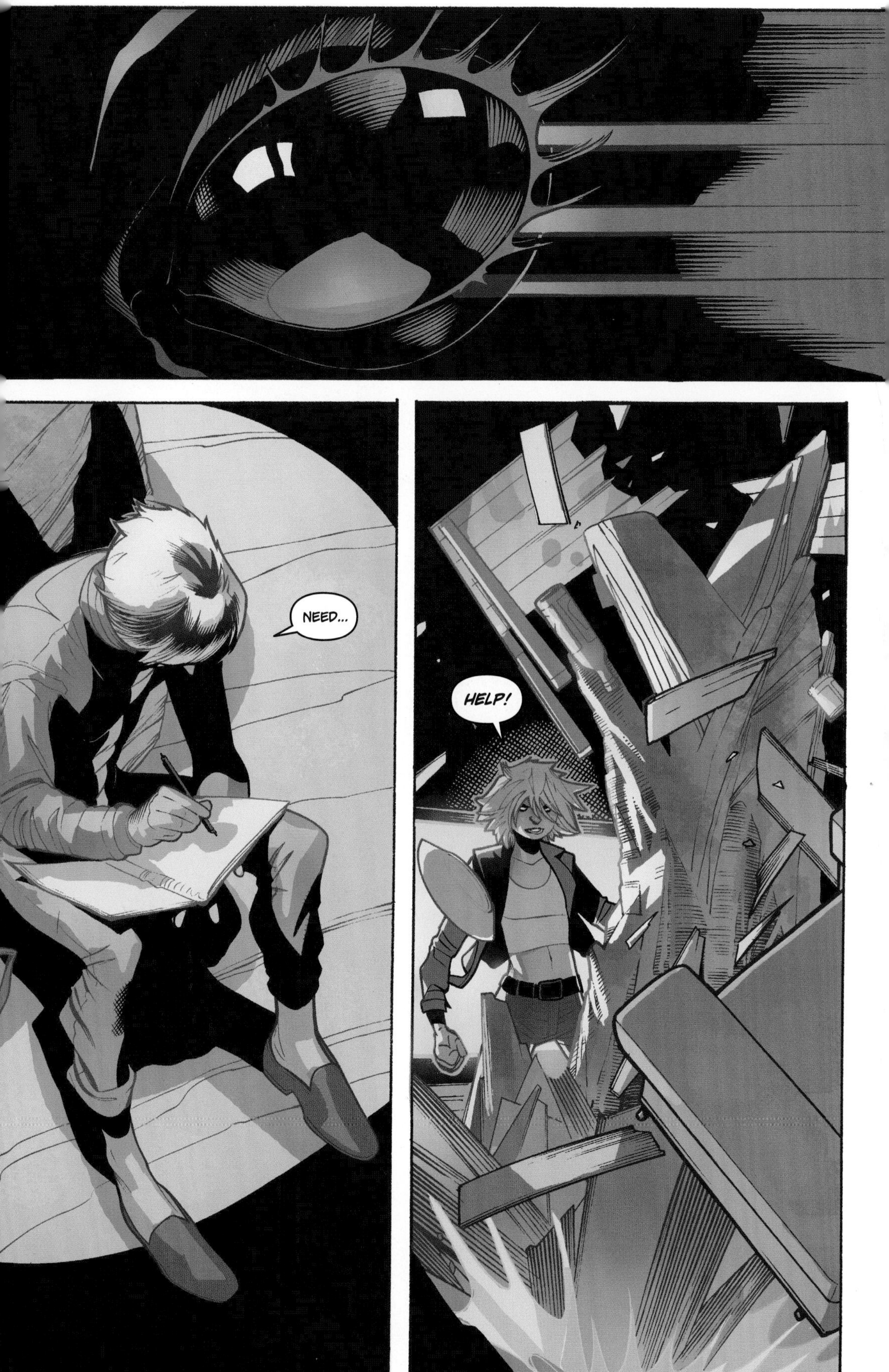
NEED...
HELP!

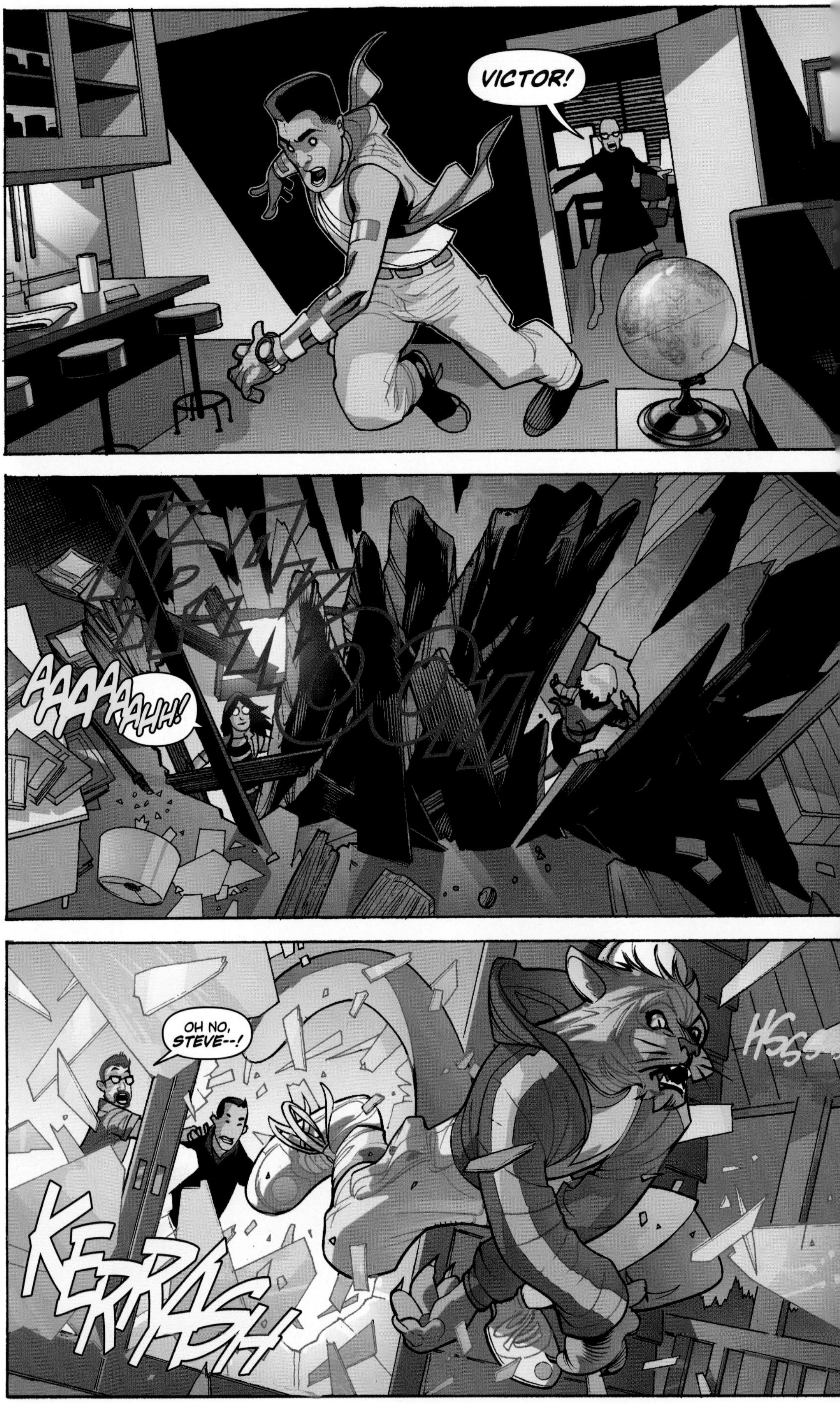
VICTOR!
AAAAAAHH!
OH NO, STEVE--!
KERRASH

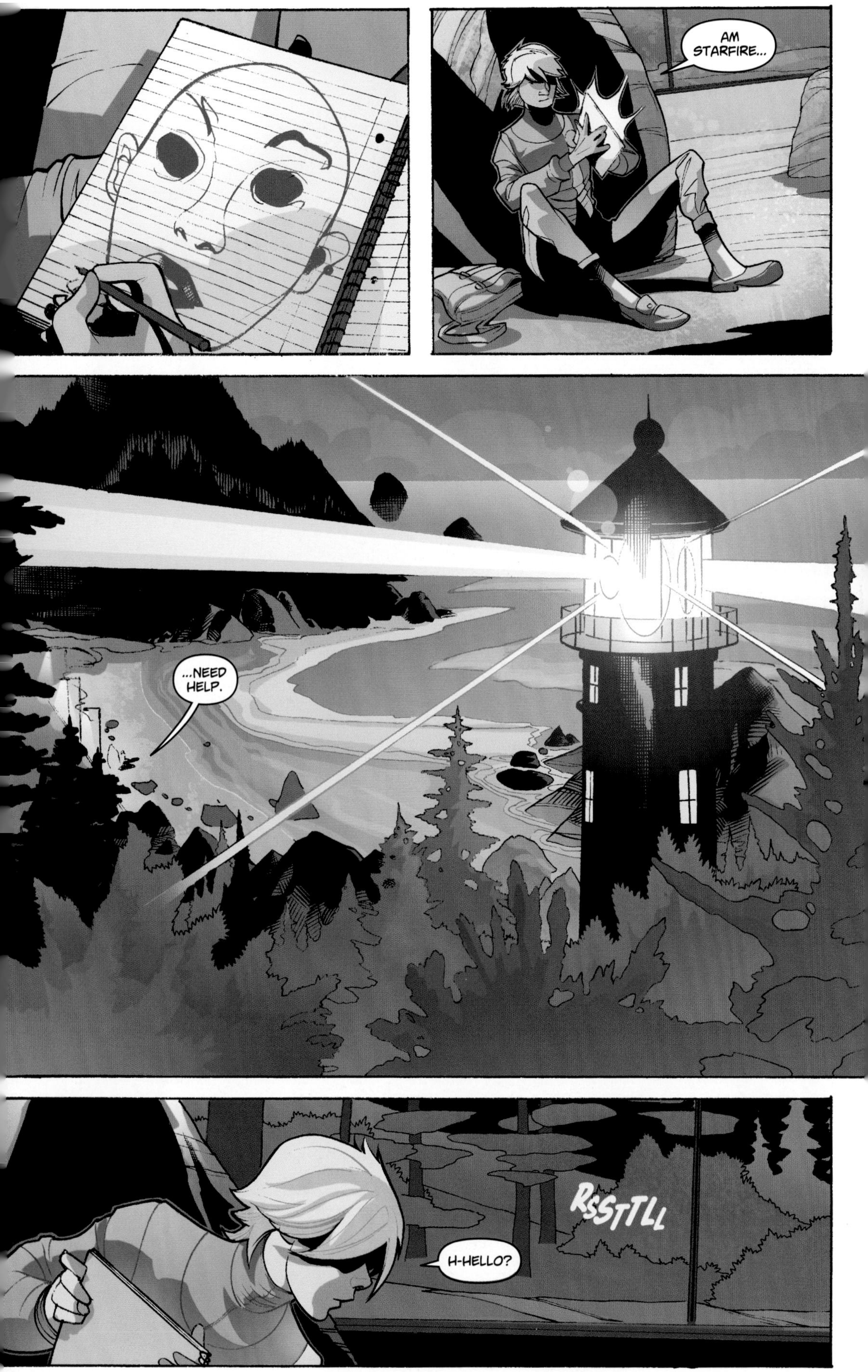
AM STARFIRE...
...NEED HELP.
RSSTTLL
H-HELLO?

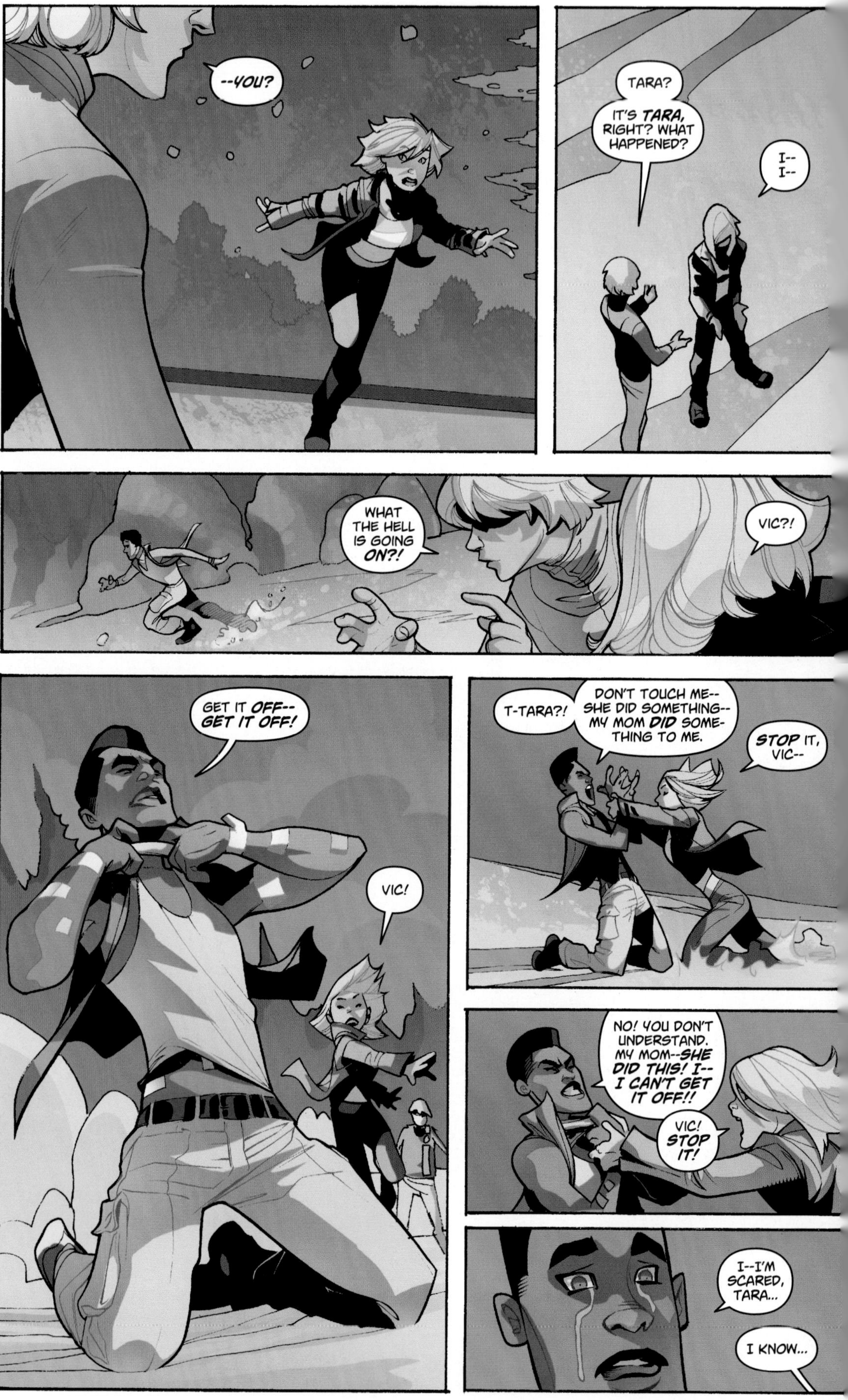

--YOU?
TARA?
IT'S TARA, RIGHT? WHAT HAPPENED?
I-- I--
WHAT THE HELL IS GOING ON?!
VIC?!
GET IT OFF-- GET IT OFF!
VIC!
T-TARA?!
DON'T TOUCH ME-- SHE DID SOMETHING-- MY MOM DID SOMETHING TO ME.
STOP IT, VIC--
NO! YOU DON'T UNDERSTAND. MY MOM--SHE DID THIS! I-- I CAN'T GET IT OFF!!
VIC! STOP IT!
I--I'M SCARED, TARA...
I KNOW...

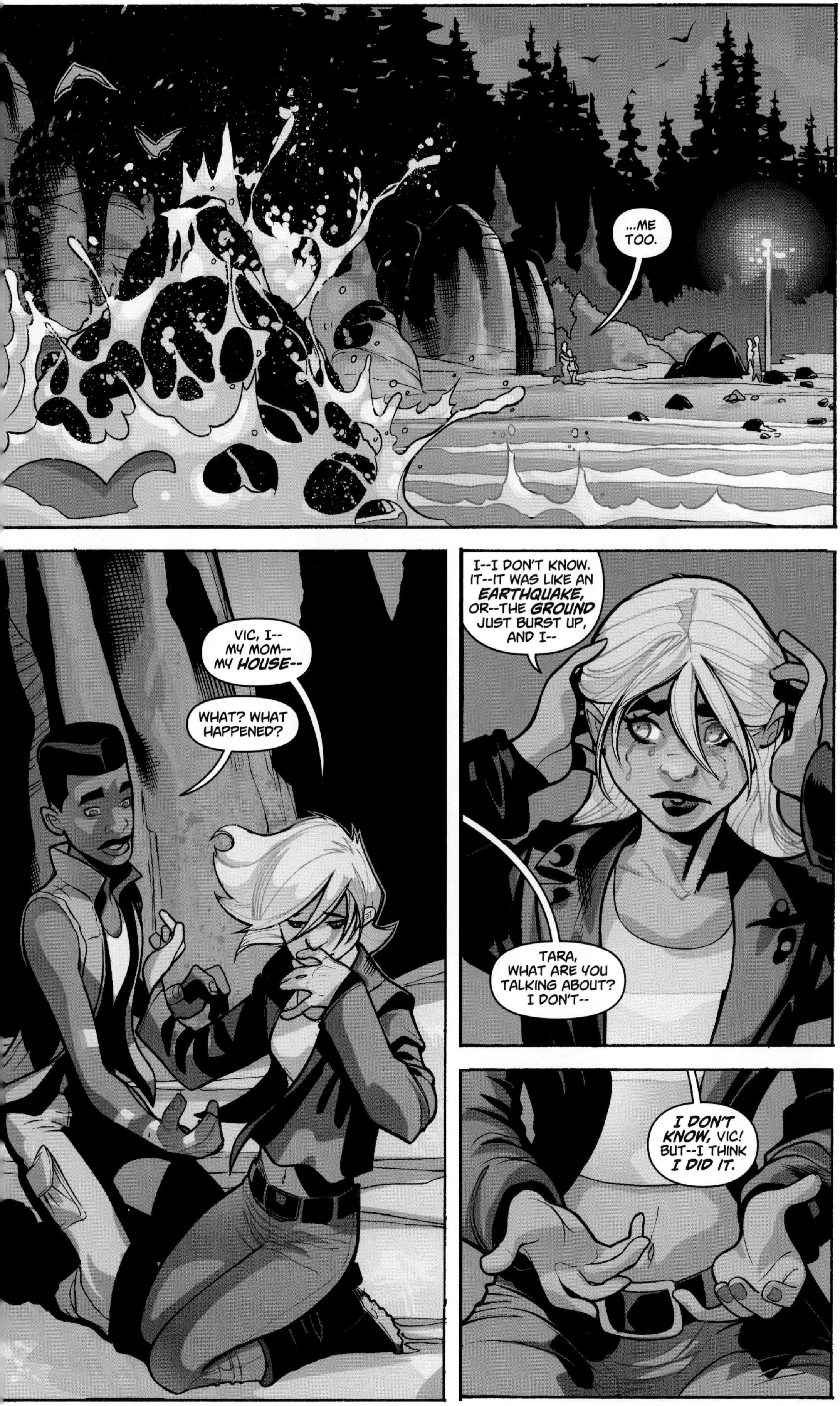
...ME TOO.
VIC, I-- MY MOM-- MY HOUSE--
WHAT? WHAT HAPPENED?
I--I DON'T KNOW. IT--IT WAS LIKE AN EARTHQUAKE, OR--THE GROUND JUST BURST UP, AND I--
TARA, WHAT ARE YOU TALKING ABOUT? I DON'T--
I DON'T KNOW, VIC! BUT--I THINK I DID IT.

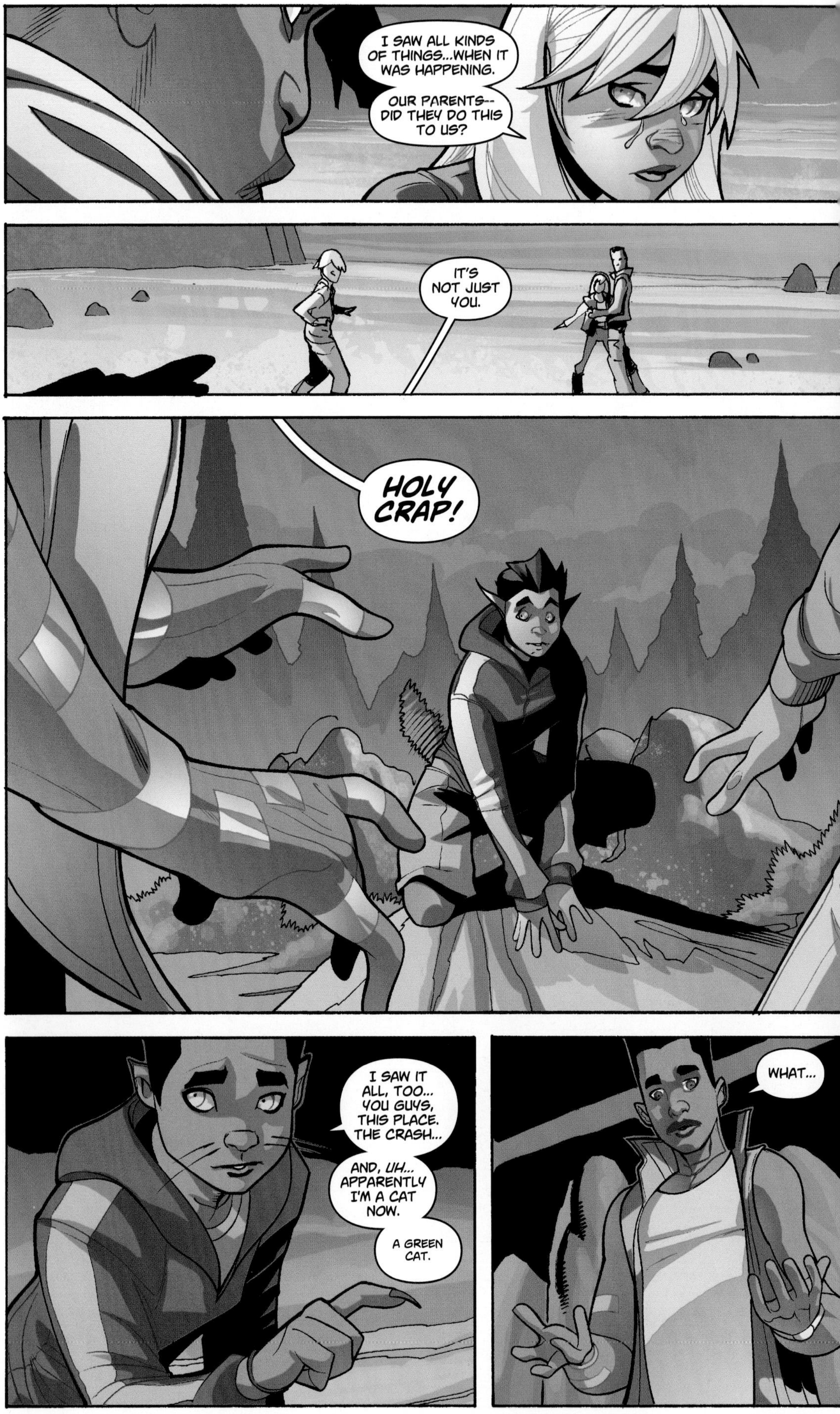
I SAW ALL KINDS OF THINGS...WHEN IT WAS HAPPENING.
OUR PARENTS-- DID THEY DO THIS TO US?
IT'S NOT JUST YOU.
HOLY CRAP!
I SAW IT ALL, TOO... YOU GUYS, THIS PLACE. THE CRASH...
AND, UH... APPARENTLY I'M A CAT NOW.
A GREEN CAT.
WHAT...

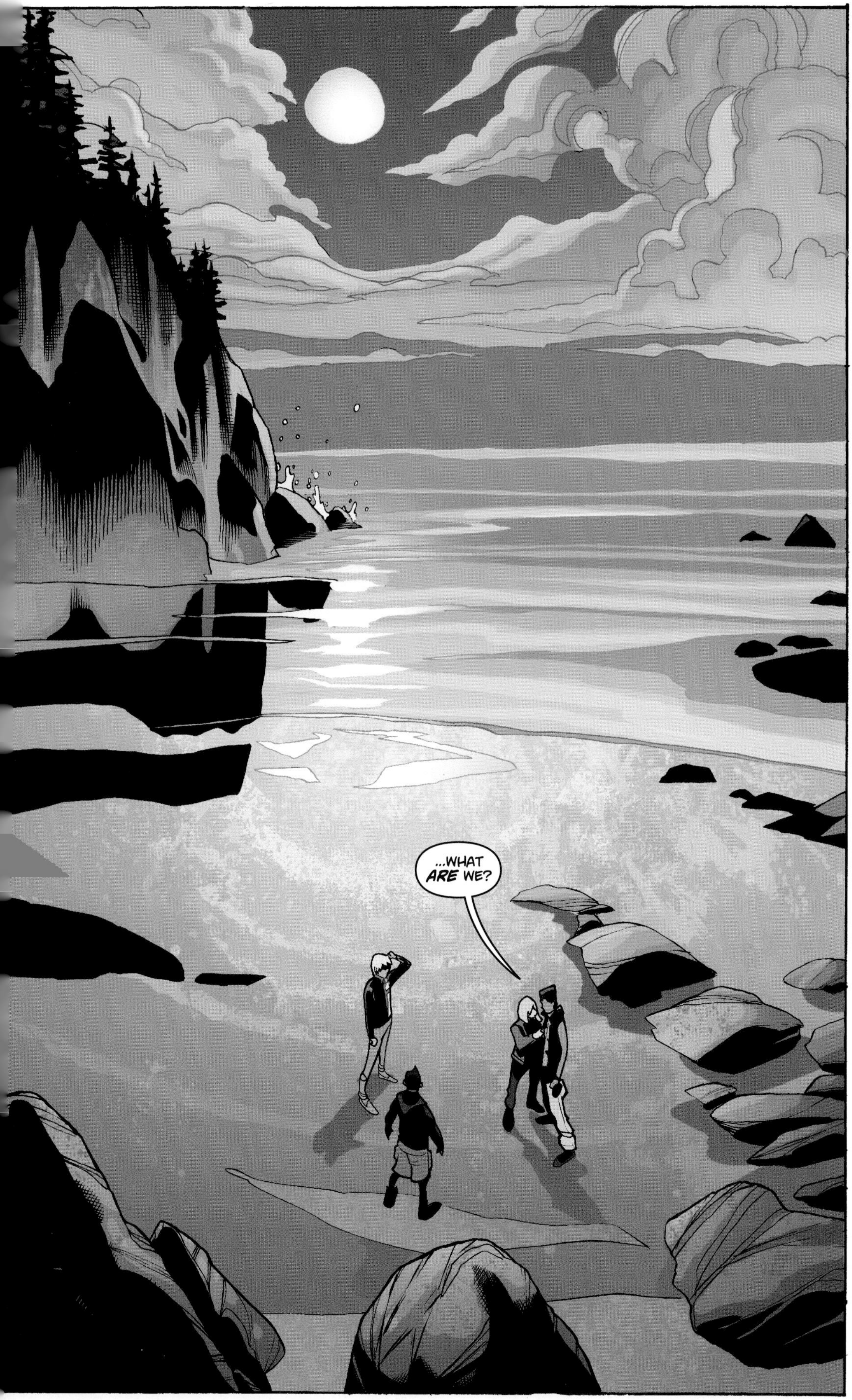
...WHAT ARE WE?

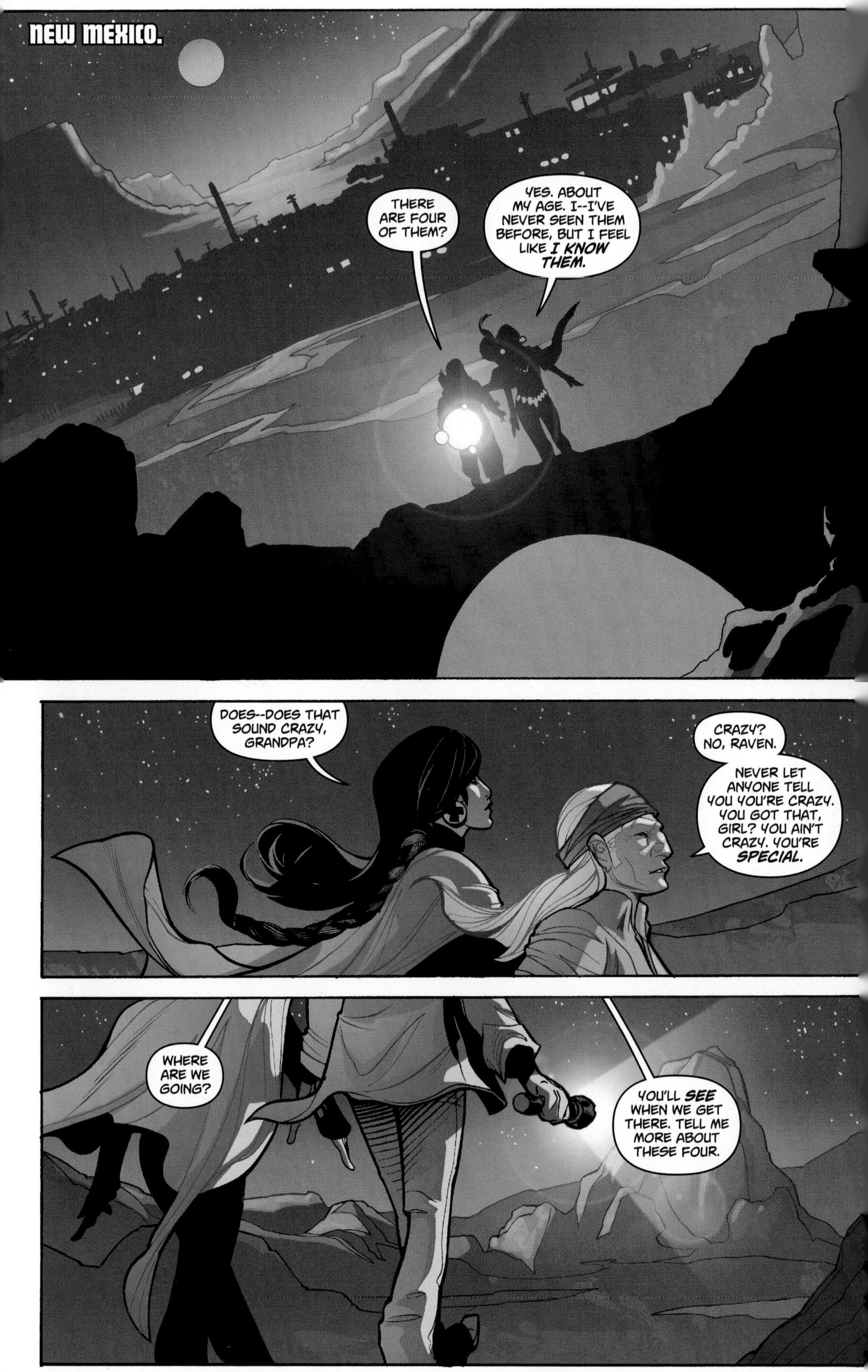
NEW MEXICO.
THERE ARE FOUR OF THEM?
YES. ABOUT MY AGE. I--I'VE NEVER SEEN THEM BEFORE, BUT I FEEL LIKE I KNOW THEM.
DOES--DOES THAT SOUND CRAZY, GRANDPA?
CRAZY? NO, RAVEN.
NEVER LET ANYONE TELL YOU YOU'RE CRAZY. YOU GOT THAT, GIRL? YOU AIN'T CRAZY. YOU'RE SPECIAL.
WHERE ARE WE GOING?
YOU'LL SEE WHEN WE GET THERE. TELL ME MORE ABOUT THESE FOUR.

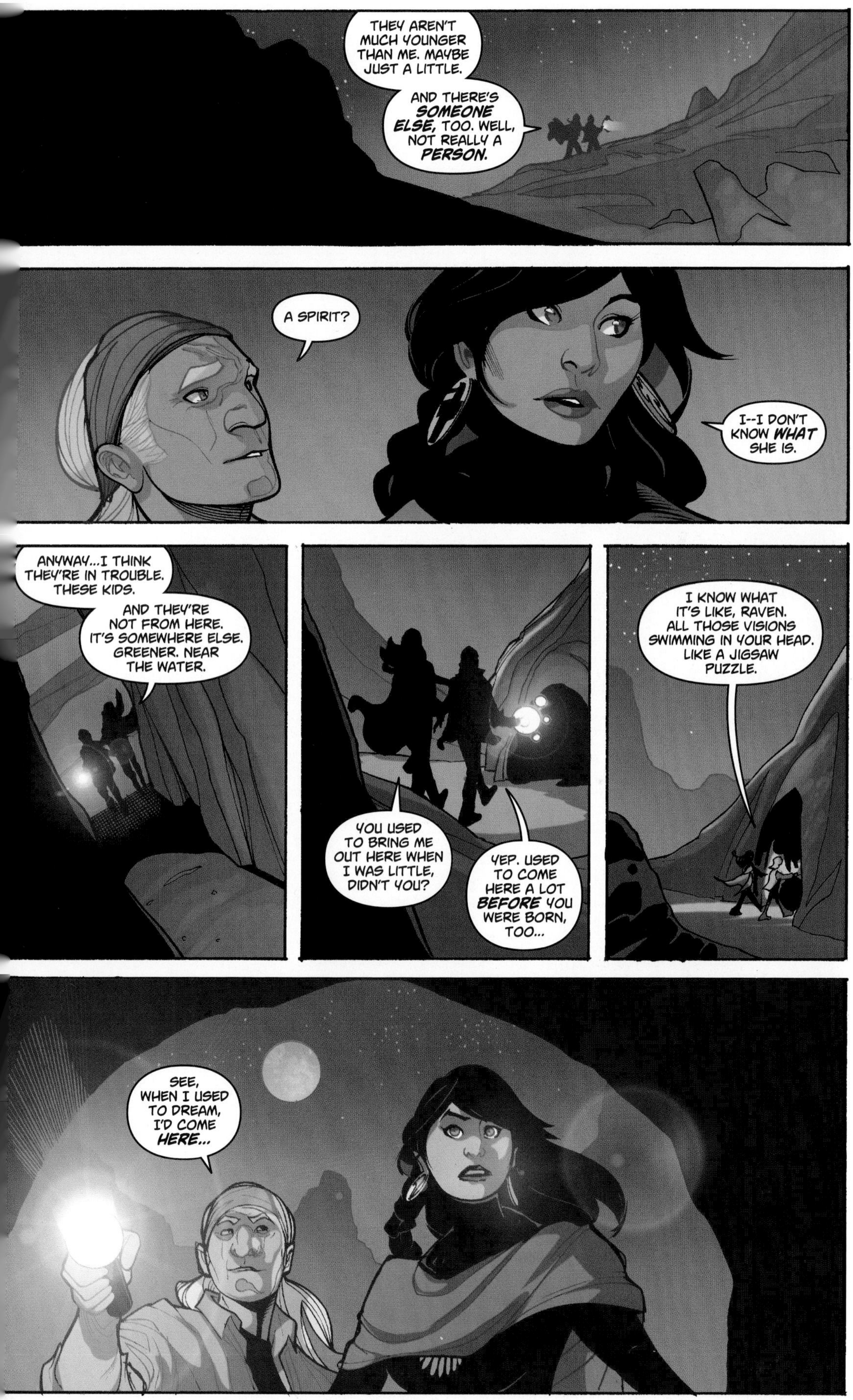
THEY AREN'T MUCH YOUNGER THAN ME. MAYBE JUST A LITTLE.
AND THERE'S SOMEONE ELSE, TOO. WELL, NOT REALLY A PERSON.
A SPIRIT?
I--I DON'T KNOW WHAT SHE IS.
ANYWAY...I THINK THEY'RE IN TROUBLE. THESE KIDS.
AND THEY'RE NOT FROM HERE. IT'S SOMEWHERE ELSE. GREENER. NEAR THE WATER.
YOU USED TO BRING ME OUT HERE WHEN I WAS LITTLE, DIDN'T YOU?
YEP. USED TO COME HERE A LOT BEFORE YOU WERE BORN, TOO...
I KNOW WHAT IT'S LIKE, RAVEN. ALL THOSE VISIONS SWIMMING IN YOUR HEAD. LIKE A JIGSAW PUZZLE.
SEE, WHEN I USED TO DREAM, I'D COME HERE...

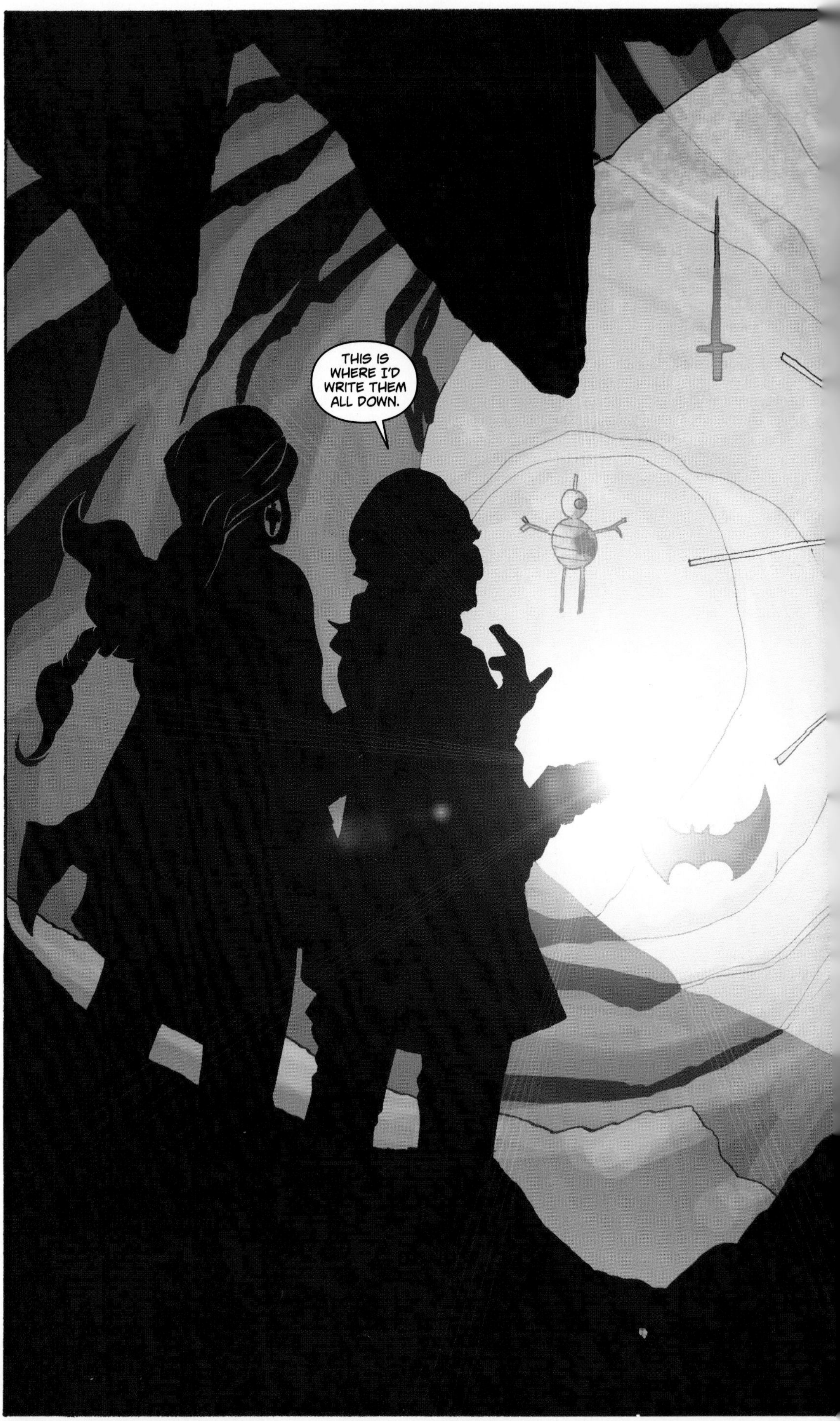
THIS IS WHERE I'D WRITE THEM ALL DOWN.

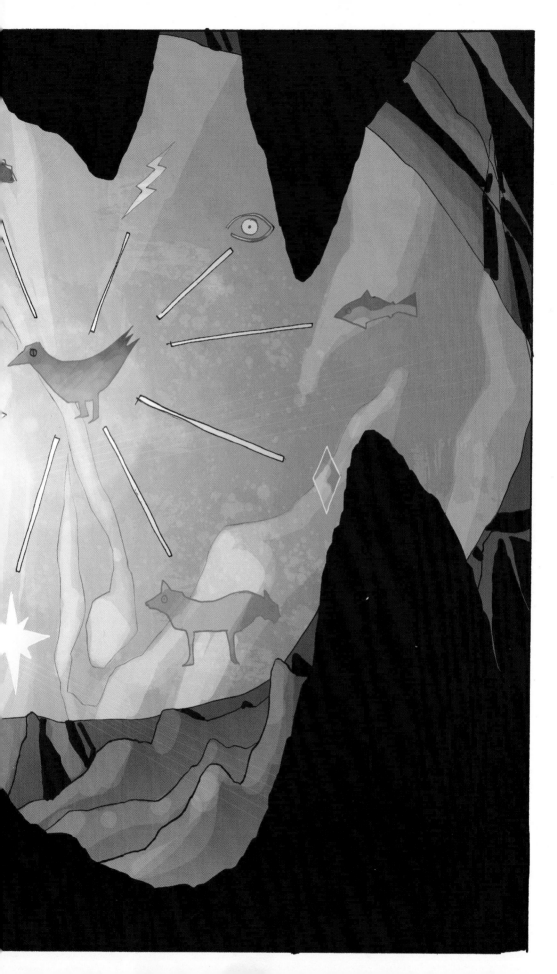

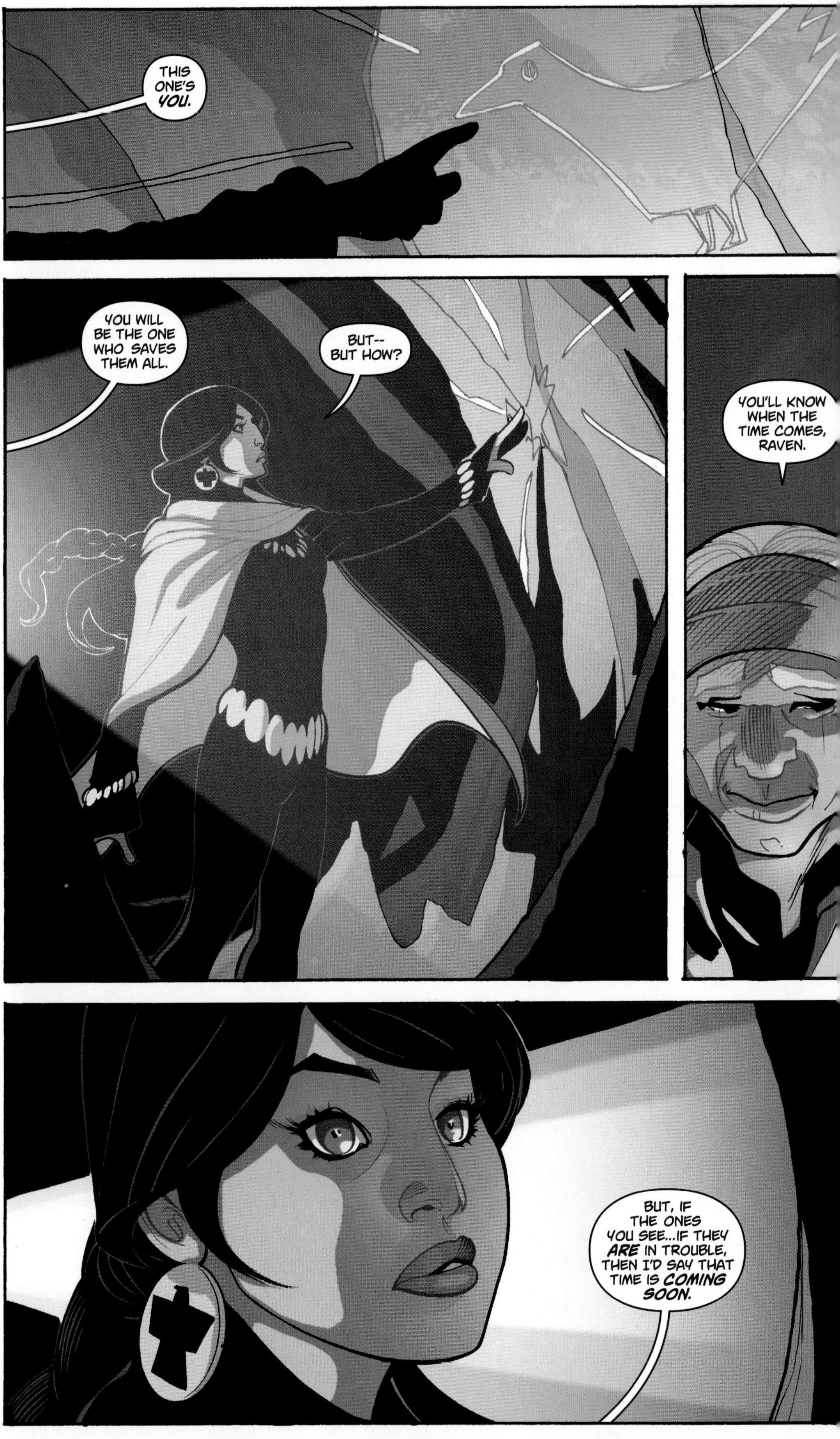
THIS ONE'S *YOU.*
YOU WILL BE THE ONE WHO SAVES THEM ALL.
BUT-- BUT HOW?
YOU'LL KNOW WHEN THE TIME COMES, RAVEN.
BUT, IF THE ONES YOU SEE...IF THEY *ARE* IN TROUBLE, THEN I'D SAY THAT TIME IS *COMING SOON.*

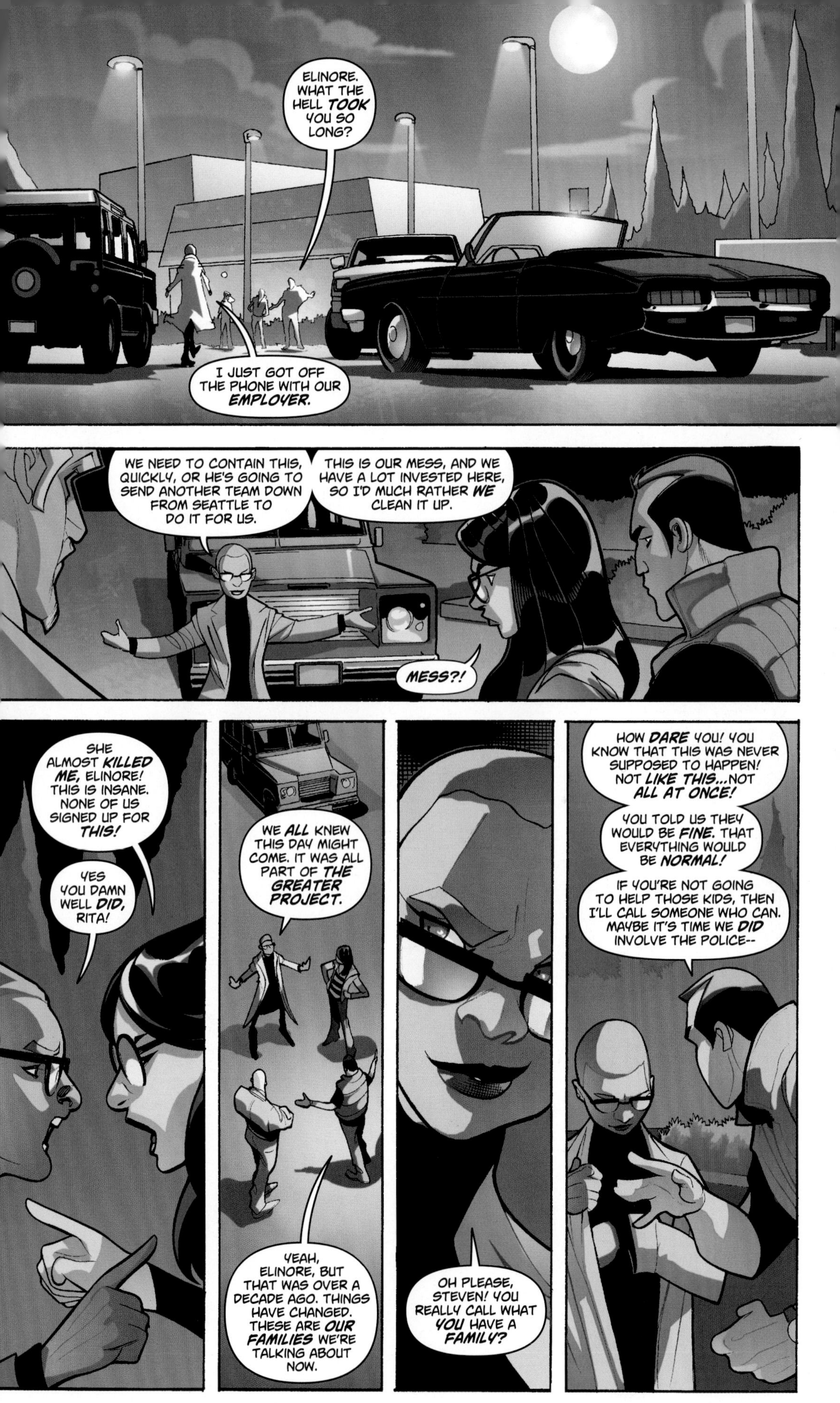

ELINORE. WHAT THE HELL TOOK YOU SO LONG?
I JUST GOT OFF THE PHONE WITH OUR EMPLOYER.
WE NEED TO CONTAIN THIS, QUICKLY, OR HE'S GOING TO SEND ANOTHER TEAM DOWN FROM SEATTLE TO DO IT FOR US.
THIS IS OUR MESS, AND WE HAVE A LOT INVESTED HERE, SO I'D MUCH RATHER WE CLEAN IT UP.
MESS?!
SHE ALMOST KILLED ME, ELINORE! THIS IS INSANE. NONE OF US SIGNED UP FOR THIS!
YES YOU DAMN WELL DID, RITA!
WE ALL KNEW THIS DAY MIGHT COME. IT WAS ALL PART OF THE GREATER PROJECT.
YEAH, ELINORE, BUT THAT WAS OVER A DECADE AGO. THINGS HAVE CHANGED. THESE ARE OUR FAMILIES WE'RE TALKING ABOUT NOW.
OH PLEASE, STEVEN! YOU REALLY CALL WHAT YOU HAVE A FAMILY?
HOW DARE YOU! YOU KNOW THAT THIS WAS NEVER SUPPOSED TO HAPPEN! NOT LIKE THIS...NOT ALL AT ONCE!
YOU TOLD US THEY WOULD BE FINE. THAT EVERYTHING WOULD BE NORMAL!
IF YOU'RE NOT GOING TO HELP THOSE KIDS, THEN I'LL CALL SOMEONE WHO CAN. MAYBE IT'S TIME WE DID INVOLVE THE POLICE--

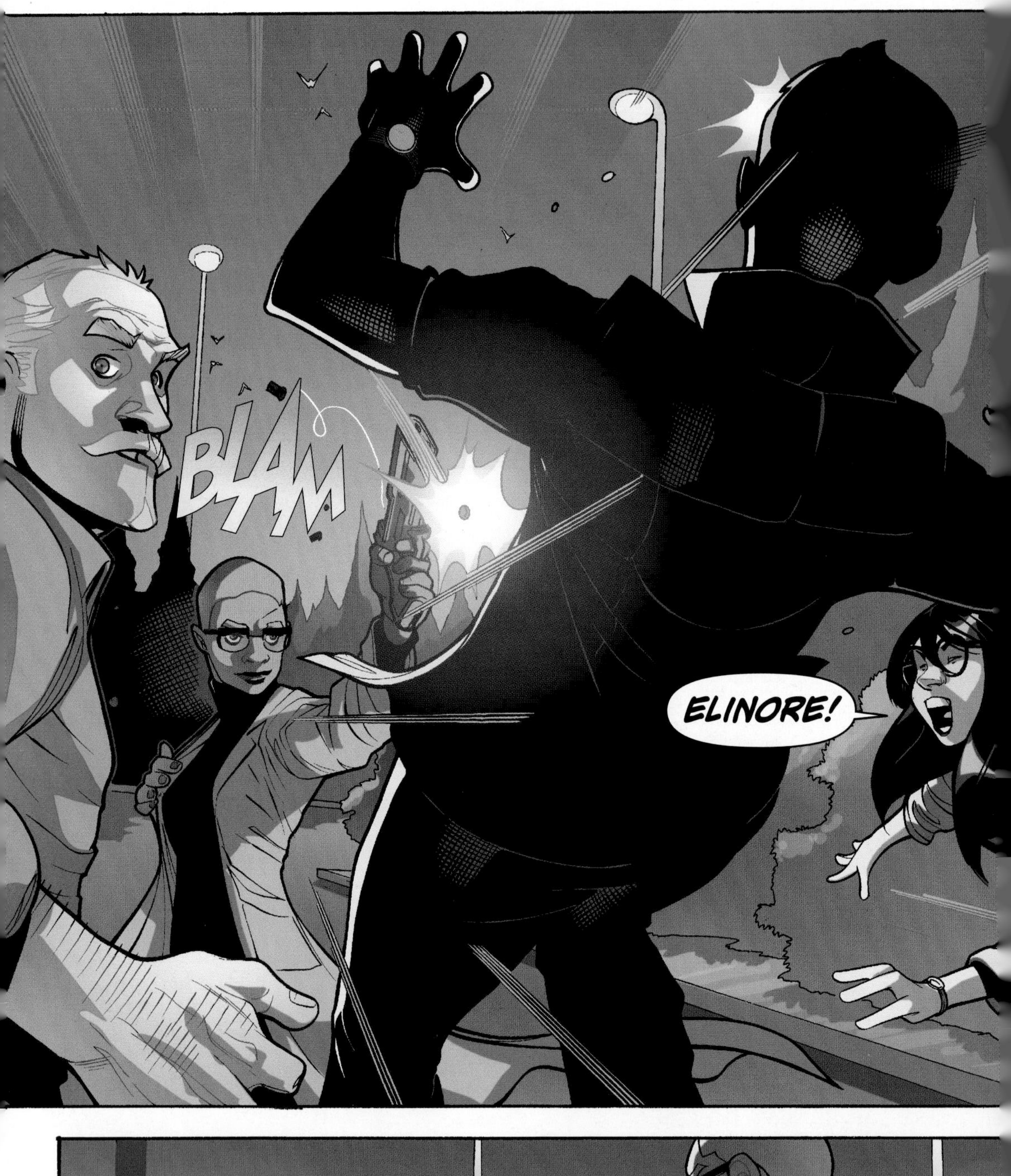
BLAM
ELINORE!

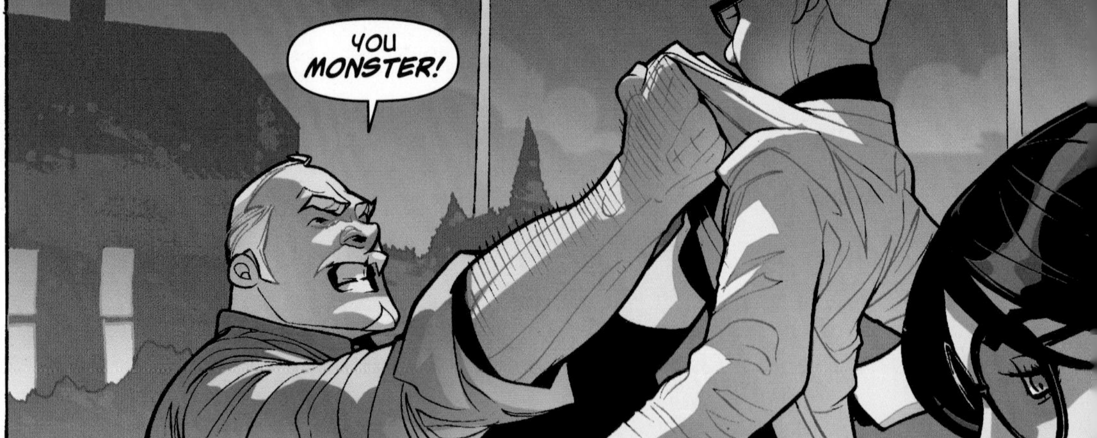
YOU MONSTER!

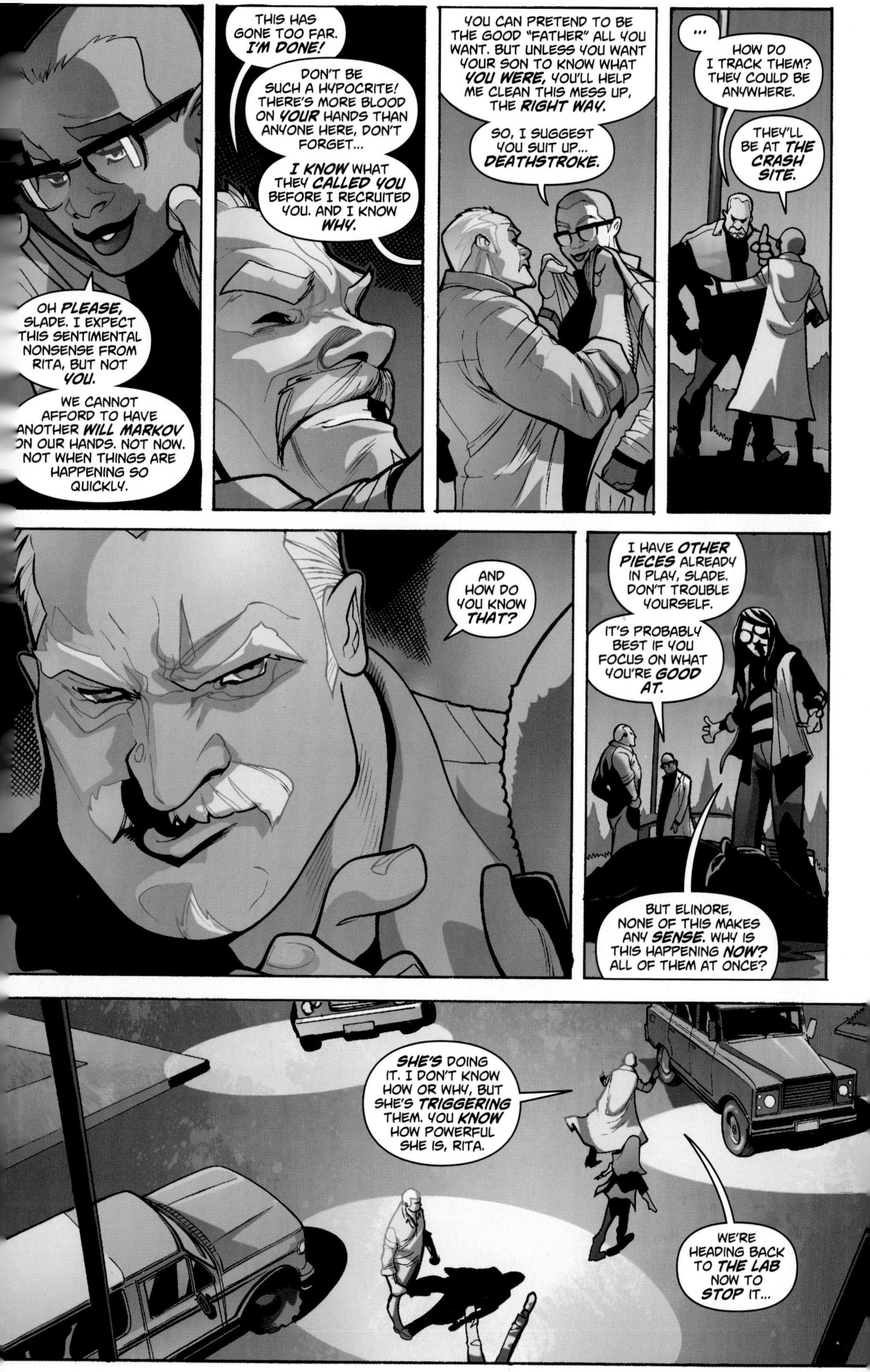
OH PLEASE, SLADE. I EXPECT THIS SENTIMENTAL NONSENSE FROM RITA, BUT NOT YOU.
WE CANNOT AFFORD TO HAVE ANOTHER WILL MARKOV ON OUR HANDS. NOT NOW. NOT WHEN THINGS ARE HAPPENING SO QUICKLY.
THIS HAS GONE TOO FAR. I'M DONE!
DON'T BE SUCH A HYPOCRITE! THERE'S MORE BLOOD ON YOUR HANDS THAN ANYONE HERE, DON'T FORGET...
I KNOW WHAT THEY CALLED YOU BEFORE I RECRUITED YOU. AND I KNOW WHY.
YOU CAN PRETEND TO BE THE GOOD "FATHER" ALL YOU WANT. BUT UNLESS YOU WANT YOUR SON TO KNOW WHAT YOU WERE, YOU'LL HELP ME CLEAN THIS MESS UP, THE RIGHT WAY.
SO, I SUGGEST YOU SUIT UP... DEATHSTROKE.
...
HOW DO I TRACK THEM? THEY COULD BE ANYWHERE.
THEY'LL BE AT THE CRASH SITE.
AND HOW DO YOU KNOW THAT?
I HAVE OTHER PIECES ALREADY IN PLAY, SLADE. DON'T TROUBLE YOURSELF.
IT'S PROBABLY BEST IF YOU FOCUS ON WHAT YOU'RE GOOD AT.
BUT ELINORE, NONE OF THIS MAKES ANY SENSE. WHY IS THIS HAPPENING NOW? ALL OF THEM AT ONCE?
SHE'S DOING IT. I DON'T KNOW HOW OR WHY, BUT SHE'S TRIGGERING THEM. YOU KNOW HOW POWERFUL SHE IS, RITA.
WE'RE HEADING BACK TO THE LAB NOW TO STOP IT...

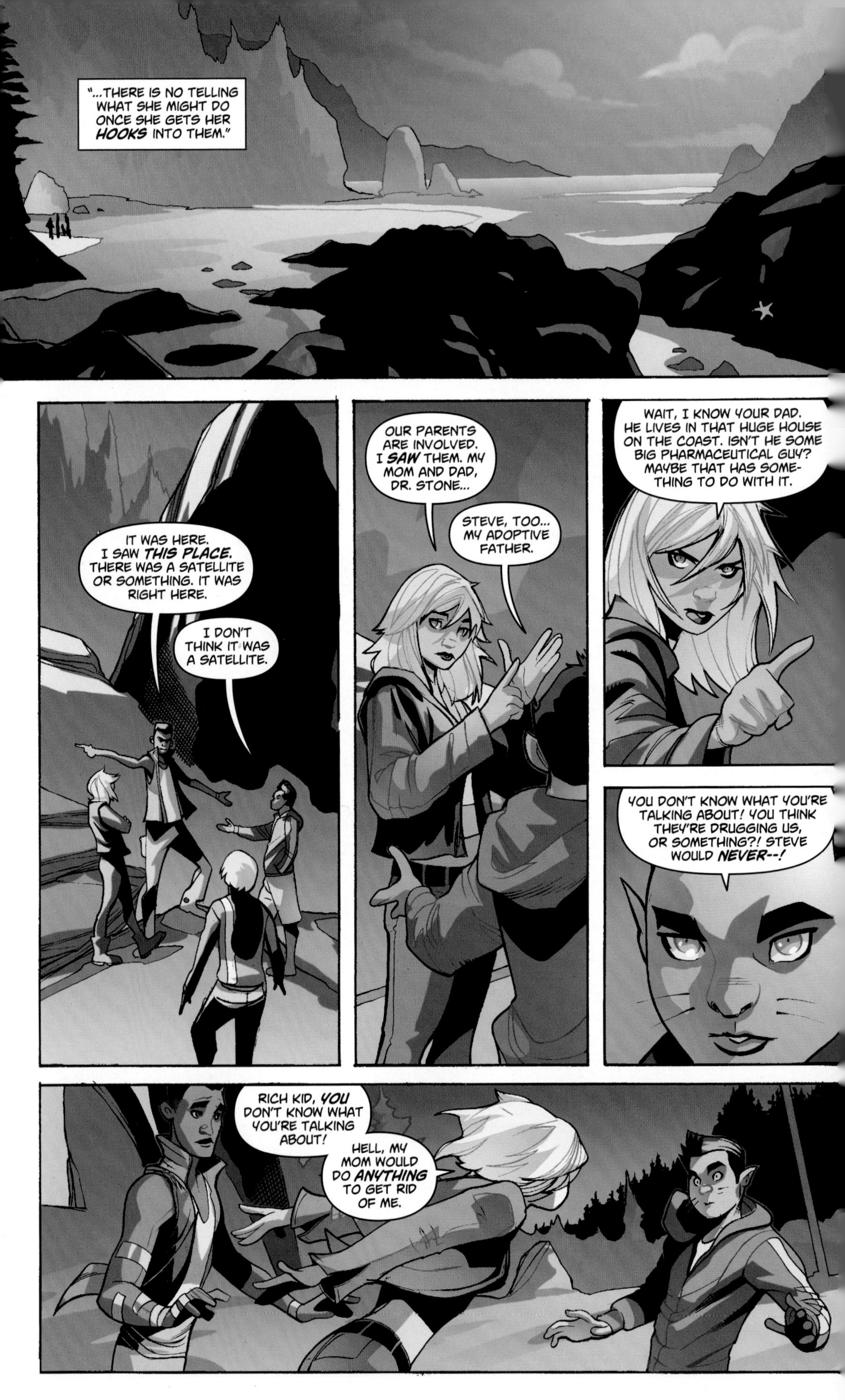
"...THERE IS NO TELLING WHAT SHE MIGHT DO ONCE SHE GETS HER HOOKS INTO THEM."
IT WAS HERE. I SAW THIS PLACE. THERE WAS A SATELLITE OR SOMETHING. IT WAS RIGHT HERE.
I DON'T THINK IT WAS A SATELLITE.
OUR PARENTS ARE INVOLVED. I SAW THEM. MY MOM AND DAD, DR. STONE...
STEVE, TOO... MY ADOPTIVE FATHER.
WAIT, I KNOW YOUR DAD. HE LIVES IN THAT HUGE HOUSE ON THE COAST. ISN'T HE SOME BIG PHARMACEUTICAL GUY? MAYBE THAT HAS SOME-THING TO DO WITH IT.
YOU DON'T KNOW WHAT YOU'RE TALKING ABOUT! YOU THINK THEY'RE DRUGGING US, OR SOMETHING?! STEVE WOULD NEVER--!
RICH KID, YOU DON'T KNOW WHAT YOU'RE TALKING ABOUT!
HELL, MY MOM WOULD DO ANYTHING TO GET RID OF ME.

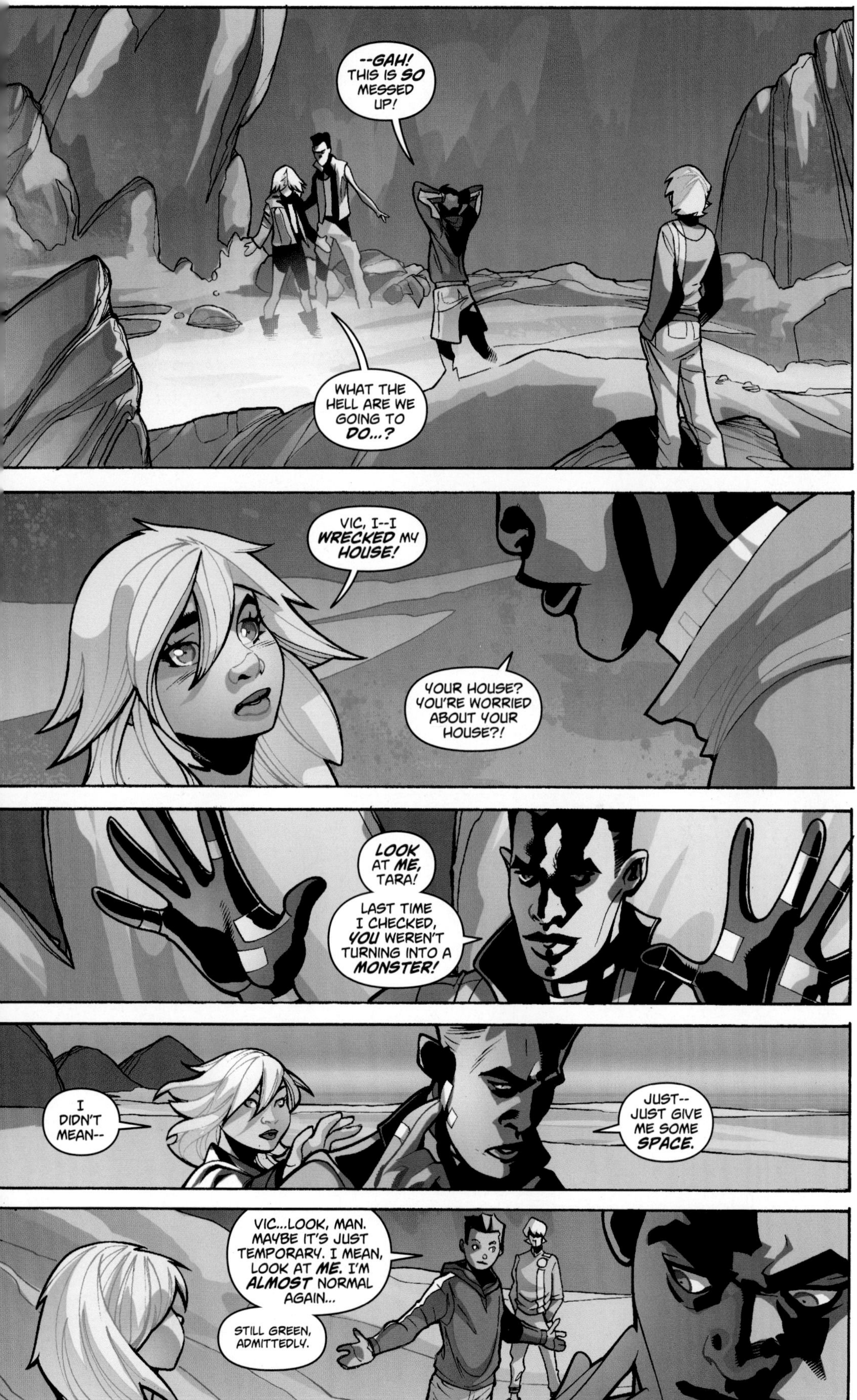
--GAH! THIS IS SO MESSED UP!
WHAT THE HELL ARE WE GOING TO DO...?
VIC, I--I WRECKED MY HOUSE!
YOUR HOUSE? YOU'RE WORRIED ABOUT YOUR HOUSE?!
LOOK AT ME, TARA!
LAST TIME I CHECKED, YOU WEREN'T TURNING INTO A MONSTER!
I DIDN'T MEAN--
JUST-- JUST GIVE ME SOME SPACE.
VIC...LOOK, MAN. MAYBE IT'S JUST TEMPORARY. I MEAN, LOOK AT ME. I'M ALMOST NORMAL AGAIN...
STILL GREEN, ADMITTEDLY.

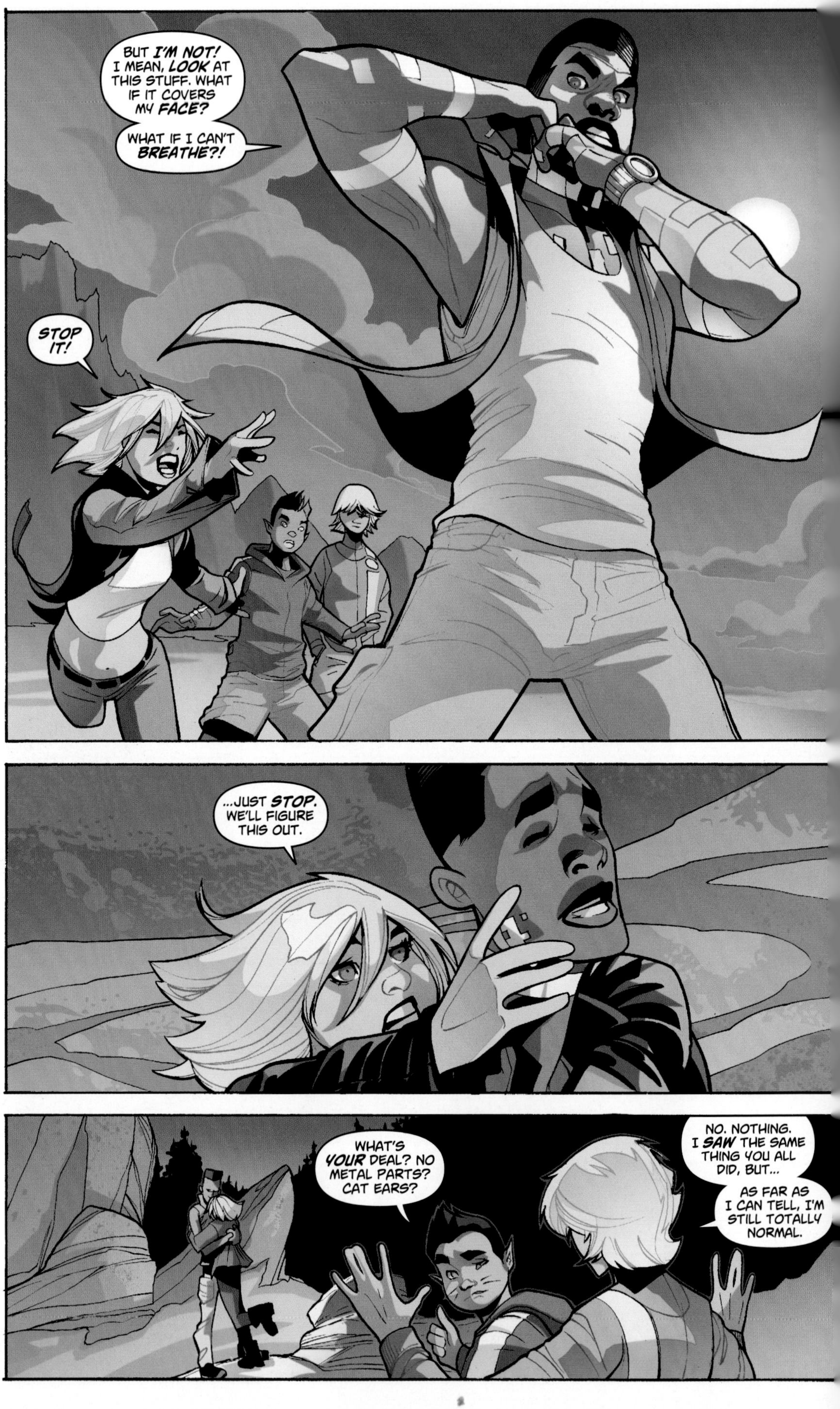
BUT I'M NOT! I MEAN, LOOK AT THIS STUFF. WHAT IF IT COVERS MY FACE?
WHAT IF I CAN'T BREATHE?!
STOP IT!
...JUST STOP. WE'LL FIGURE THIS OUT.
WHAT'S YOUR DEAL? NO METAL PARTS? CAT EARS?
NO. NOTHING. I SAW THE SAME THING YOU ALL DID, BUT...
AS FAR AS I CAN TELL, I'M STILL TOTALLY NORMAL.

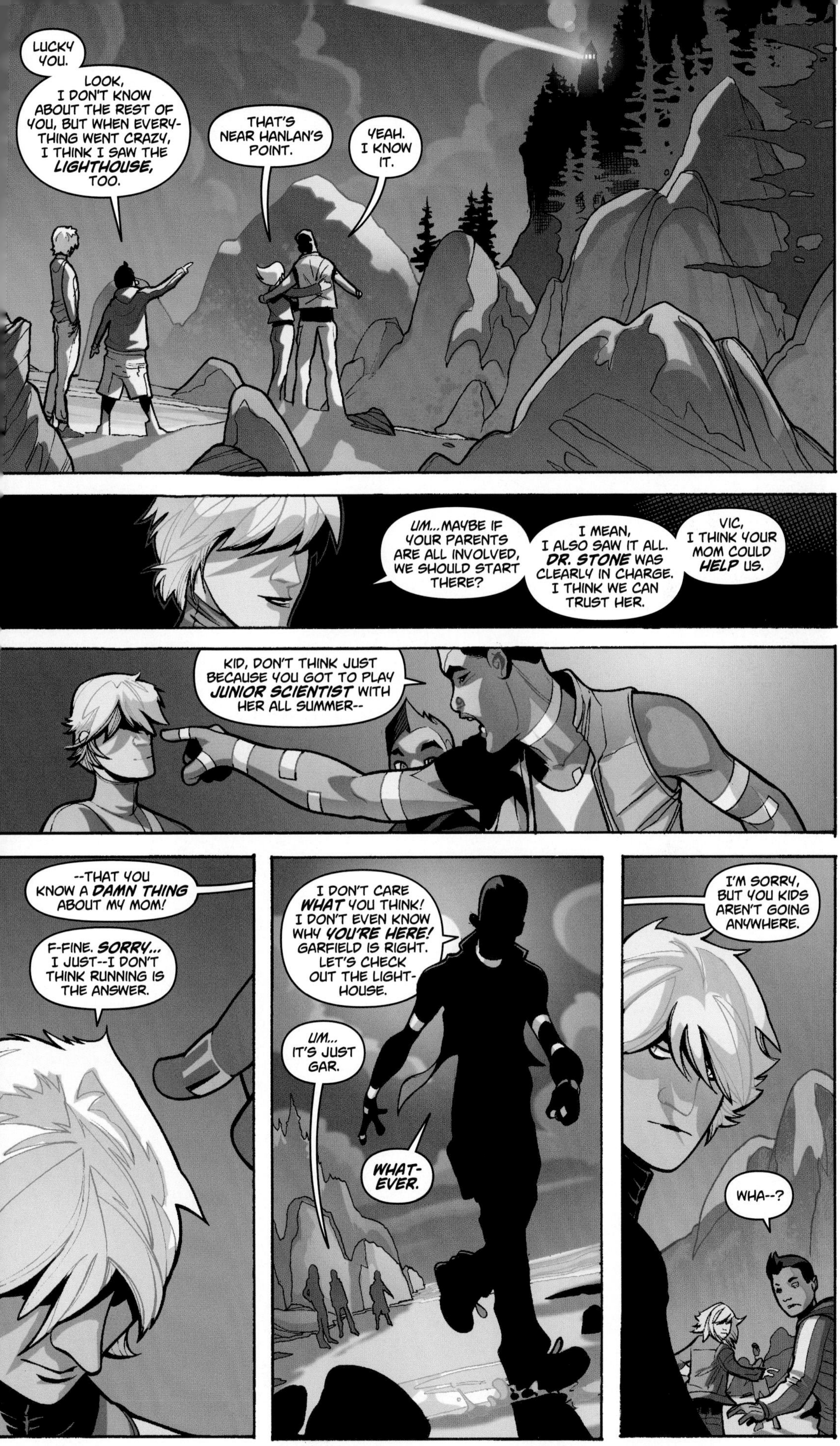
LUCKY YOU.
LOOK, I DON'T KNOW ABOUT THE REST OF YOU, BUT WHEN EVERYTHING WENT CRAZY, I THINK I SAW THE **LIGHTHOUSE,** TOO.
THAT'S NEAR HANLAN'S POINT.
YEAH. I KNOW IT.
UM...MAYBE IF YOUR PARENTS ARE ALL INVOLVED, WE SHOULD START THERE?
I MEAN, I ALSO SAW IT ALL. **DR. STONE** WAS CLEARLY IN CHARGE. I THINK WE CAN TRUST HER.
VIC, I THINK YOUR MOM COULD **HELP** US.
KID, DON'T THINK JUST BECAUSE YOU GOT TO PLAY **JUNIOR SCIENTIST** WITH HER ALL SUMMER--
--THAT YOU KNOW A **DAMN THING** ABOUT MY MOM!
F-FINE. **SORRY...** I JUST--I DON'T THINK RUNNING IS THE ANSWER.
I DON'T CARE **WHAT** YOU THINK! I DON'T EVEN KNOW WHY **YOU'RE HERE!** GARFIELD IS RIGHT. LET'S CHECK OUT THE LIGHTHOUSE.
UM... IT'S JUST GAR.
WHATEVER.
I'M SORRY, BUT YOU KIDS AREN'T GOING ANYWHERE.
WHA--?

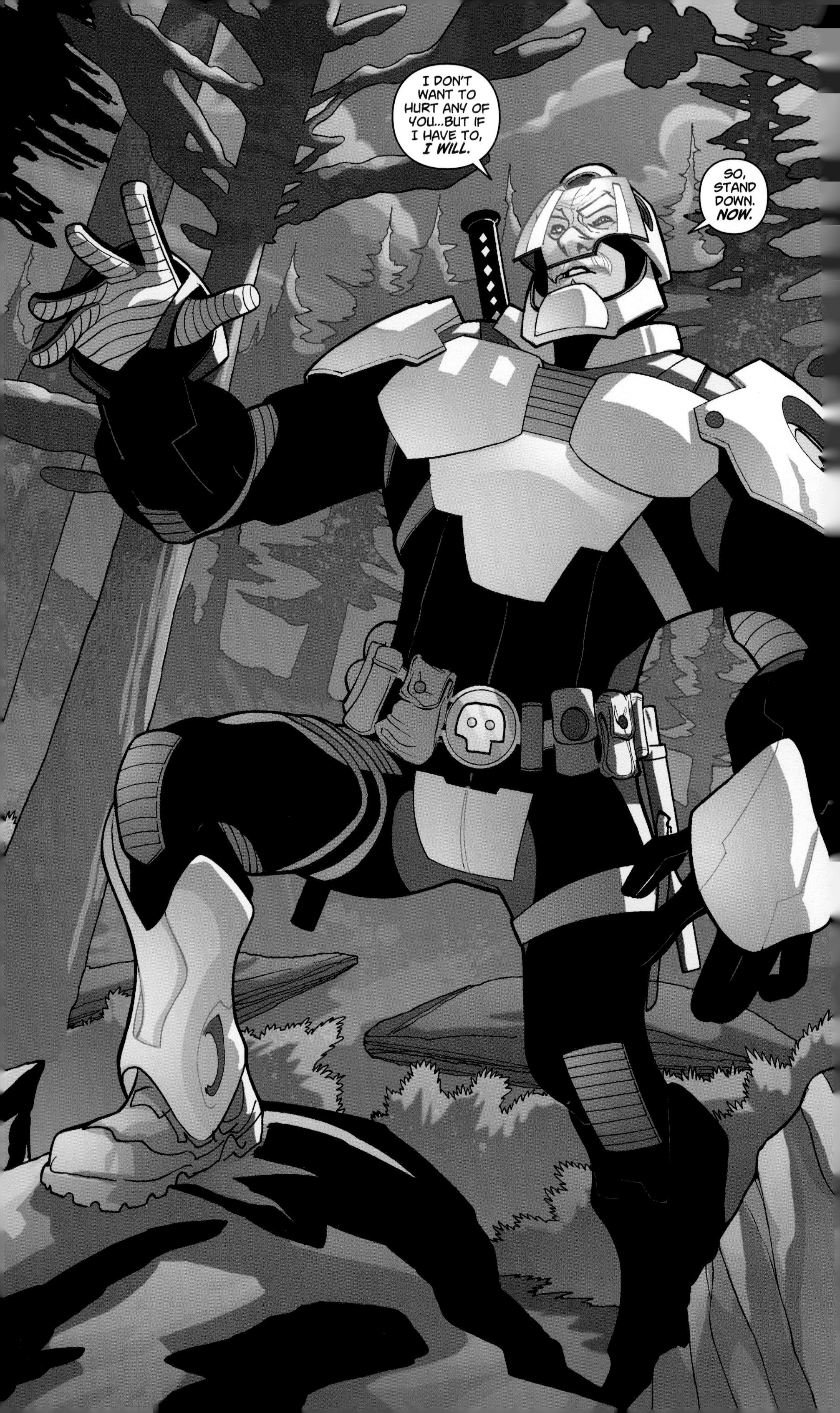
I DON'T WANT TO HURT ANY OF YOU...BUT IF I HAVE TO, *I WILL.*
SO, STAND DOWN. *NOW.*

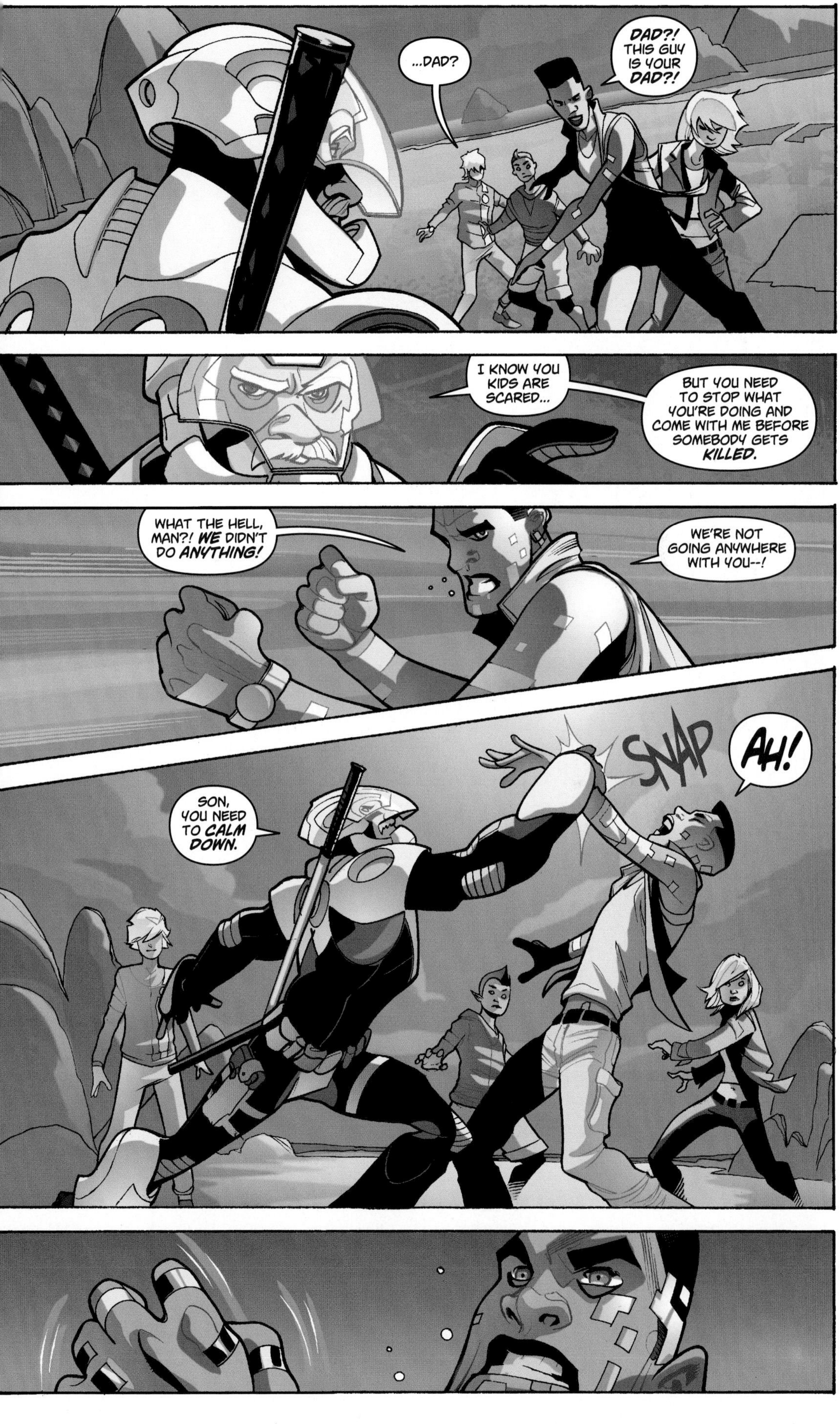
...DAD?
DAD?! THIS GUY IS YOUR DAD?!
I KNOW YOU KIDS ARE SCARED...
BUT YOU NEED TO STOP WHAT YOU'RE DOING AND COME WITH ME BEFORE SOMEBODY GETS KILLED.
WHAT THE HELL, MAN?! WE DIDN'T DO ANYTHING!
WE'RE NOT GOING ANYWHERE WITH YOU--!
SNAP
AH!
SON, YOU NEED TO CALM DOWN.

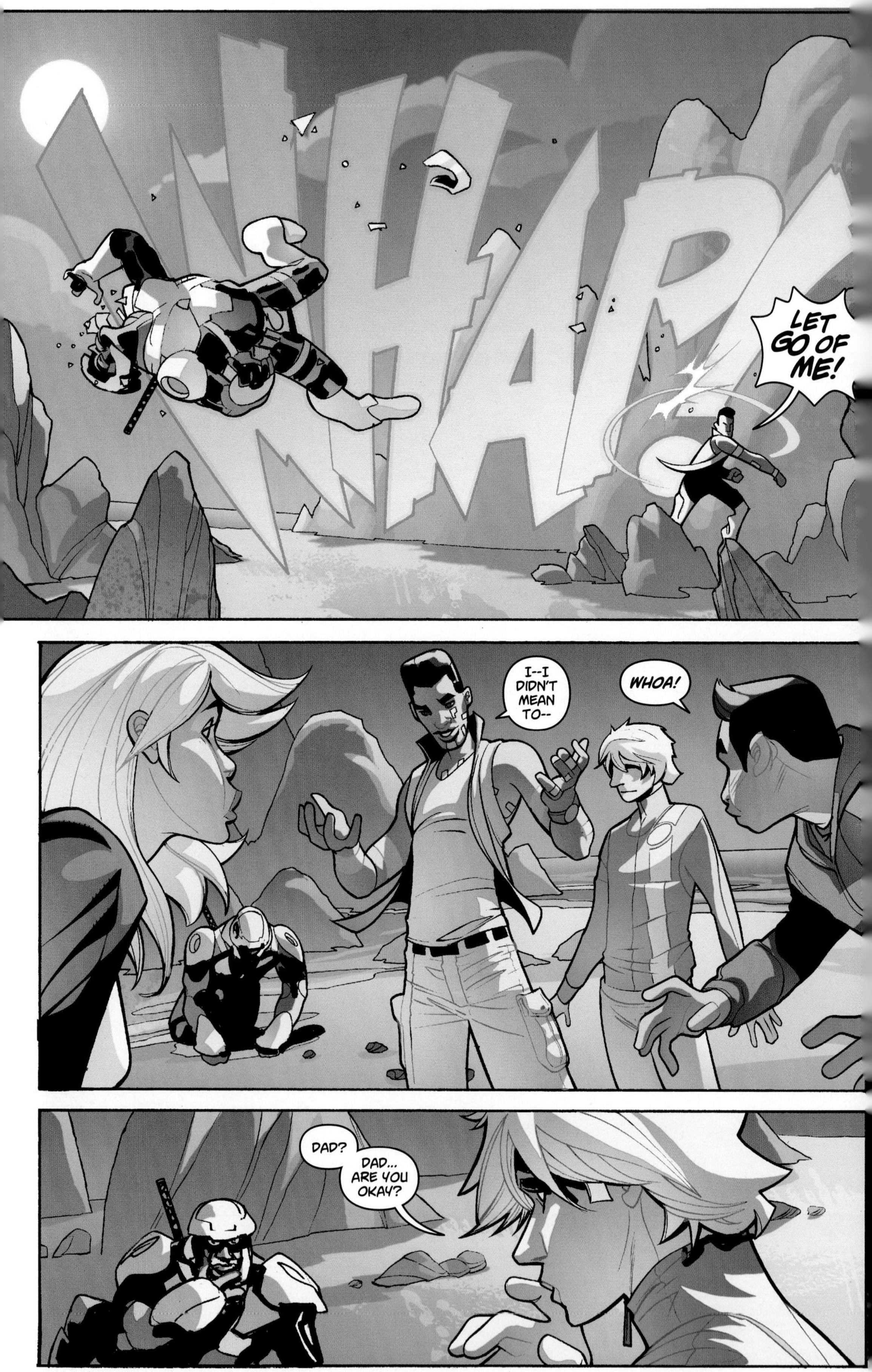
WHAP!
LET GO OF ME!
I--I DIDN'T MEAN TO--
WHOA!
DAD?
DAD... ARE YOU OKAY?

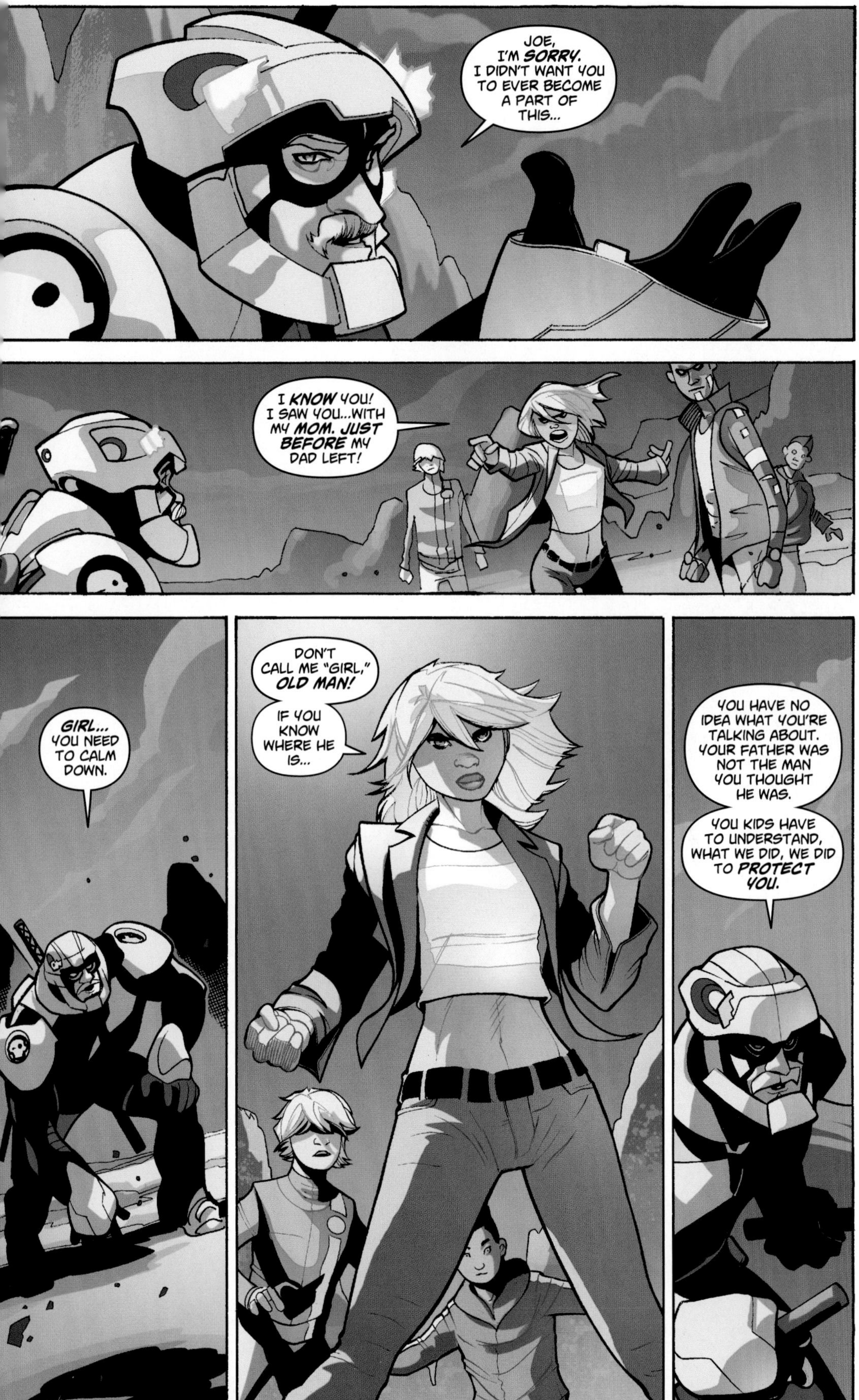
JOE, I'M SORRY. I DIDN'T WANT YOU TO EVER BECOME A PART OF THIS...
I KNOW YOU! I SAW YOU...WITH MY MOM. JUST BEFORE MY DAD LEFT!
GIRL... YOU NEED TO CALM DOWN.
DON'T CALL ME "GIRL," OLD MAN!
IF YOU KNOW WHERE HE IS...
YOU HAVE NO IDEA WHAT YOU'RE TALKING ABOUT. YOUR FATHER WAS NOT THE MAN YOU THOUGHT HE WAS.
YOU KIDS HAVE TO UNDERSTAND, WHAT WE DID, WE DID TO PROTECT YOU.

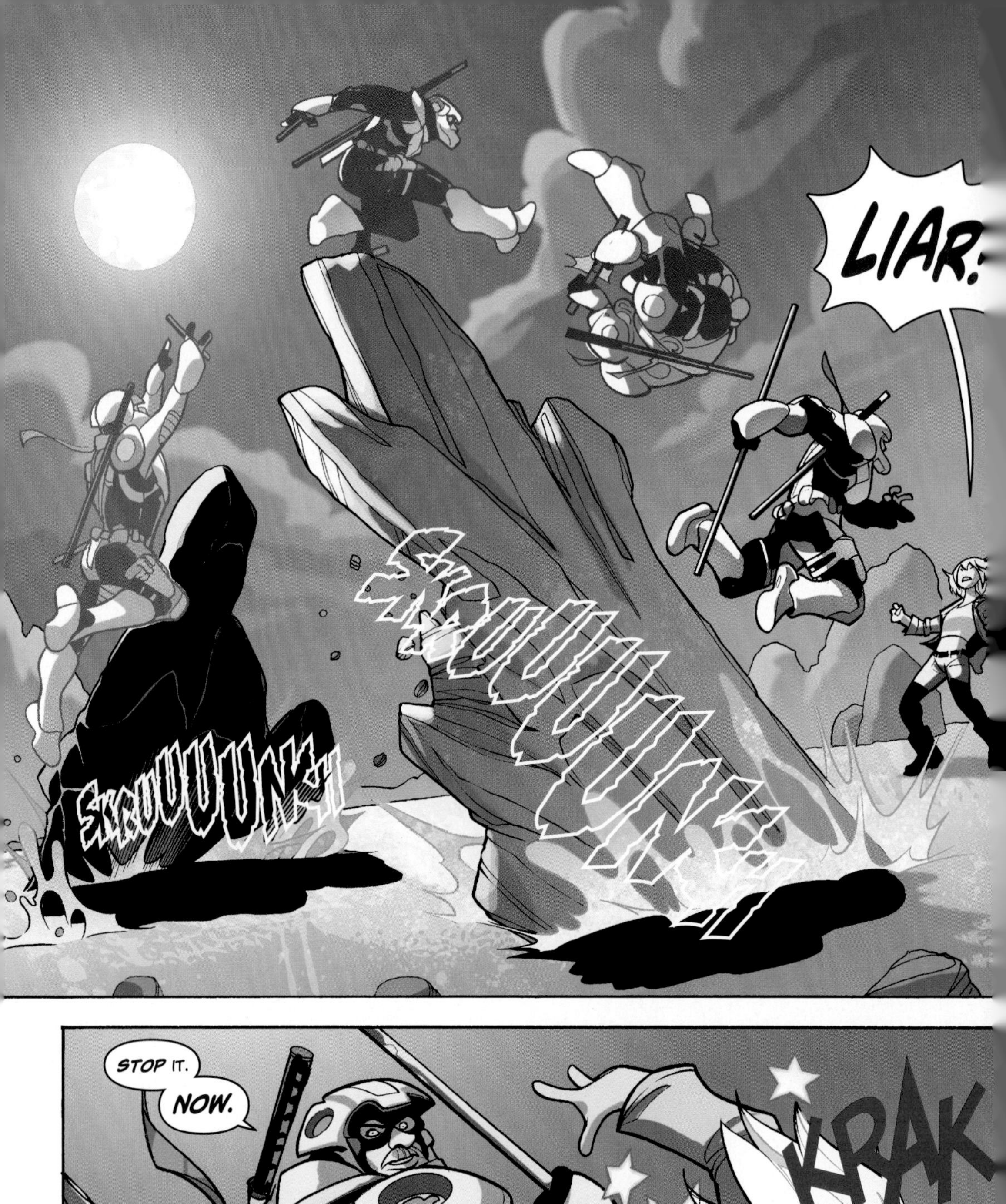
LIAR!
SKRUUUUNK!
SKRUUUUNK!

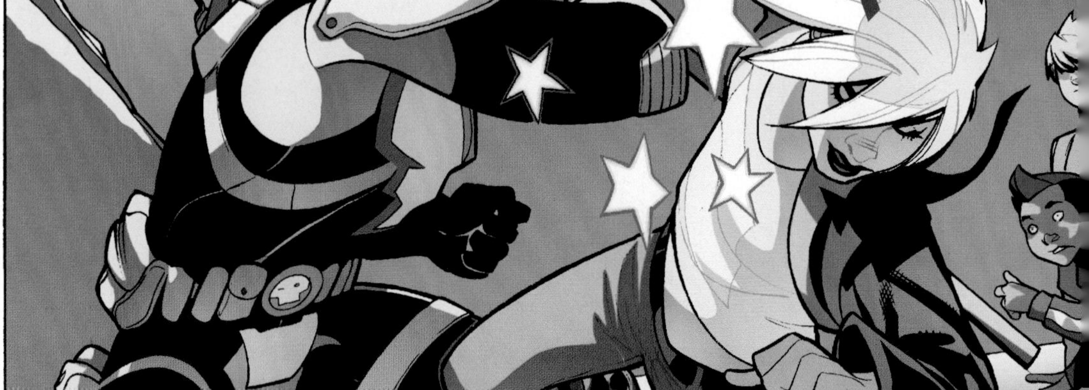
STOP IT.
NOW.
KRAK

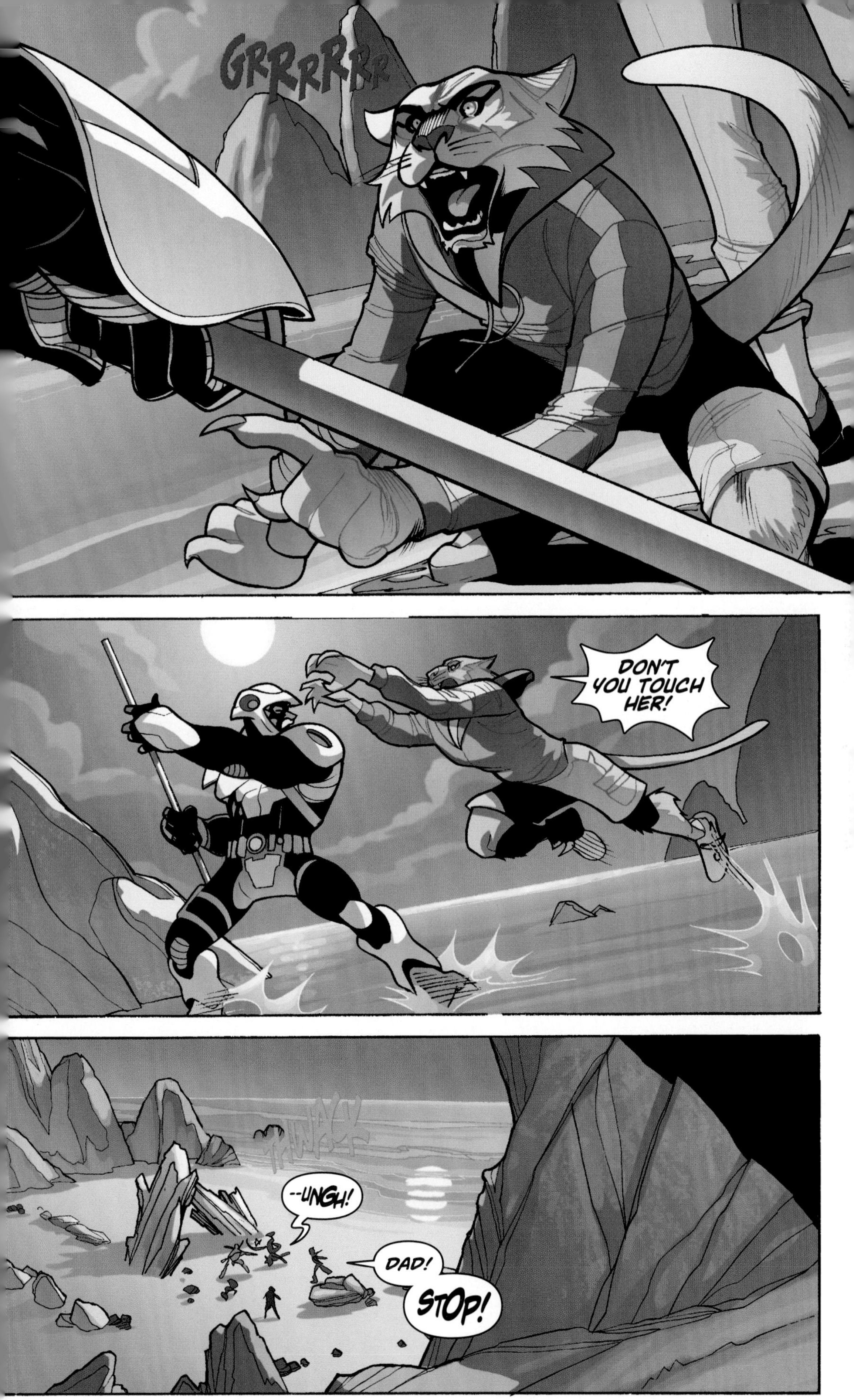
GRRRRRR
DON'T YOU TOUCH HER!
THWACK
--UNGH!
DAD!
STOP!

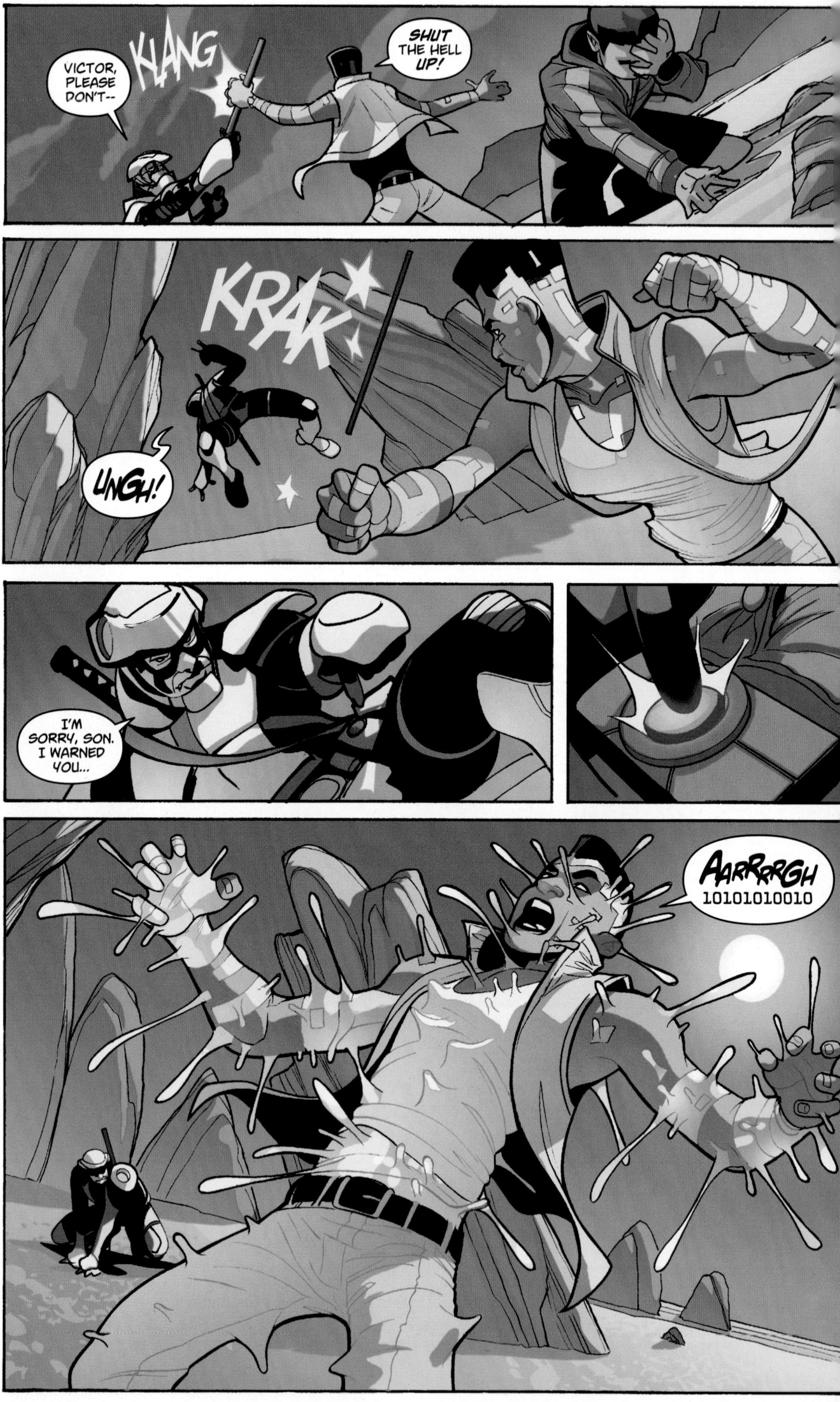
VICTOR, PLEASE DON'T--
KLANG
SHUT THE HELL UP!
KRAK
UNGH!
I'M SORRY, SON. I WARNED YOU...
AARRRRGH
10101010010

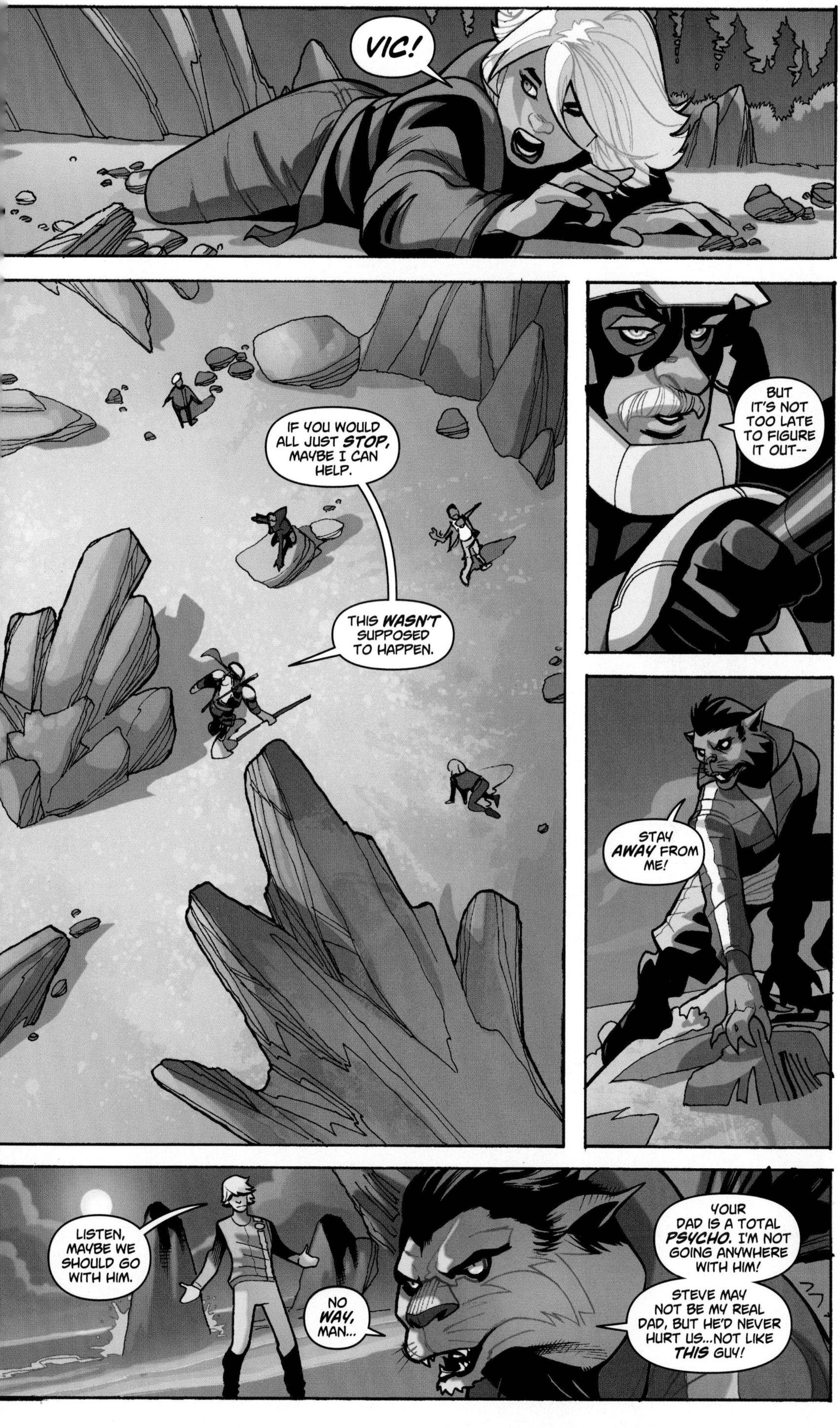
VIC!
IF YOU WOULD ALL JUST STOP, MAYBE I CAN HELP.
THIS WASN'T SUPPOSED TO HAPPEN.
BUT IT'S NOT TOO LATE TO FIGURE IT OUT--
STAY AWAY FROM ME!
LISTEN, MAYBE WE SHOULD GO WITH HIM.
NO WAY, MAN...
YOUR DAD IS A TOTAL PSYCHO. I'M NOT GOING ANYWHERE WITH HIM!
STEVE MAY NOT BE MY REAL DAD, BUT HE'D NEVER HURT US...NOT LIKE THIS GUY!

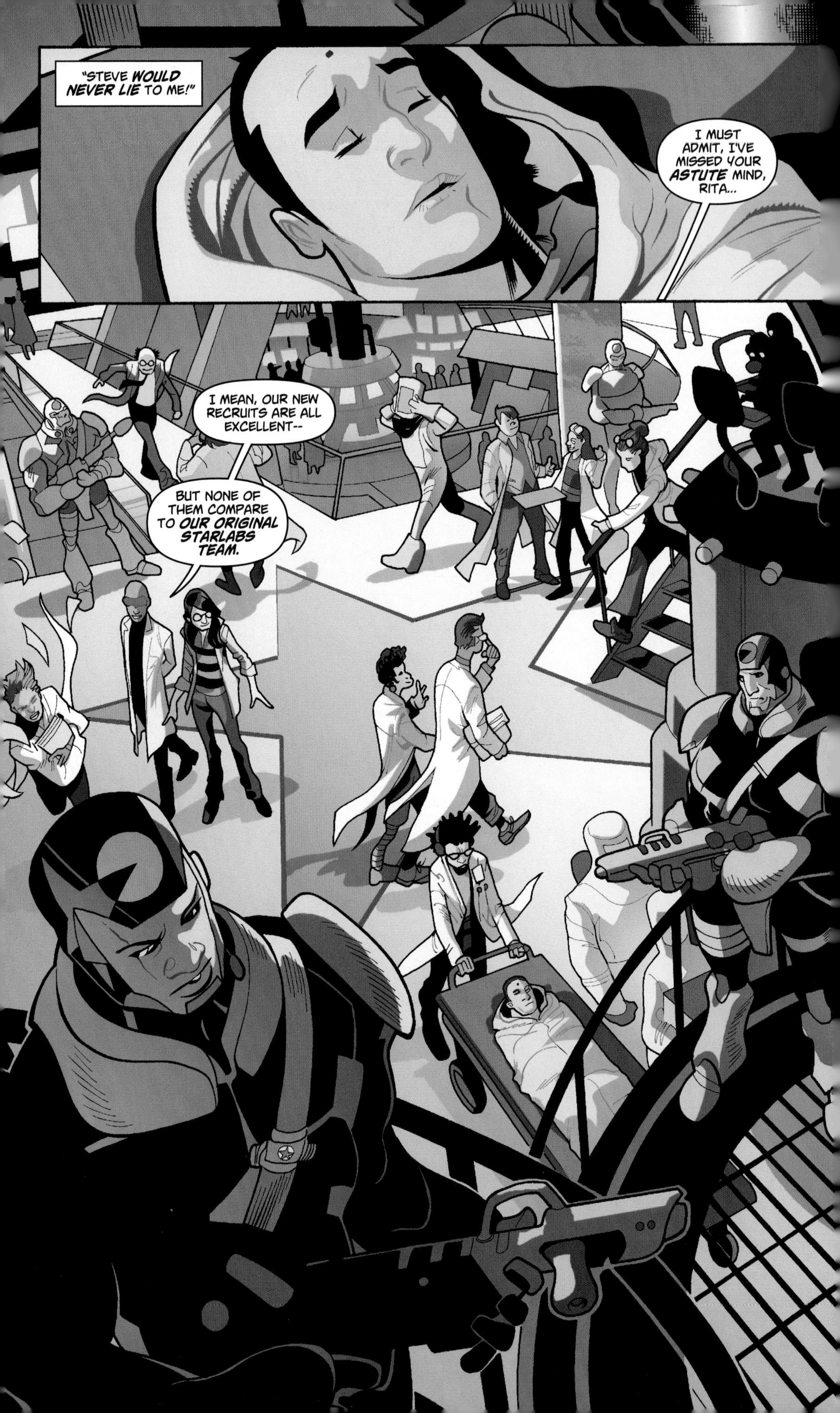
"STEVE WOULD NEVER LIE TO ME!"
I MUST ADMIT, I'VE MISSED YOUR ASTUTE MIND, RITA...
I MEAN, OUR NEW RECRUITS ARE ALL EXCELLENT--
BUT NONE OF THEM COMPARE TO OUR ORIGINAL STARLABS TEAM.

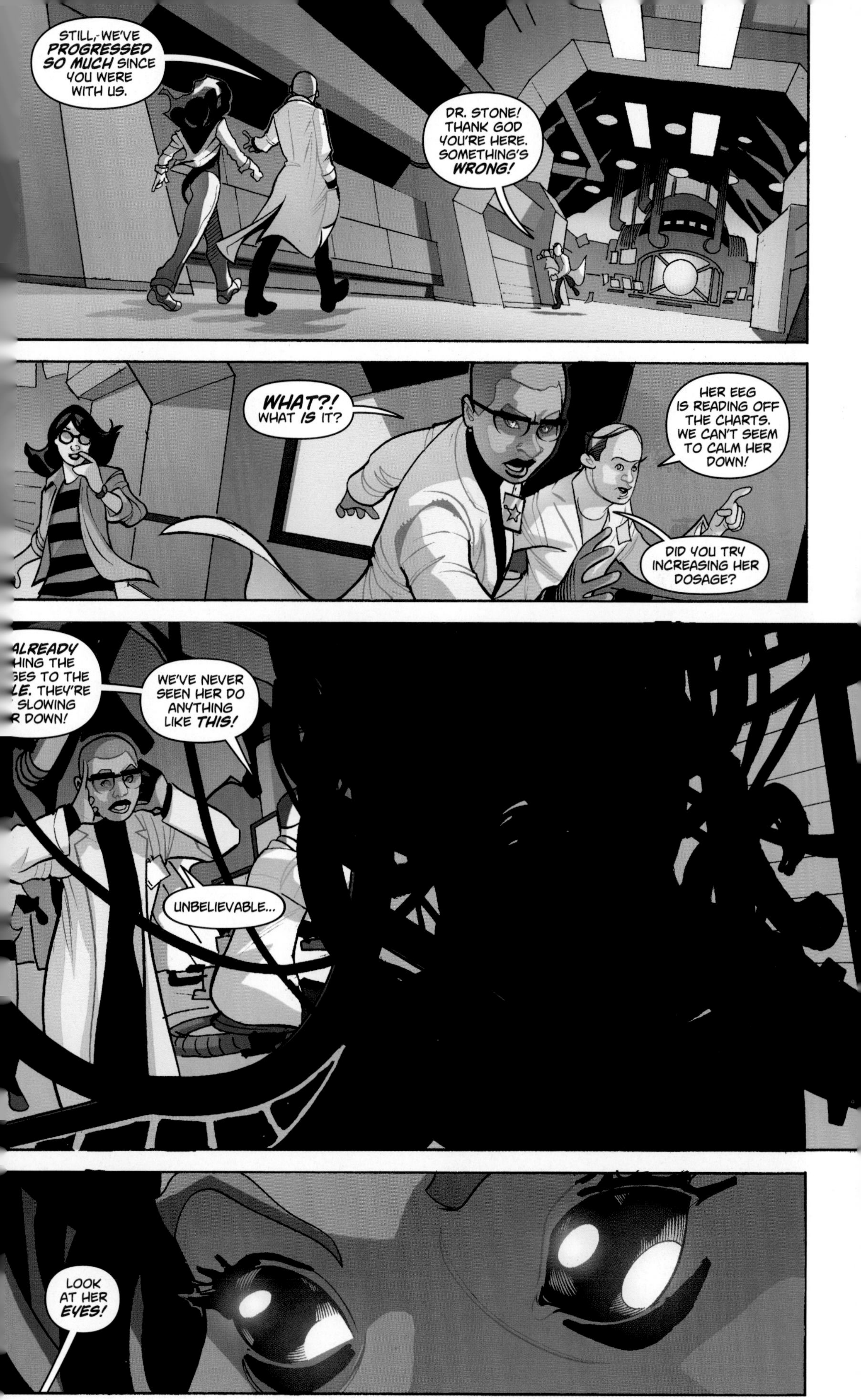
STILL, WE'VE PROGRESSED SO MUCH SINCE YOU WERE WITH US.
DR. STONE! THANK GOD YOU'RE HERE. SOMETHING'S WRONG!
WHAT?! WHAT IS IT?
HER EEG IS READING OFF THE CHARTS. WE CAN'T SEEM TO CALM HER DOWN!
DID YOU TRY INCREASING HER DOSAGE?
WE'VE NEVER SEEN HER DO ANYTHING LIKE THIS!
UNBELIEVABLE...
LOOK AT HER EYES!

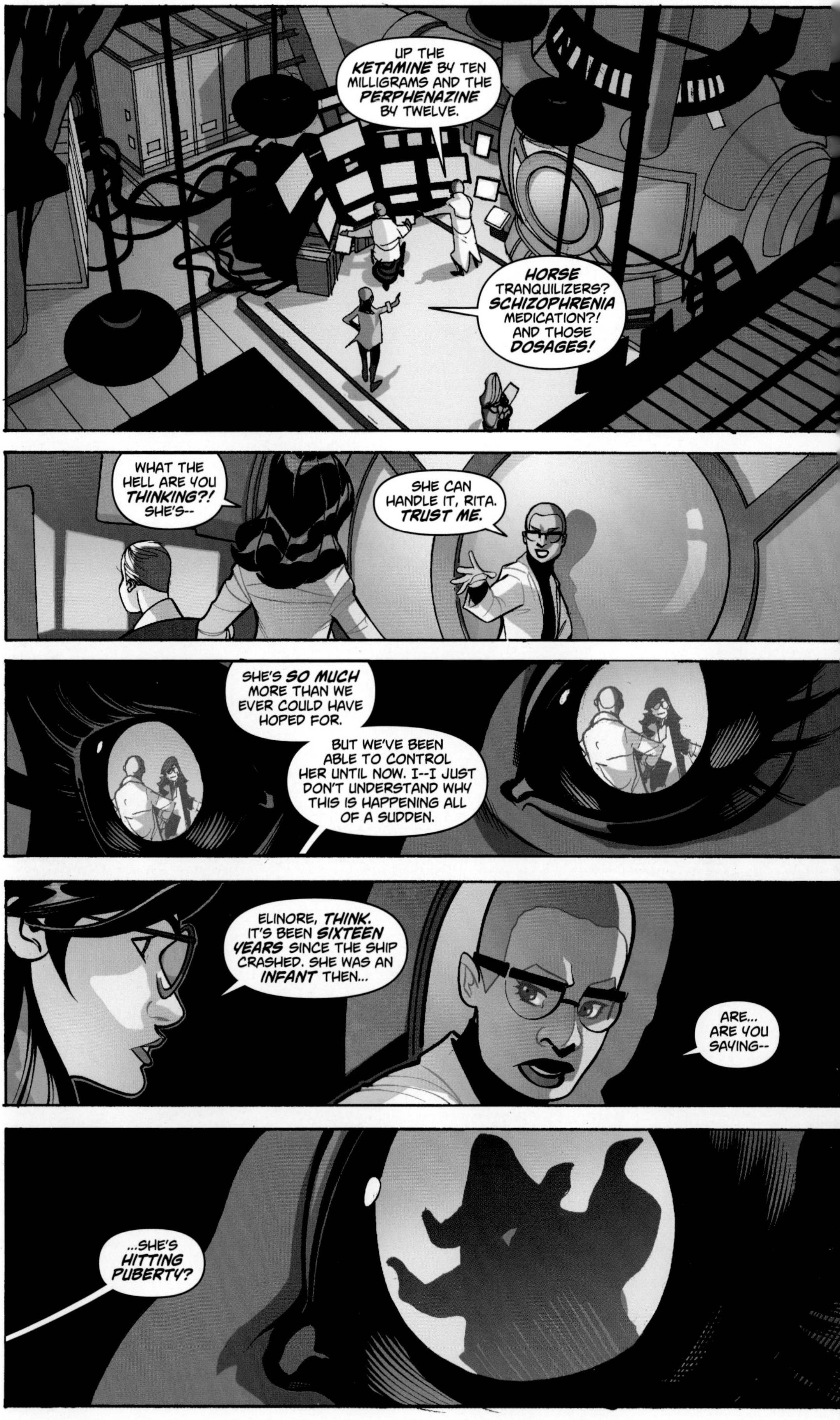
UP THE KETAMINE BY TEN MILLIGRAMS AND THE PERPHENAZINE BY TWELVE.
HORSE TRANQUILIZERS? SCHIZOPHRENIA MEDICATION?! AND THOSE DOSAGES!
WHAT THE HELL ARE YOU THINKING?! SHE'S--
SHE CAN HANDLE IT, RITA. TRUST ME.
SHE'S SO MUCH MORE THAN WE EVER COULD HAVE HOPED FOR.
BUT WE'VE BEEN ABLE TO CONTROL HER UNTIL NOW. I--I JUST DON'T UNDERSTAND WHY THIS IS HAPPENING ALL OF A SUDDEN.
ELINORE, THINK. IT'S BEEN SIXTEEN YEARS SINCE THE SHIP CRASHED. SHE WAS AN INFANT THEN...
ARE... ARE YOU SAYING--
...SHE'S HITTING PUBERTY?

AM STARFIRE...
...NEED HELP.
RAVEN?
RAVEN!
J--JUST HOLD ON, GRANDDAUGHTER... HOLD ON!

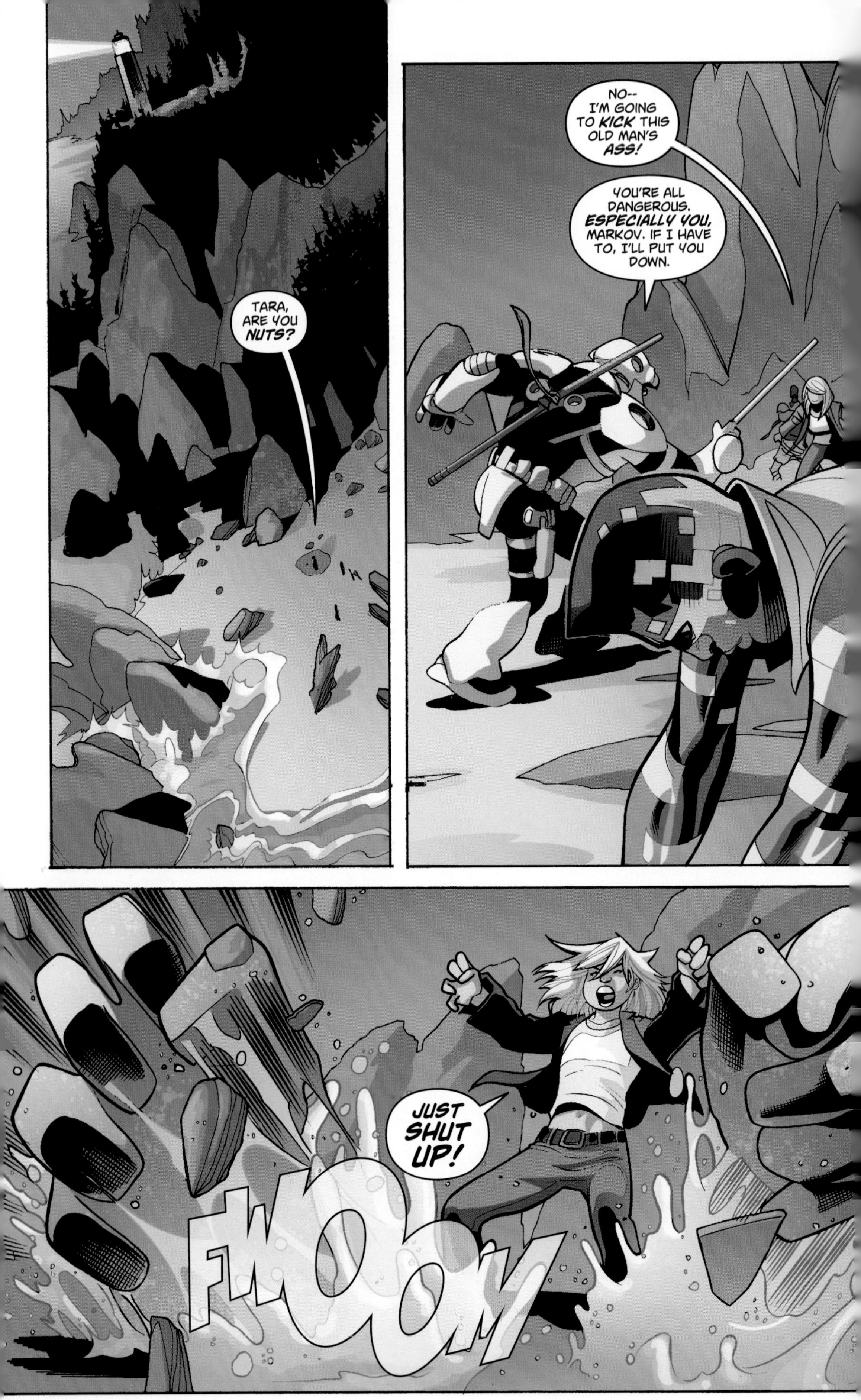
TARA, ARE YOU NUTS?
NO-- I'M GOING TO KICK THIS OLD MAN'S ASS!
YOU'RE ALL DANGEROUS. ESPECIALLY YOU, MARKOV. IF I HAVE TO, I'LL PUT YOU DOWN.
JUST SHUT UP!
FWOOOM

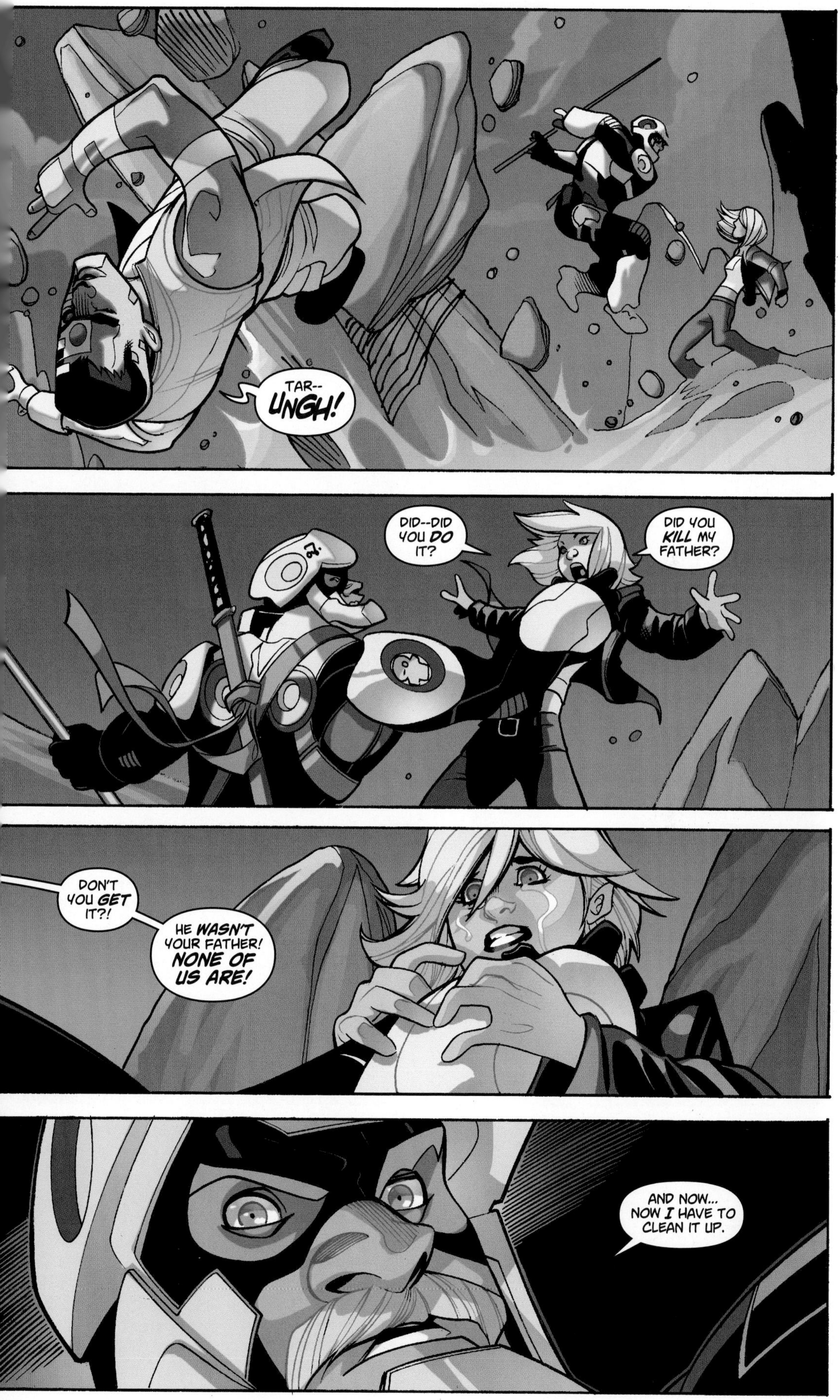
TAR--
UNGH!
DID--DID YOU DO IT?
DID YOU KILL MY FATHER?
DON'T YOU GET IT?!
HE WASN'T YOUR FATHER! NONE OF US ARE!
AND NOW... NOW I HAVE TO CLEAN IT UP.

THE SPIRIT HAS YOU NOW, GIRL. BUT DO NOT BE SCARED. COURAGE IS ITS DOORWAY.

LET MY BLOOD GUIDE YOU.

FEEL IT IN YOU, RAVEN. THE *OLD* WAYS. THE *NAVAJO* WAY.

LET IT CLEANSE YOU.

NEED HELP.

I--I'M TRYING TO HELP YOU, GRANDDAUGHTER.

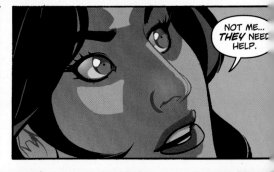

NOT ME... *THEY* NEED HELP.

...

THEN IT IS TIME. *YOU* NEED TO HELP THEM.

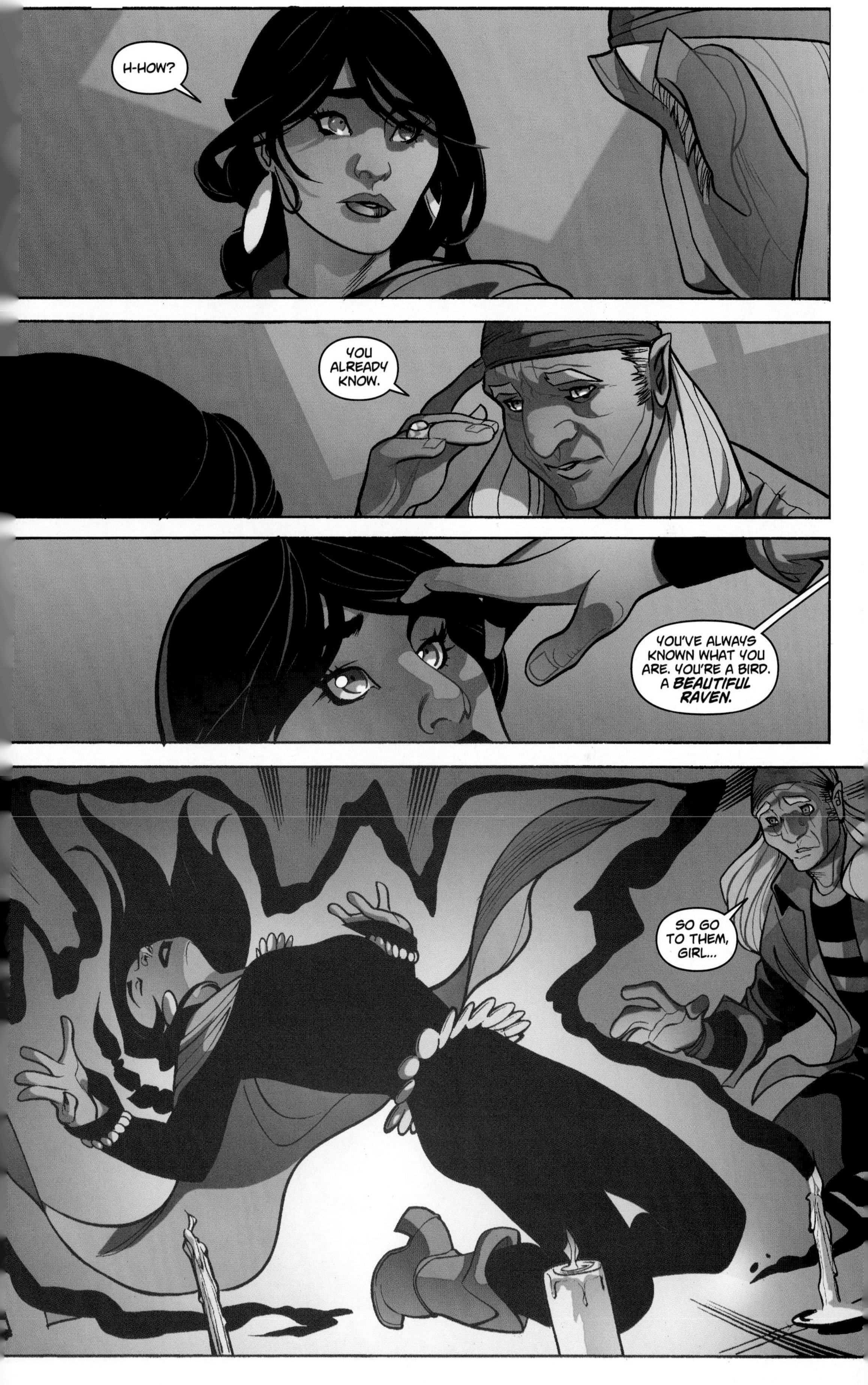
H-HOW?
YOU ALREADY KNOW.
YOU'VE ALWAYS KNOWN WHAT YOU ARE. YOU'RE A BIRD. A ***BEAUTIFUL RAVEN.***
SO GO TO THEM, GIRL...

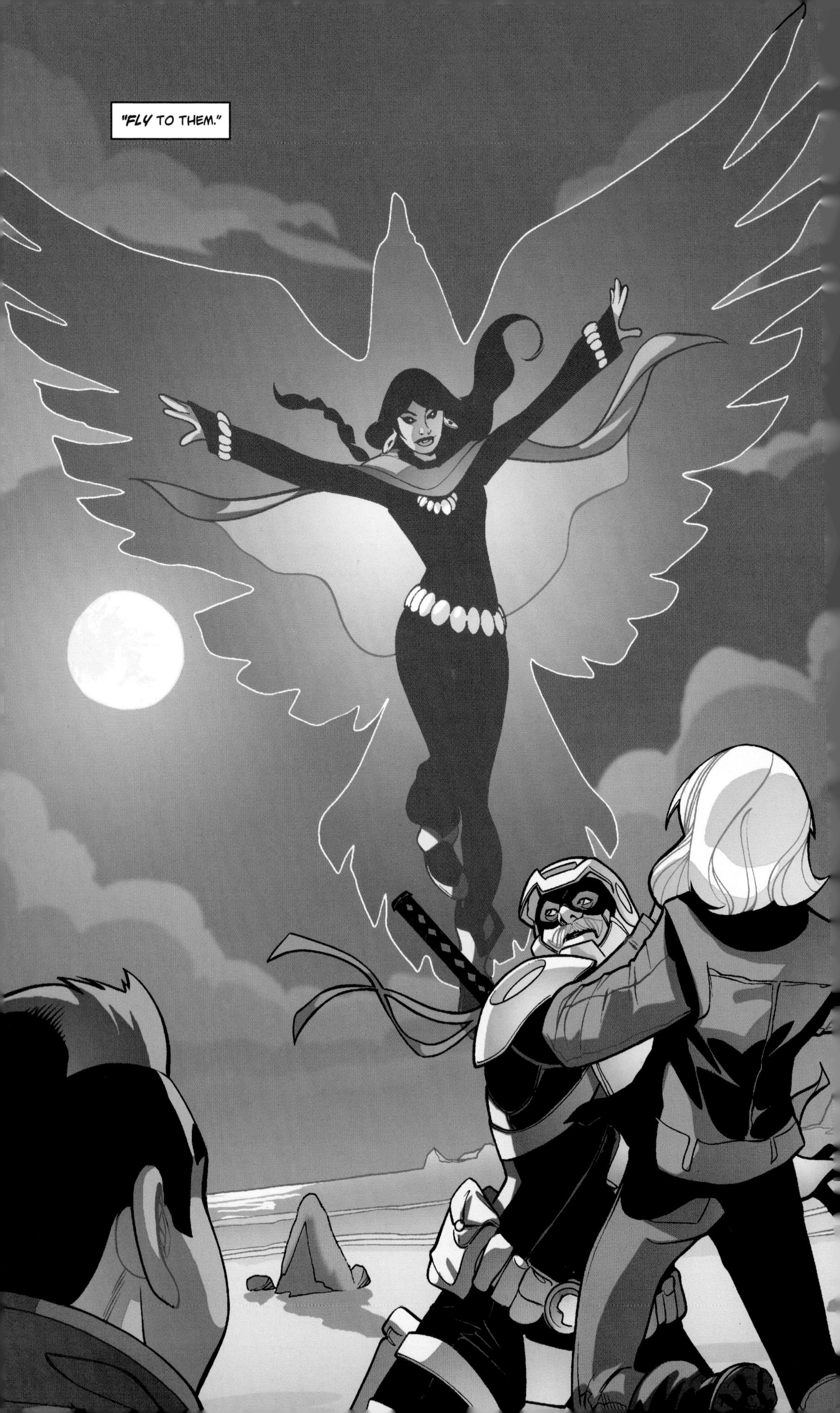
"FLY TO THEM."

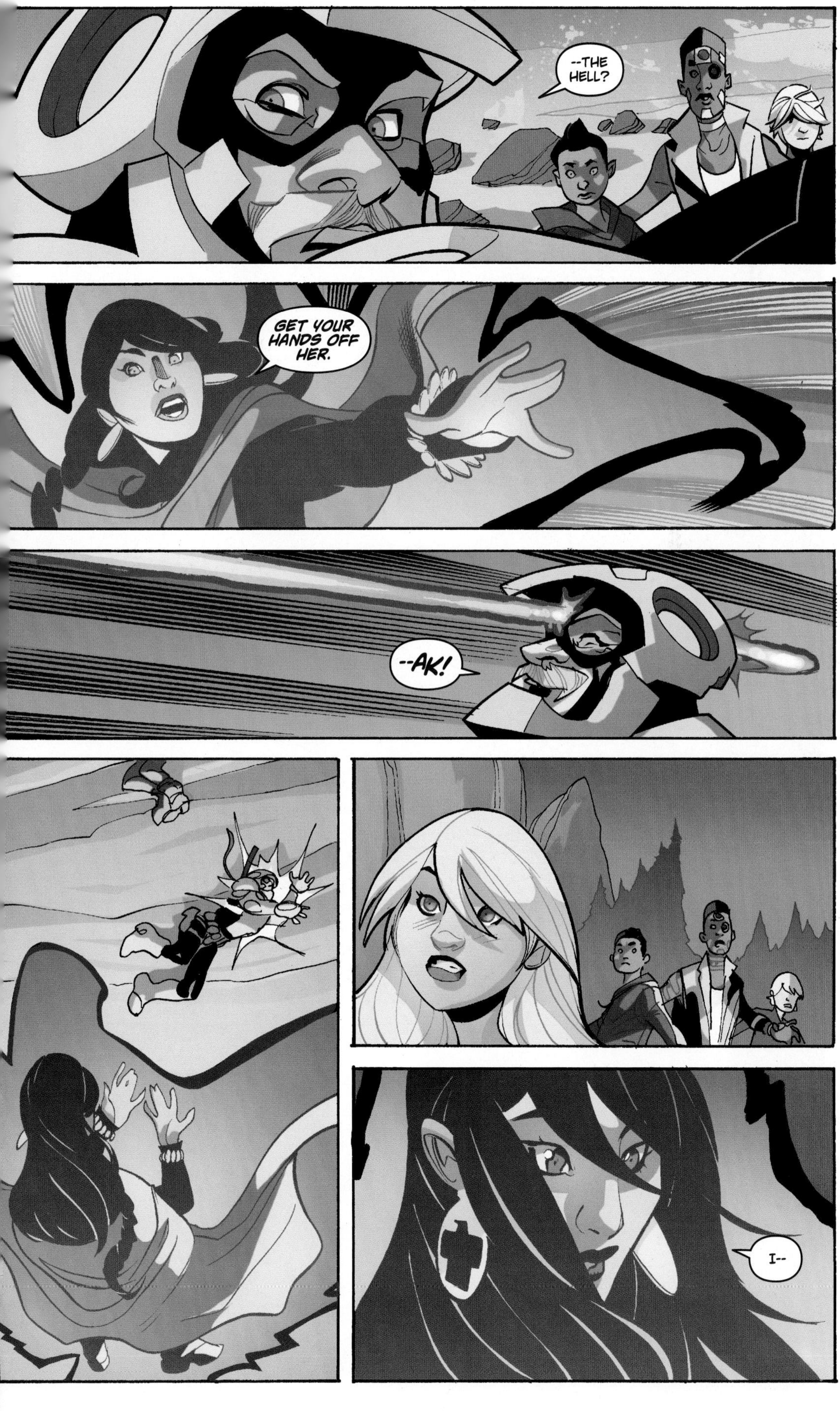
--THE HELL?
GET YOUR HANDS OFF HER.
--AK!
I--

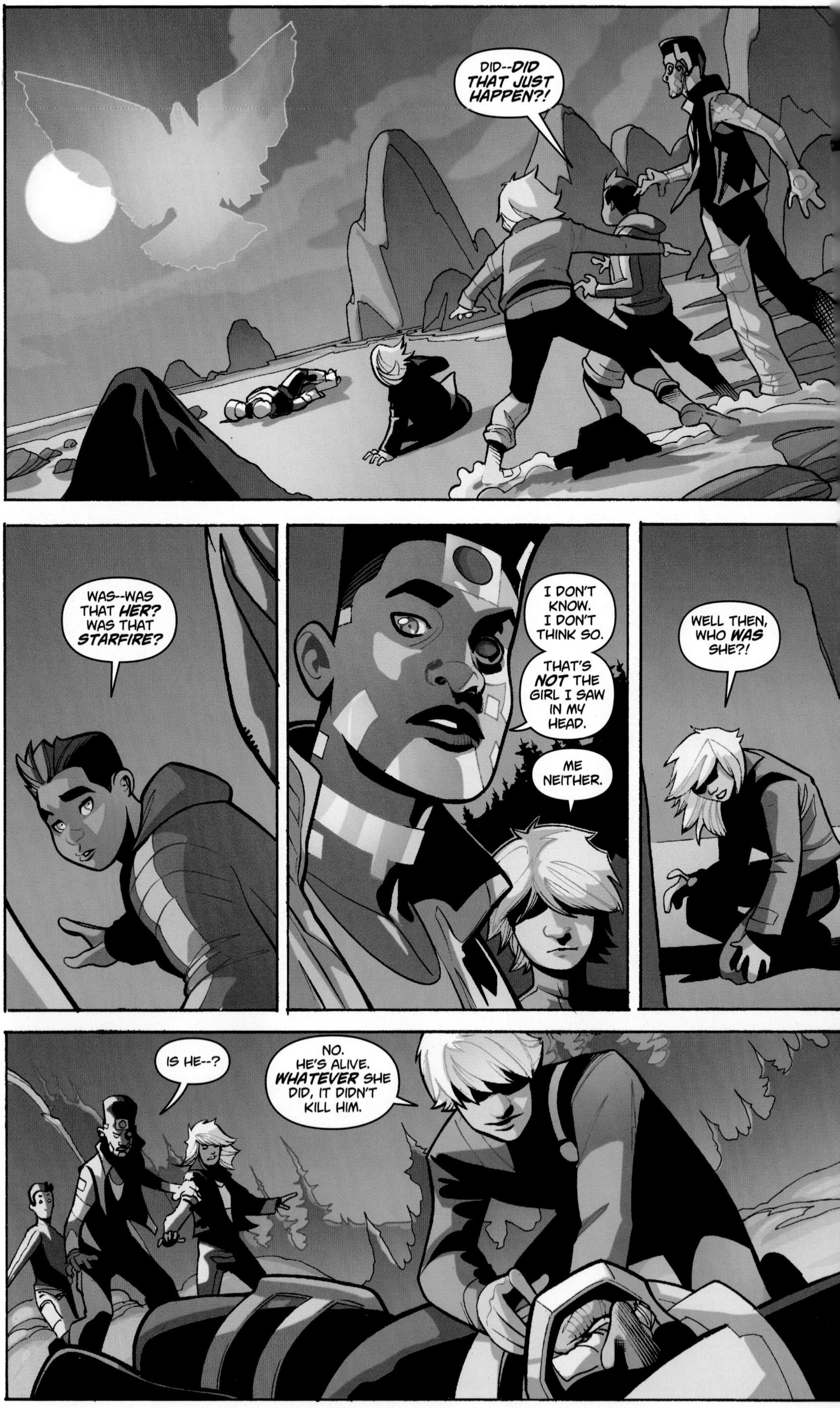
DID--DID THAT JUST HAPPEN?!
WAS--WAS THAT HER? WAS THAT STARFIRE?
I DON'T KNOW. I DON'T THINK SO.
THAT'S NOT THE GIRL I SAW IN MY HEAD.
ME NEITHER.
WELL THEN, WHO WAS SHE?!
IS HE--?
NO. HE'S ALIVE. WHATEVER SHE DID, IT DIDN'T KILL HIM.

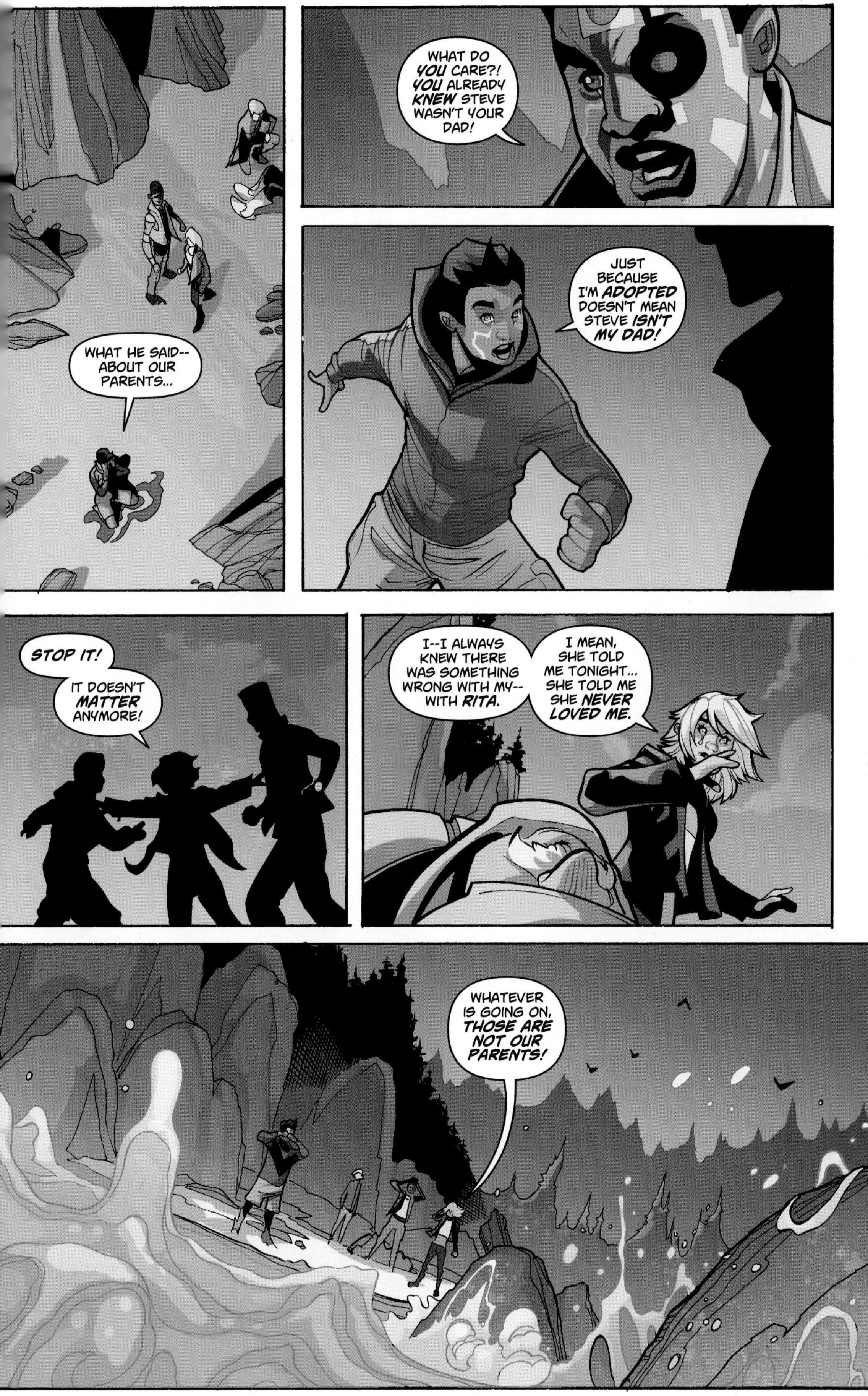
WHAT DO YOU CARE?! YOU ALREADY KNEW STEVE WASN'T YOUR DAD!
JUST BECAUSE I'M ADOPTED DOESN'T MEAN STEVE ISN'T MY DAD!
WHAT HE SAID-- ABOUT OUR PARENTS...
STOP IT!
IT DOESN'T MATTER ANYMORE!
I--I ALWAYS KNEW THERE WAS SOMETHING WRONG WITH MY-- WITH RITA.
I MEAN, SHE TOLD ME TONIGHT... SHE TOLD ME SHE NEVER LOVED ME.
WHATEVER IS GOING ON, THOSE ARE NOT OUR PARENTS!

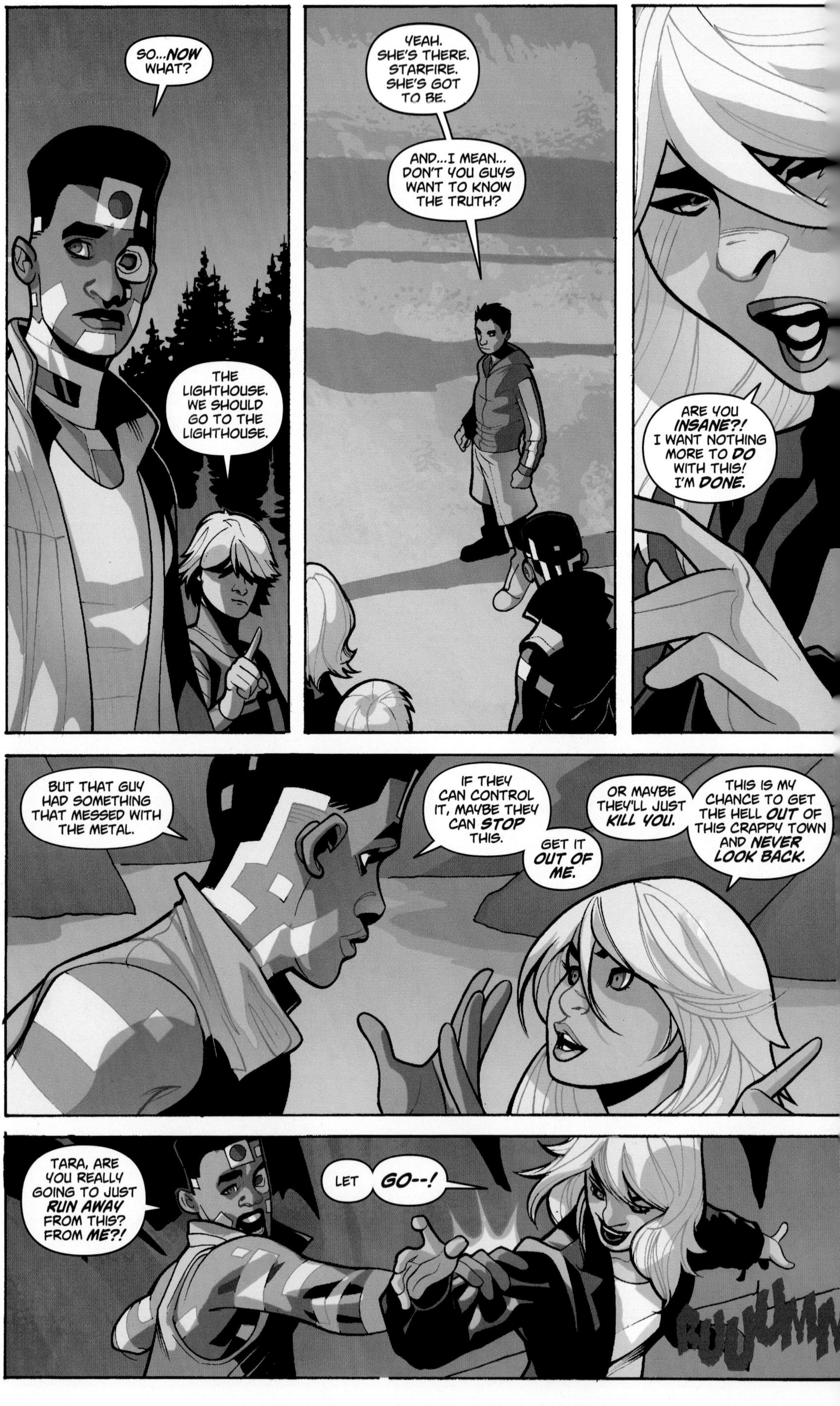
SO...NOW WHAT?
THE LIGHTHOUSE. WE SHOULD GO TO THE LIGHTHOUSE.
YEAH. SHE'S THERE. STARFIRE. SHE'S GOT TO BE.
AND...I MEAN... DON'T YOU GUYS WANT TO KNOW THE TRUTH?
ARE YOU INSANE?! I WANT NOTHING MORE TO DO WITH THIS! I'M DONE.
BUT THAT GUY HAD SOMETHING THAT MESSED WITH THE METAL.
IF THEY CAN CONTROL IT, MAYBE THEY CAN STOP THIS.
GET IT OUT OF ME.
OR MAYBE THEY'LL JUST KILL YOU.
THIS IS MY CHANCE TO GET THE HELL OUT OF THIS CRAPPY TOWN AND NEVER LOOK BACK.
TARA, ARE YOU REALLY GOING TO JUST RUN AWAY FROM THIS? FROM ME?!
LET GO--!
RUUUMM

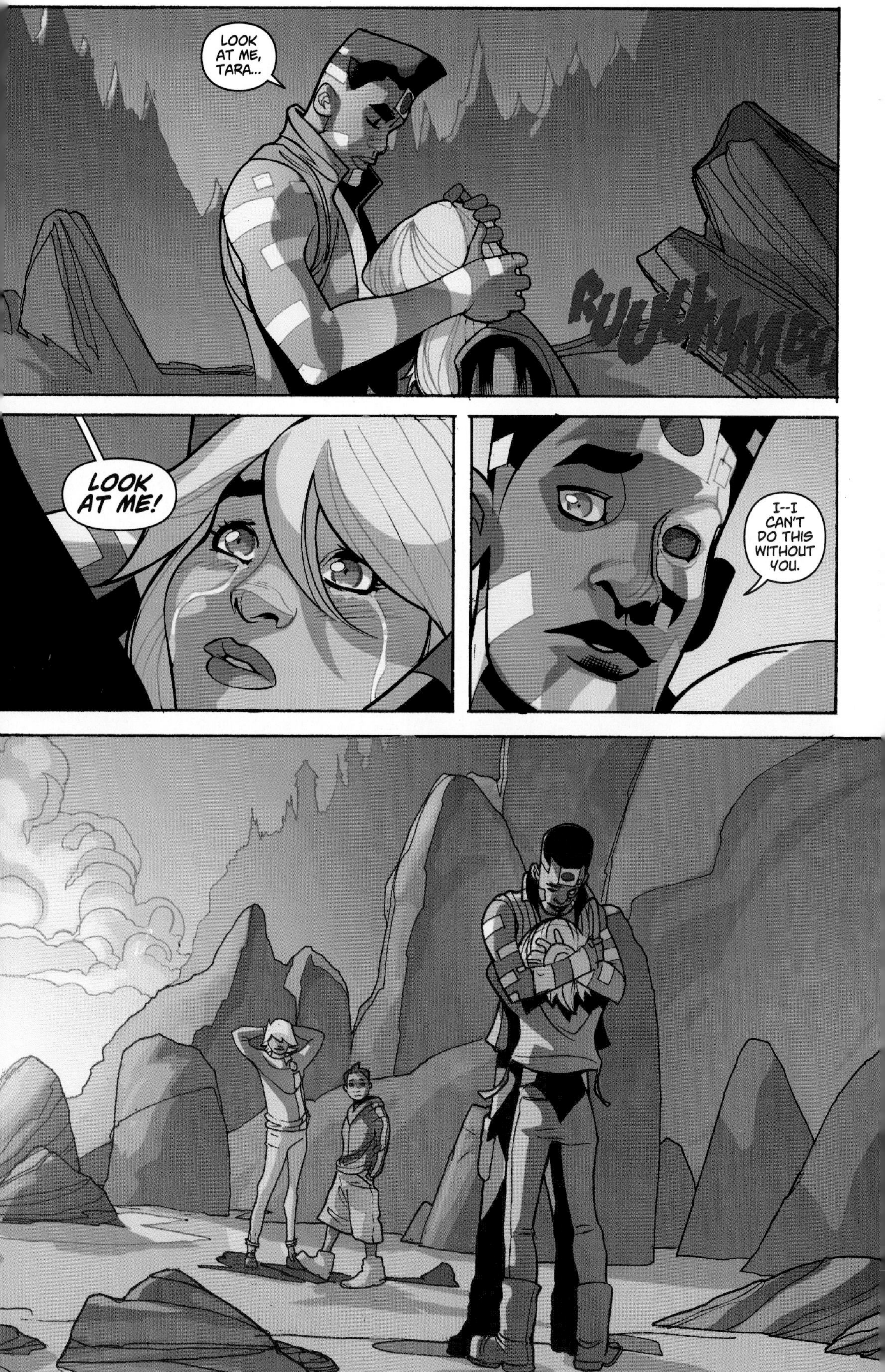
LOOK AT ME, TARA...
RUUUMMMBL
LOOK AT ME!
I--I CAN'T DO THIS WITHOUT YOU.

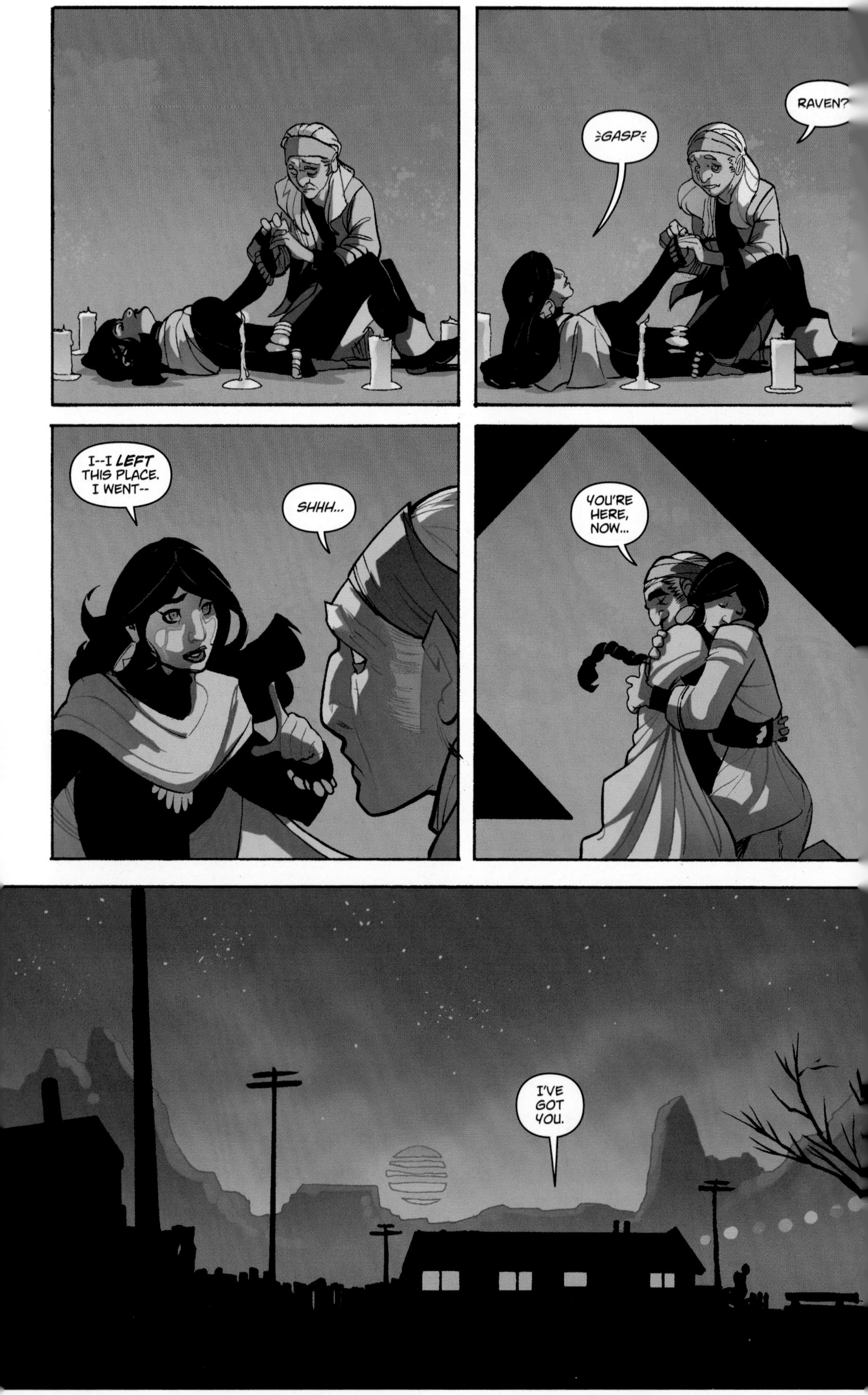

GASP
RAVEN?
I--I LEFT THIS PLACE. I WENT--
SHHH...
YOU'RE HERE, NOW...
I'VE GOT YOU.

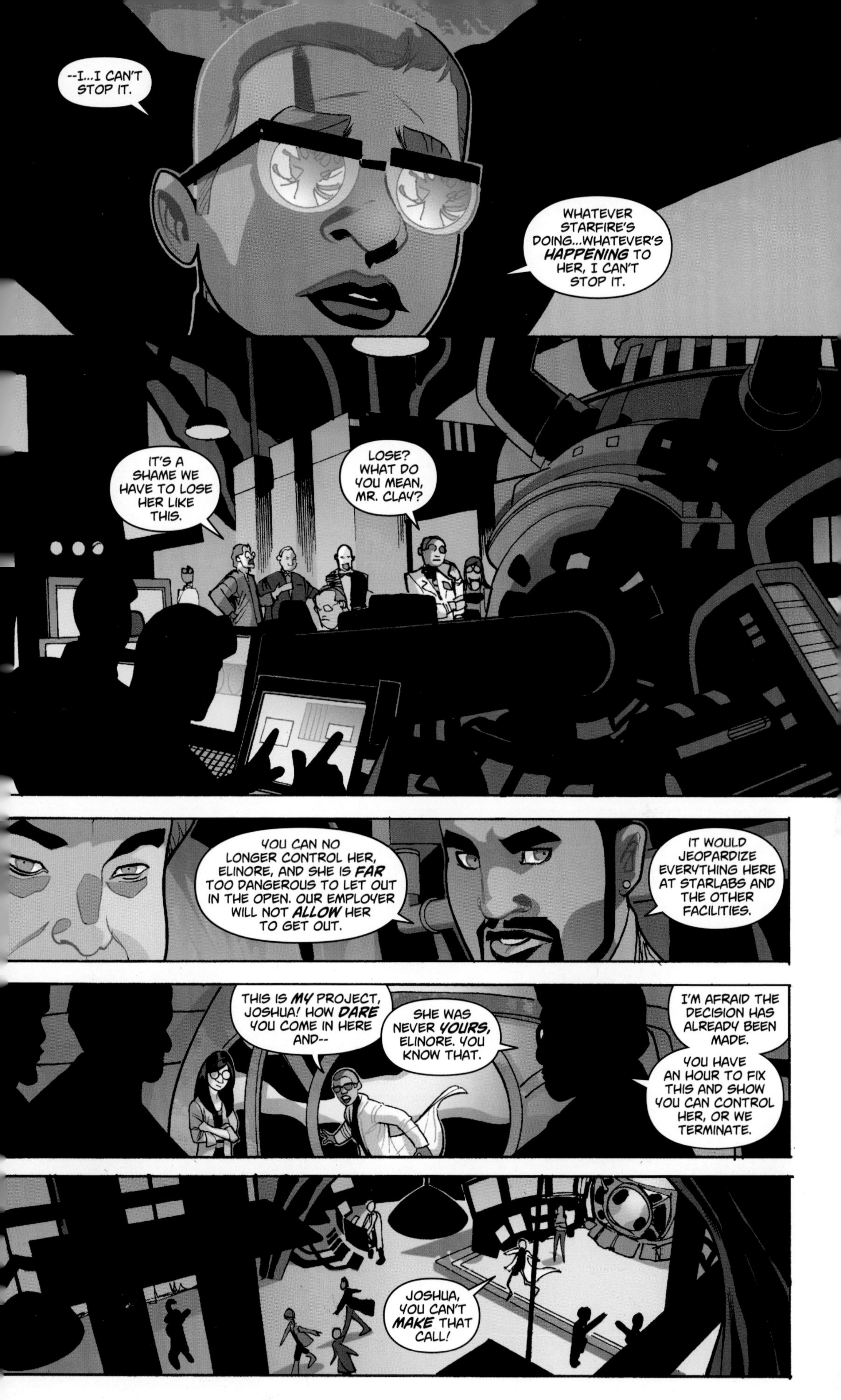
--I...I CAN'T STOP IT.
WHATEVER STARFIRE'S DOING...WHATEVER'S HAPPENING TO HER, I CAN'T STOP IT.
IT'S A SHAME WE HAVE TO LOSE HER LIKE THIS.
LOSE? WHAT DO YOU MEAN, MR. CLAY?
YOU CAN NO LONGER CONTROL HER, ELINORE, AND SHE IS FAR TOO DANGEROUS TO LET OUT IN THE OPEN. OUR EMPLOYER WILL NOT ALLOW HER TO GET OUT.
IT WOULD JEOPARDIZE EVERYTHING HERE AT STARLABS AND THE OTHER FACILITIES.
THIS IS MY PROJECT, JOSHUA! HOW DARE YOU COME IN HERE AND--
SHE WAS NEVER YOURS, ELINORE. YOU KNOW THAT.
I'M AFRAID THE DECISION HAS ALREADY BEEN MADE.
YOU HAVE AN HOUR TO FIX THIS AND SHOW YOU CAN CONTROL HER, OR WE TERMINATE.
JOSHUA, YOU CAN'T MAKE THAT CALL!

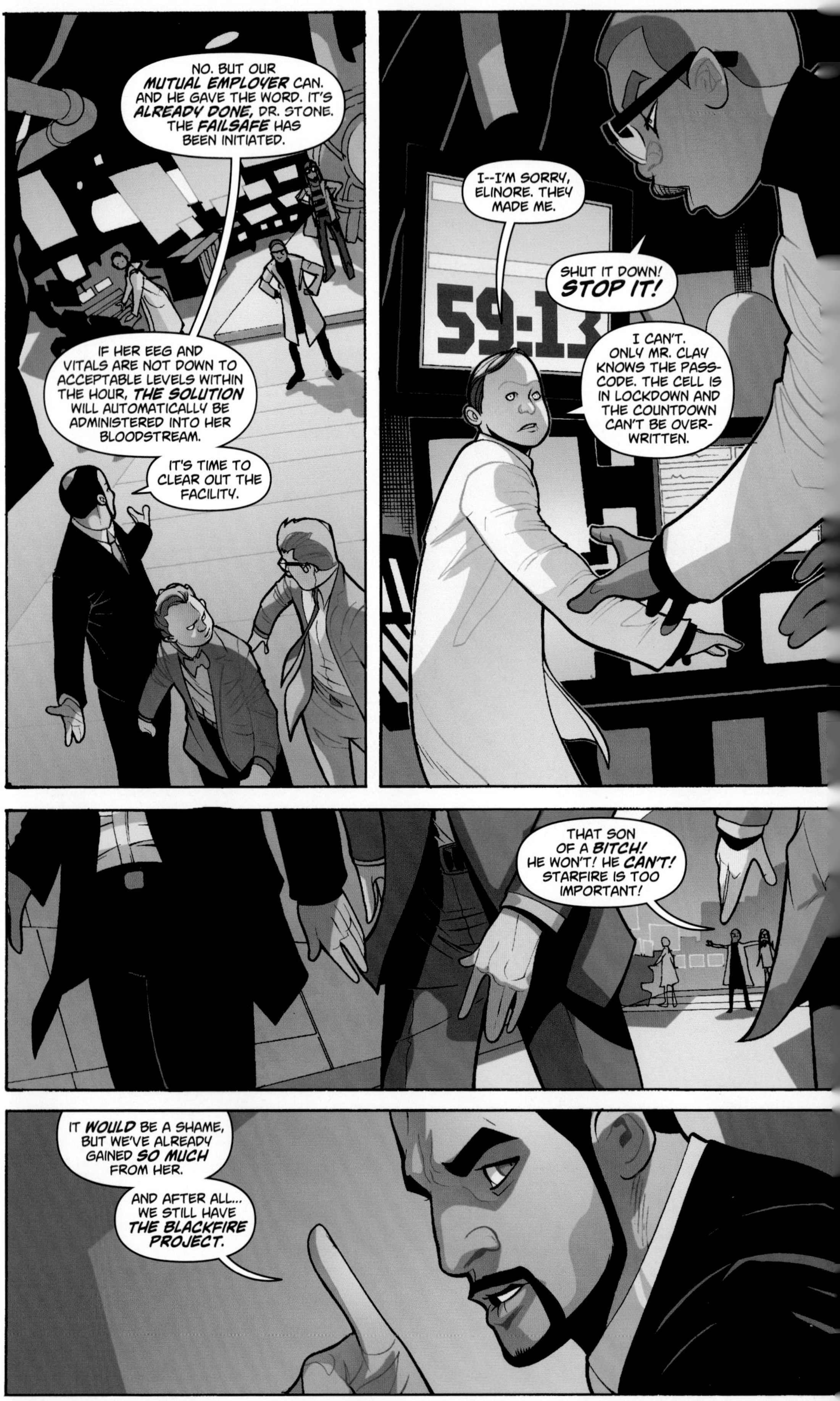
NO. BUT OUR MUTUAL EMPLOYER CAN. AND HE GAVE THE WORD. IT'S ALREADY DONE, DR. STONE. THE FAILSAFE HAS BEEN INITIATED.
IF HER EEG AND VITALS ARE NOT DOWN TO ACCEPTABLE LEVELS WITHIN THE HOUR, THE SOLUTION WILL AUTOMATICALLY BE ADMINISTERED INTO HER BLOODSTREAM.
IT'S TIME TO CLEAR OUT THE FACILITY.
I--I'M SORRY, ELINORE. THEY MADE ME.
SHUT IT DOWN! STOP IT!
59:13
I CAN'T. ONLY MR. CLAY KNOWS THE PASS-CODE. THE CELL IS IN LOCKDOWN AND THE COUNTDOWN CAN'T BE OVER-WRITTEN.
THAT SON OF A BITCH! HE WON'T! HE CAN'T! STARFIRE IS TOO IMPORTANT!
IT WOULD BE A SHAME, BUT WE'VE ALREADY GAINED SO MUCH FROM HER.
AND AFTER ALL... WE STILL HAVE THE BLACKFIRE PROJECT.

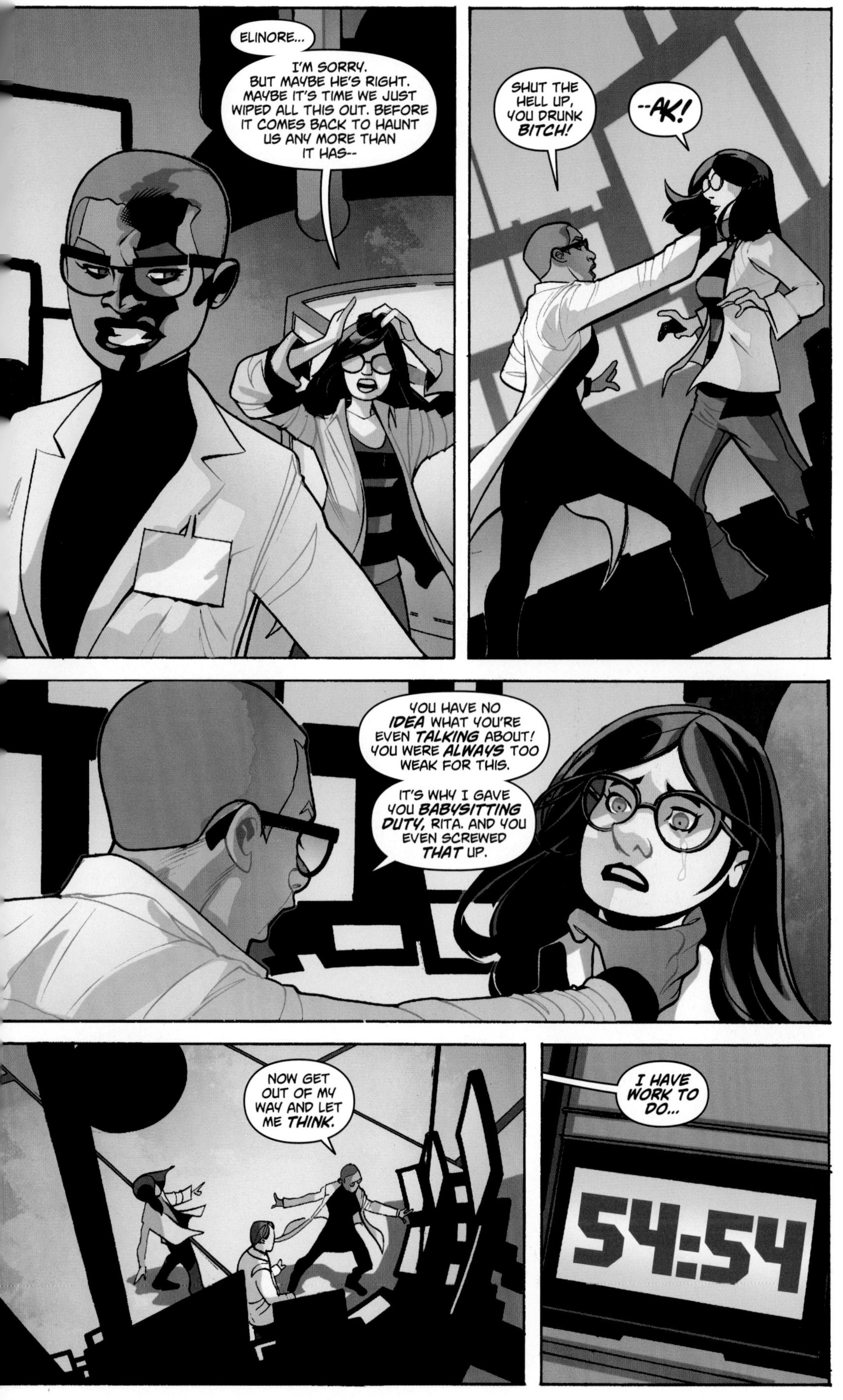

ELINORE...
I'M SORRY. BUT MAYBE HE'S RIGHT. MAYBE IT'S TIME WE JUST WIPED ALL THIS OUT. BEFORE IT COMES BACK TO HAUNT US ANY MORE THAN IT HAS--
SHUT THE HELL UP, YOU DRUNK *BITCH!*
--AK!
YOU HAVE NO *IDEA* WHAT YOU'RE EVEN *TALKING* ABOUT! YOU WERE *ALWAYS* TOO WEAK FOR THIS.
IT'S WHY I GAVE YOU *BABYSITTING DUTY,* RITA. AND YOU EVEN SCREWED *THAT* UP.
NOW GET OUT OF MY WAY AND LET ME *THINK.*
I HAVE WORK TO DO...
54:54

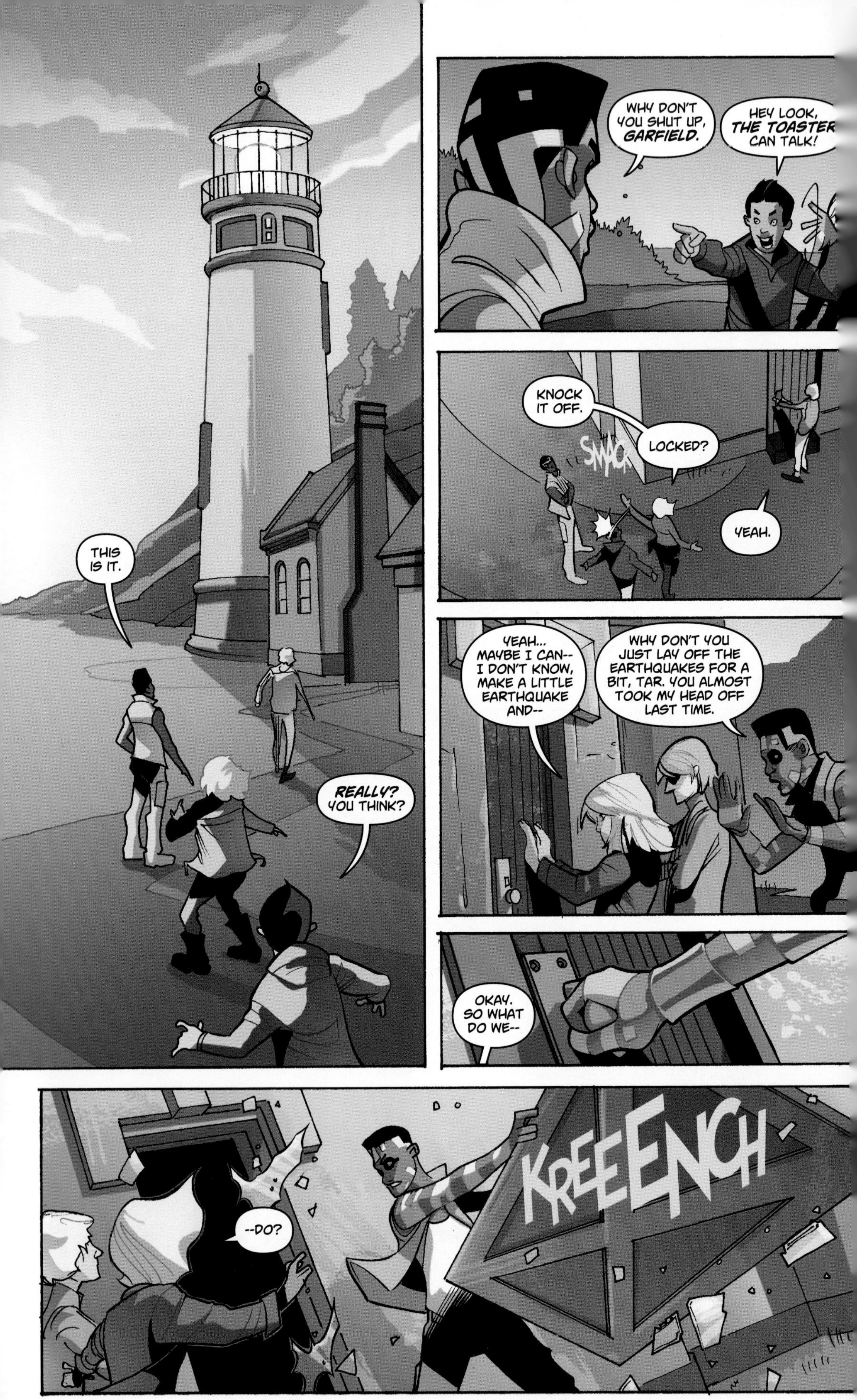

THIS IS IT.
REALLY? YOU THINK?
WHY DON'T YOU SHUT UP, GARFIELD.
HEY LOOK, THE TOASTER CAN TALK!
KNOCK IT OFF.
SMACK
LOCKED?
YEAH.
YEAH... MAYBE I CAN-- I DON'T KNOW, MAKE A LITTLE EARTHQUAKE AND--
WHY DON'T YOU JUST LAY OFF THE EARTHQUAKES FOR A BIT, TAR. YOU ALMOST TOOK MY HEAD OFF LAST TIME.
OKAY. SO WHAT DO WE--
--DO?
KREEENCH

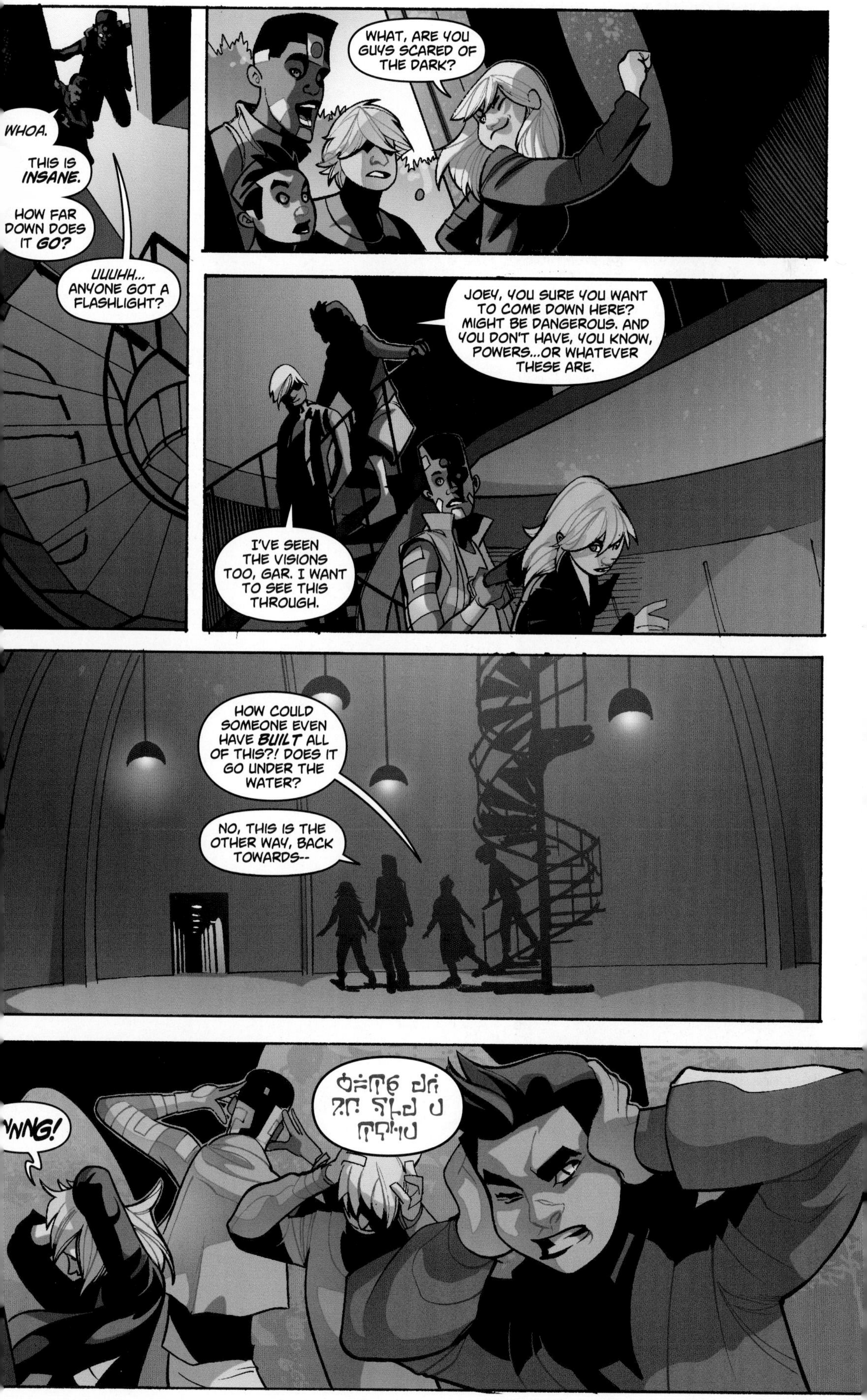
WHOA.
THIS IS *INSANE*.
HOW FAR DOWN DOES IT *GO*?
UUUHH... ANYONE GOT A FLASHLIGHT?
WHAT, ARE YOU GUYS SCARED OF THE DARK?
JOEY, YOU SURE YOU WANT TO COME DOWN HERE? MIGHT BE DANGEROUS. AND YOU DON'T HAVE, YOU KNOW, POWERS...OR WHATEVER THESE ARE.
I'VE SEEN THE VISIONS TOO, GAR. I WANT TO SEE THIS THROUGH.
HOW COULD SOMEONE EVEN HAVE *BUILT* ALL OF THIS?! DOES IT GO UNDER THE WATER?
NO, THIS IS THE OTHER WAY, BACK TOWARDS--
NNNG!

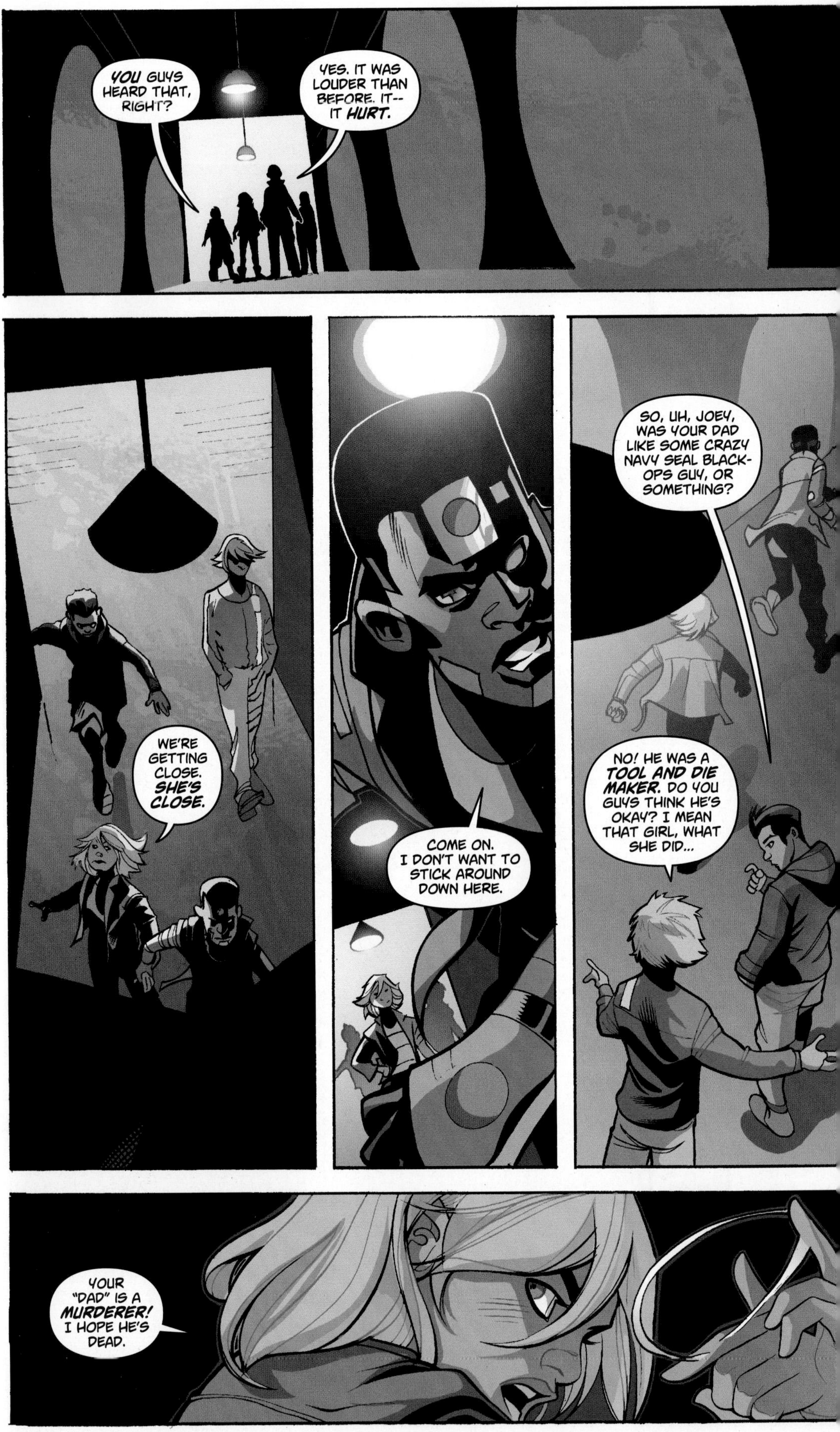
YOU GUYS HEARD THAT, RIGHT?
YES. IT WAS LOUDER THAN BEFORE. IT-- IT HURT.
WE'RE GETTING CLOSE. SHE'S CLOSE.
COME ON. I DON'T WANT TO STICK AROUND DOWN HERE.
SO, UH, JOEY, WAS YOUR DAD LIKE SOME CRAZY NAVY SEAL BLACK-OPS GUY, OR SOMETHING?
NO! HE WAS A TOOL AND DIE MAKER. DO YOU GUYS THINK HE'S OKAY? I MEAN THAT GIRL, WHAT SHE DID...
YOUR "DAD" IS A MURDERER! I HOPE HE'S DEAD.

ARE YOU *KIDDING ME*, TARA?

NO MATTER *WHAT* HE DID, THAT GUY STILL *RAISED* HIM!

NOT *ALL* OF US HATE OUR PARENTS--

OH, THAT'S JUST *SO SWEET*, GARFIELD. REALLY. IT'S TRULY HEART-WARMING.

WOULD YOU GUYS *COOL* IT?

LOOK...

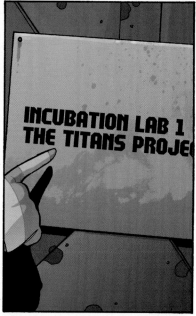

INCUBATION LAB 1
THE TITANS PROJE

I--I DON'T THINK THIS IS A GOOD IDEA, YOU GUYS.

THERE'S NO TELLING *WHAT* COULD BE IN THERE. MAYBE WE SHOULD--

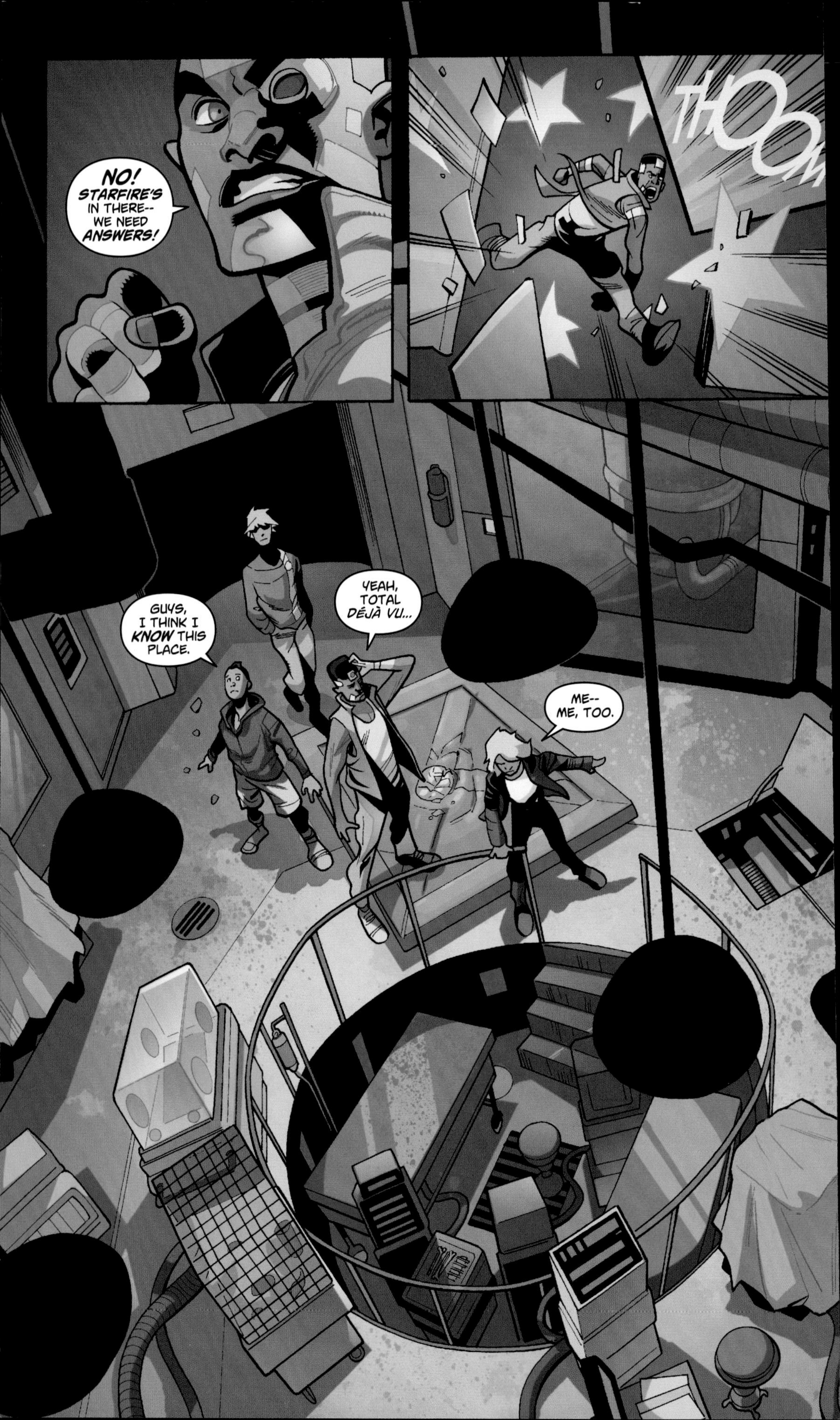
NO! STARFIRE'S IN THERE-- WE NEED ANSWERS!
THOOM
GUYS, I THINK I KNOW THIS PLACE.
YEAH, TOTAL DÉJÀ VU...
ME-- ME, TOO.

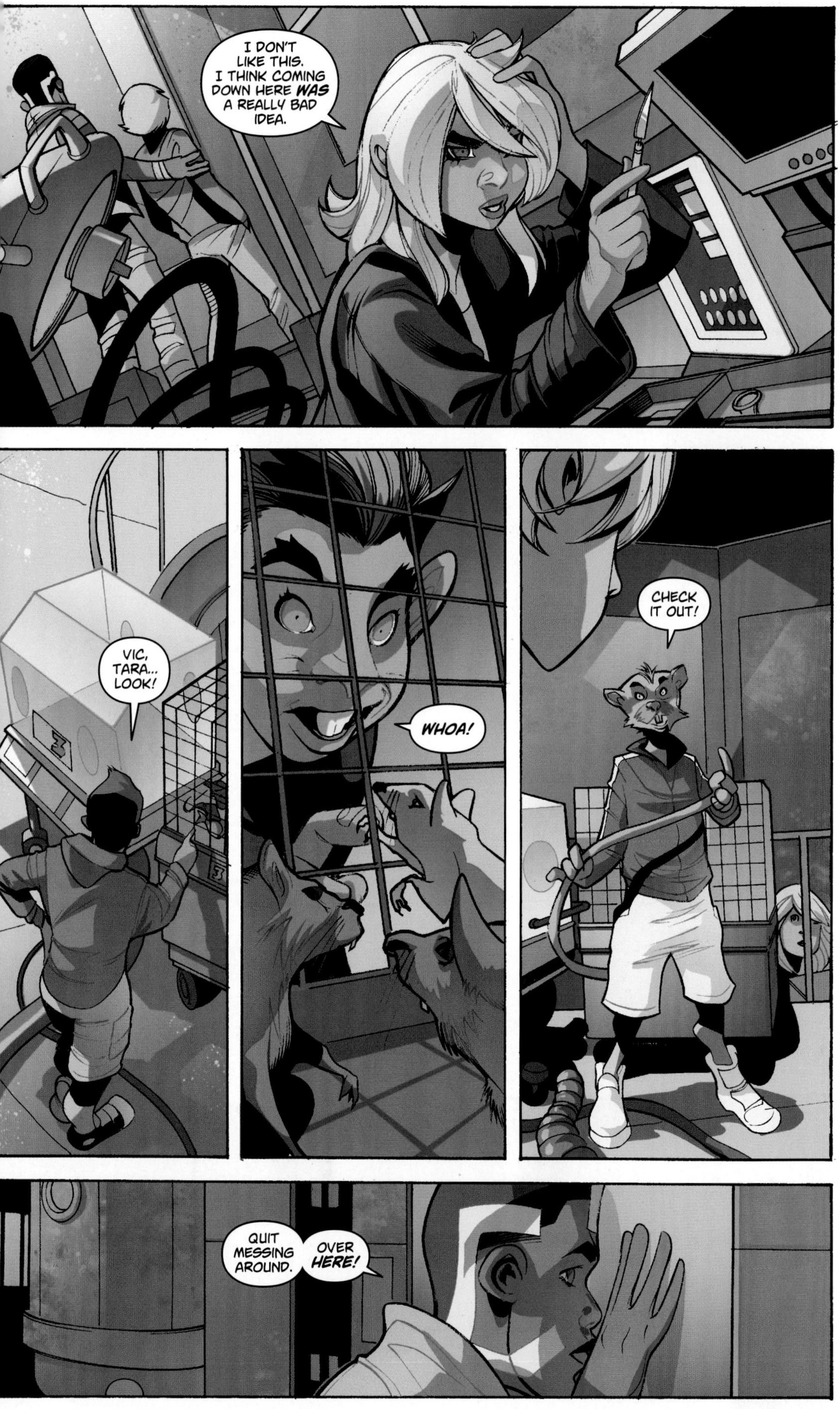
I DON'T LIKE THIS. I THINK COMING DOWN HERE *WAS* A REALLY BAD IDEA.
VIC, TARA... LOOK!
WHOA!
CHECK IT OUT!
QUIT MESSING AROUND.
OVER *HERE!*

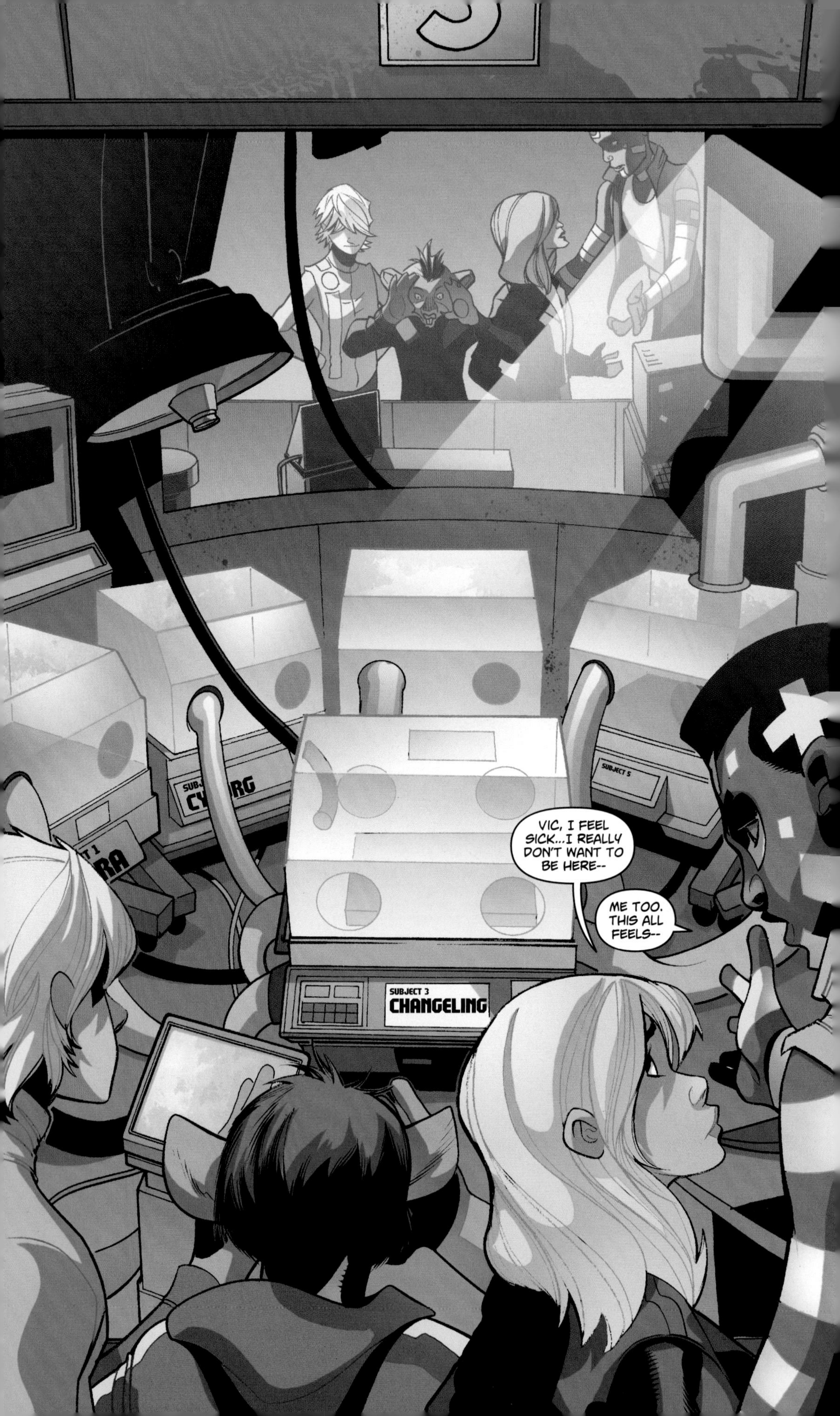
SUBJECT 5
VIC, I FEEL SICK...I REALLY DON'T WANT TO BE HERE--
ME TOO. THIS ALL FEELS--
SUBJECT 3
CHANGELING

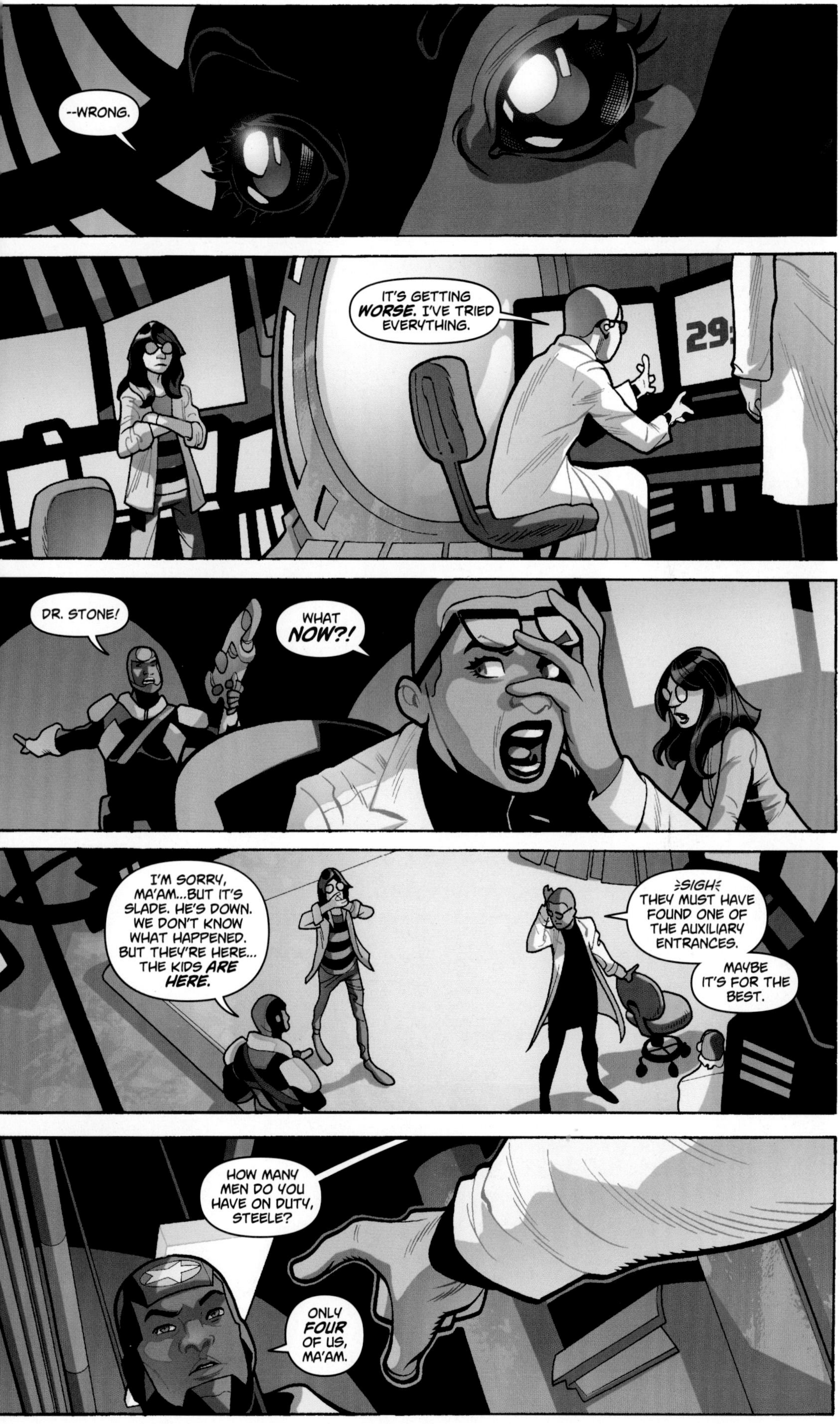
--WRONG.
IT'S GETTING WORSE. I'VE TRIED EVERYTHING.
29:
DR. STONE!
WHAT NOW?!
I'M SORRY, MA'AM...BUT IT'S SLADE. HE'S DOWN. WE DON'T KNOW WHAT HAPPENED. BUT THEY'RE HERE... THE KIDS ARE HERE.
SIGH THEY MUST HAVE FOUND ONE OF THE AUXILIARY ENTRANCES.
MAYBE IT'S FOR THE BEST.
HOW MANY MEN DO YOU HAVE ON DUTY, STEELE?
ONLY FOUR OF US, MA'AM.

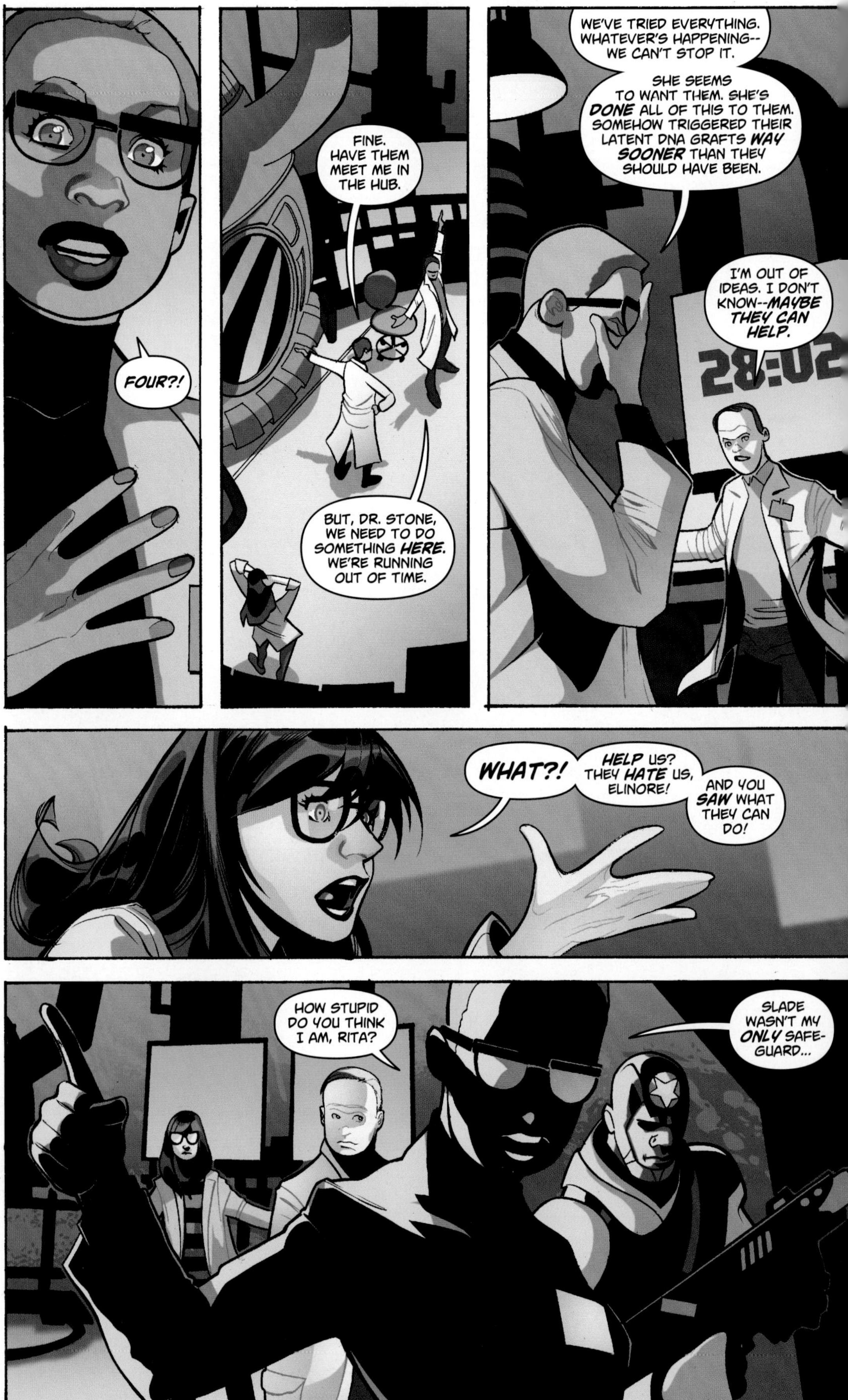
FOUR?!
FINE. HAVE THEM MEET ME IN THE HUB.
BUT, DR. STONE, WE NEED TO DO SOMETHING HERE. WE'RE RUNNING OUT OF TIME.
WE'VE TRIED EVERYTHING. WHATEVER'S HAPPENING-- WE CAN'T STOP IT.
SHE SEEMS TO WANT THEM. SHE'S DONE ALL OF THIS TO THEM. SOMEHOW TRIGGERED THEIR LATENT DNA GRAFTS WAY SOONER THAN THEY SHOULD HAVE BEEN.
I'M OUT OF IDEAS. I DON'T KNOW--MAYBE THEY CAN HELP.
28:02
WHAT?!
HELP US? THEY HATE US, ELINORE!
AND YOU SAW WHAT THEY CAN DO!
HOW STUPID DO YOU THINK I AM, RITA?
SLADE WASN'T MY ONLY SAFE-GUARD...

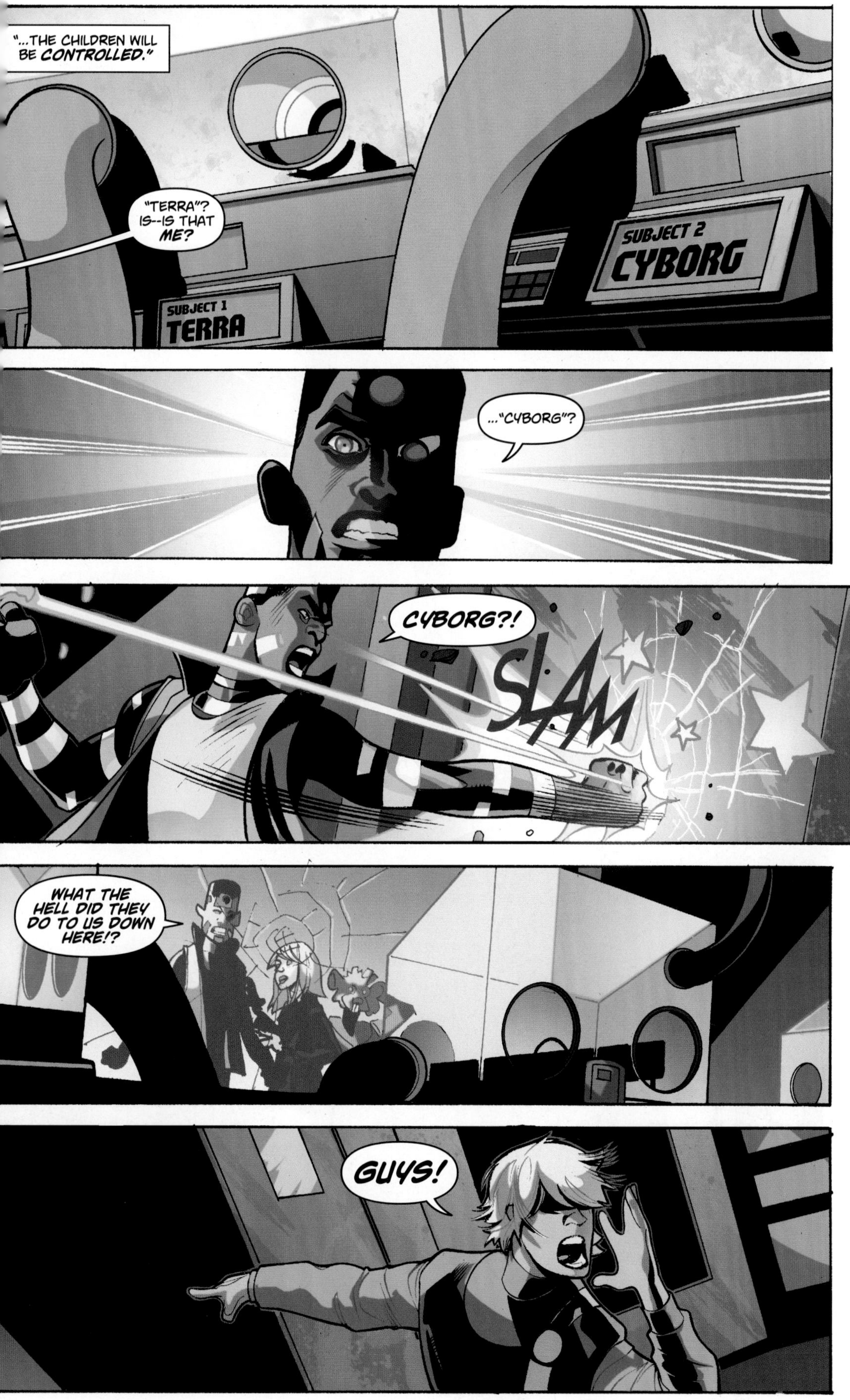
"...THE CHILDREN WILL BE CONTROLLED."
"TERRA"? IS--IS THAT ME?
SUBJECT 2 CYBORG
SUBJECT 1 TERRA
..."CYBORG"?
CYBORG?!
SLAM
WHAT THE HELL DID THEY DO TO US DOWN HERE!?
GUYS!

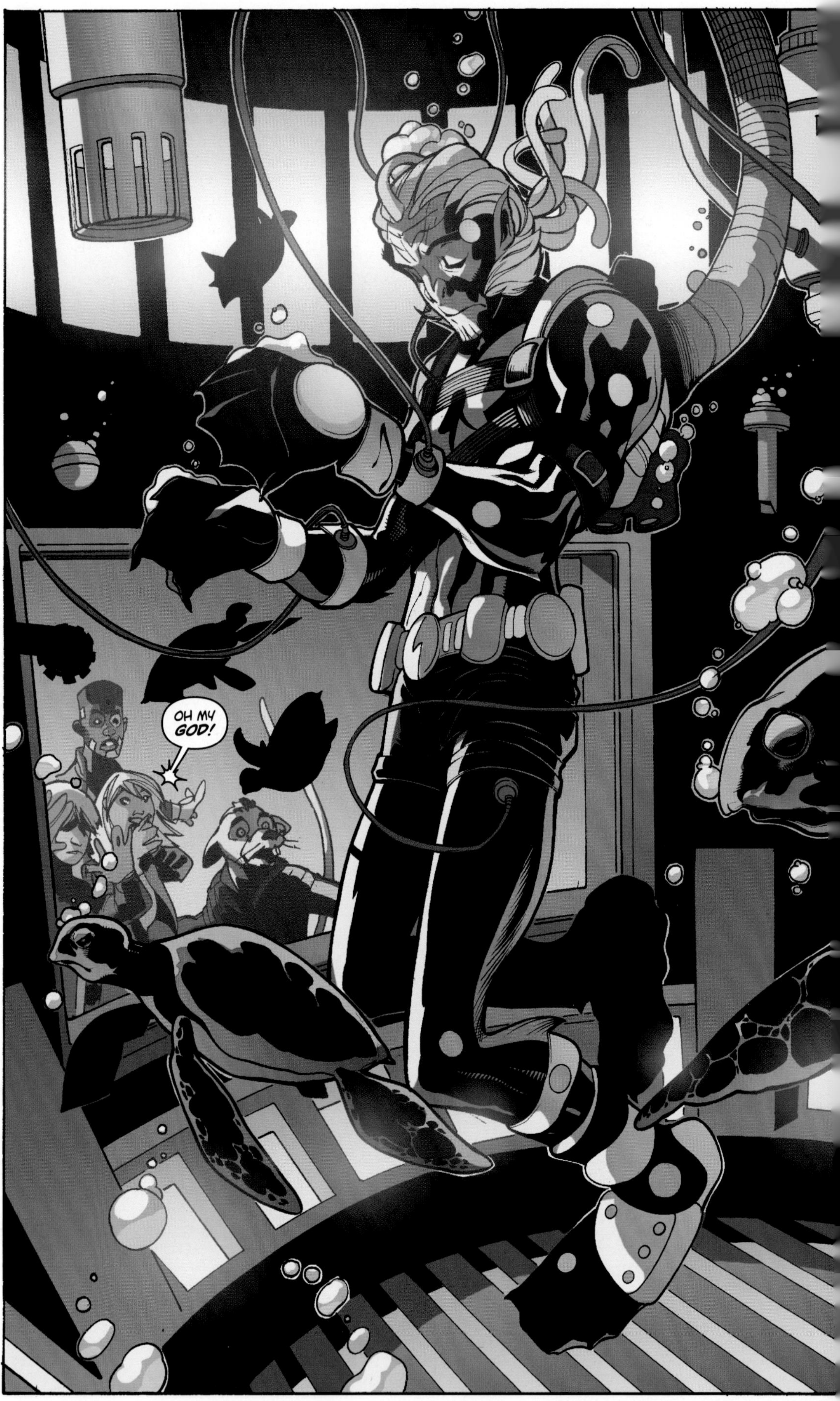
OH MY GOD!

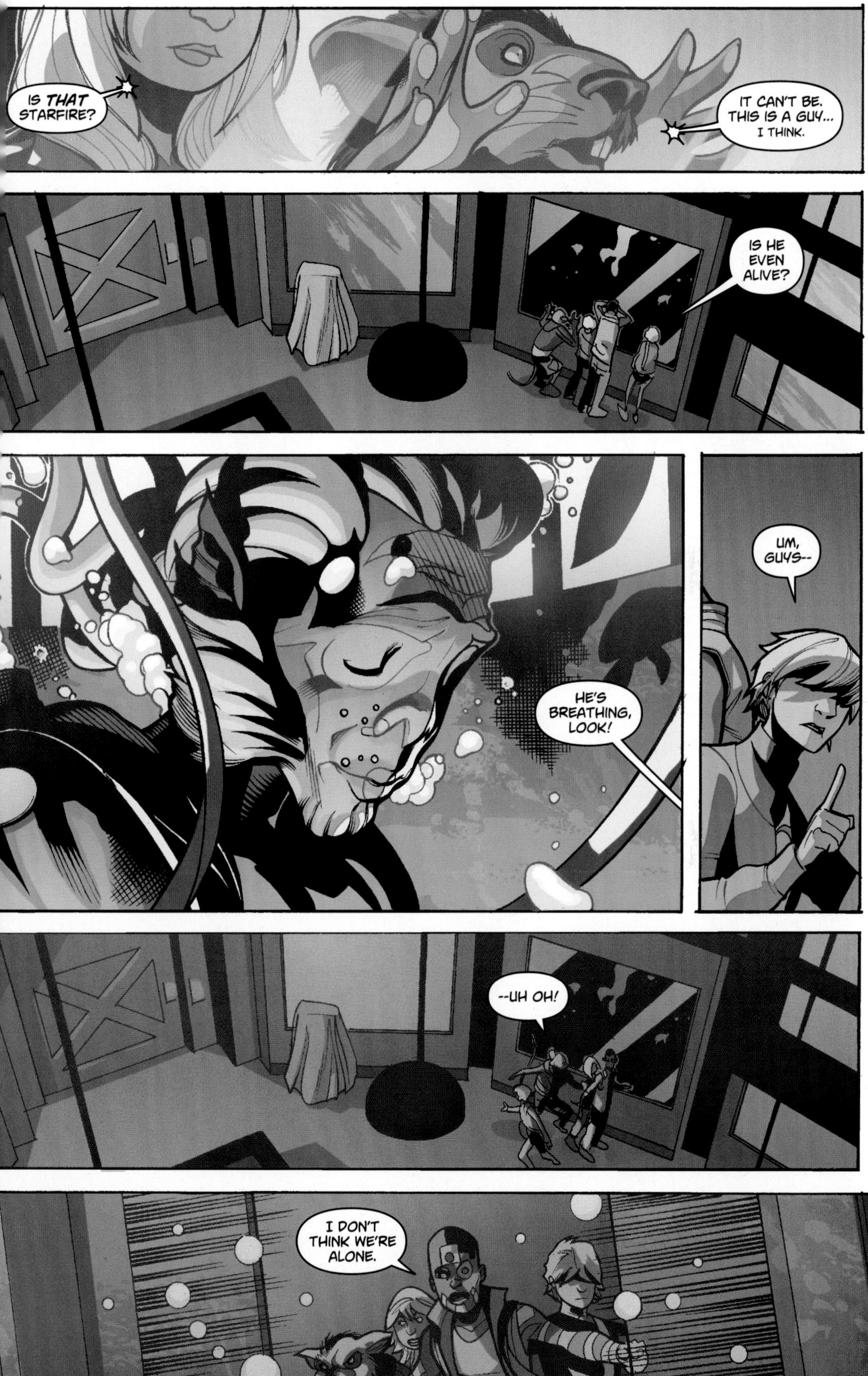
IS THAT STARFIRE?
IT CAN'T BE. THIS IS A GUY... I THINK.
IS HE EVEN ALIVE?
HE'S BREATHING, LOOK!
UM, GUYS--
--UH OH!
I DON'T THINK WE'RE ALONE.

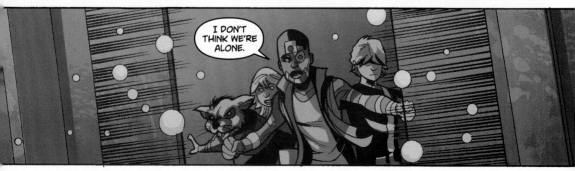

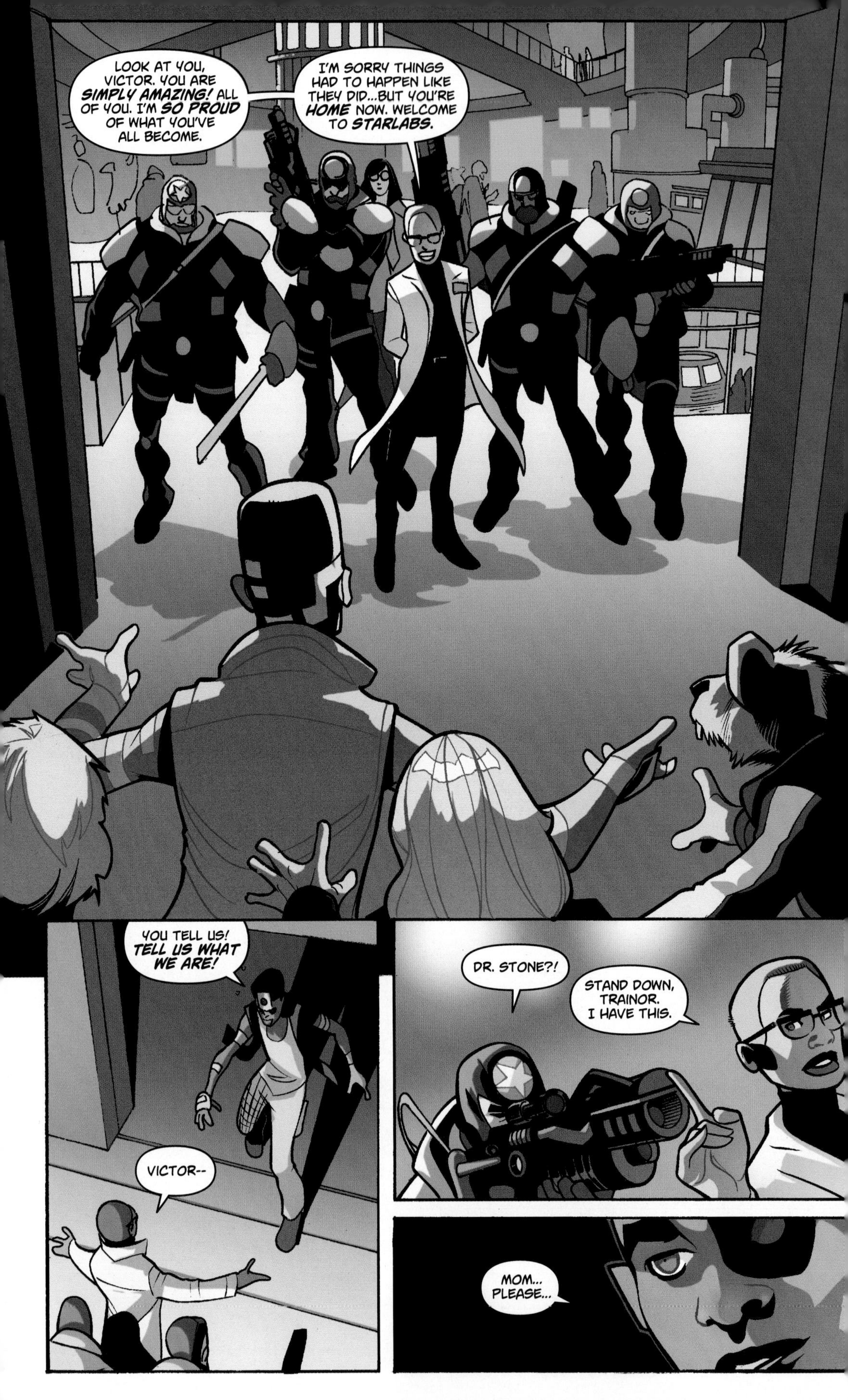
LOOK AT YOU, VICTOR. YOU ARE SIMPLY AMAZING! ALL OF YOU. I'M SO PROUD OF WHAT YOU'VE ALL BECOME.
I'M SORRY THINGS HAD TO HAPPEN LIKE THEY DID...BUT YOU'RE HOME NOW. WELCOME TO STARLABS.
YOU TELL US! TELL US WHAT WE ARE!
VICTOR--
DR. STONE?!
STAND DOWN, TRAINOR. I HAVE THIS.
MOM... PLEASE...

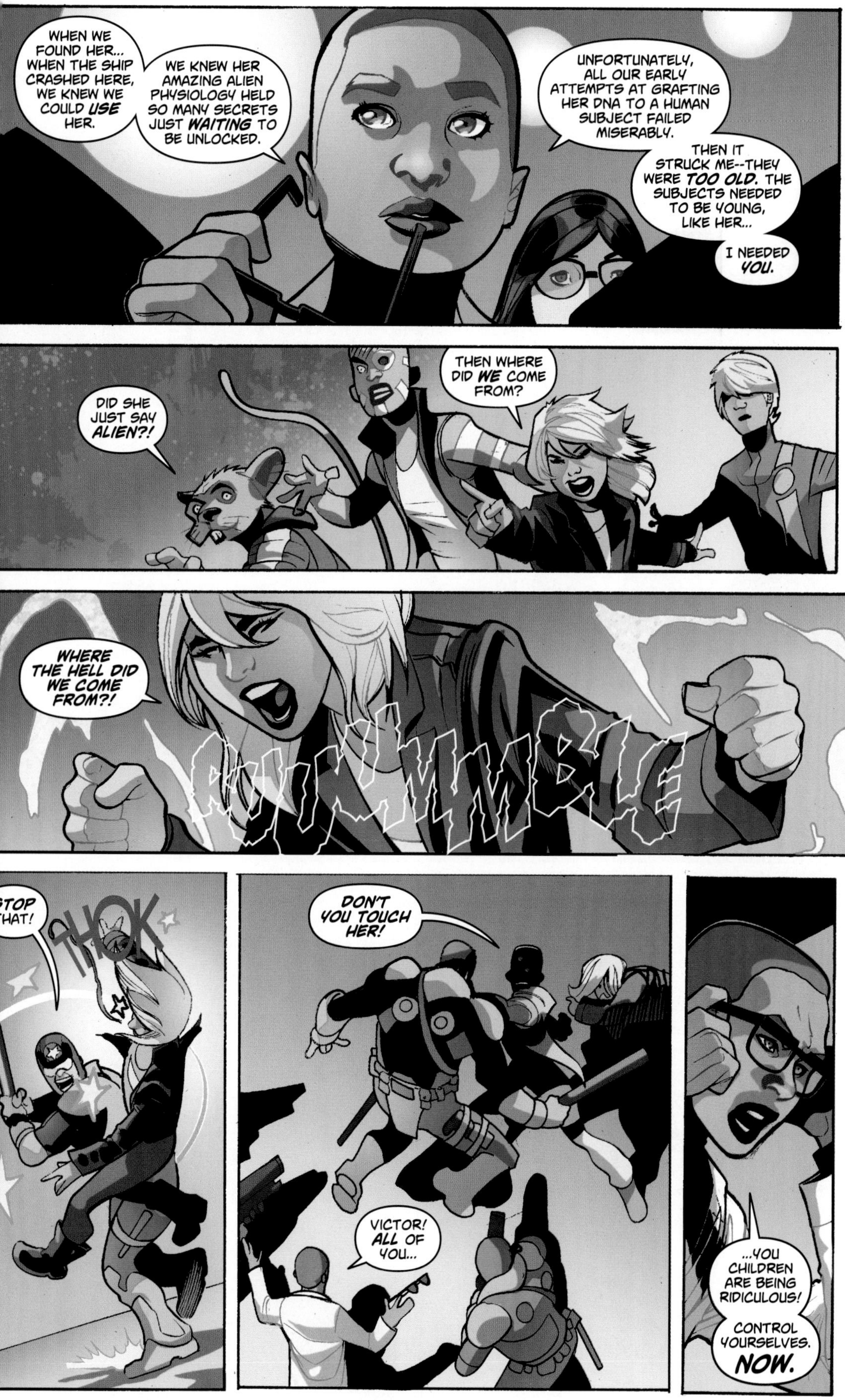
WHEN WE FOUND HER... WHEN THE SHIP CRASHED HERE, WE KNEW WE COULD USE HER.
WE KNEW HER AMAZING ALIEN PHYSIOLOGY HELD SO MANY SECRETS JUST WAITING TO BE UNLOCKED.
UNFORTUNATELY, ALL OUR EARLY ATTEMPTS AT GRAFTING HER DNA TO A HUMAN SUBJECT FAILED MISERABLY.
THEN IT STRUCK ME--THEY WERE TOO OLD. THE SUBJECTS NEEDED TO BE YOUNG, LIKE HER...
I NEEDED YOU.
DID SHE JUST SAY ALIEN?!
THEN WHERE DID WE COME FROM?
WHERE THE HELL DID WE COME FROM?!
STOP THAT!
THOK
DON'T YOU TOUCH HER!
VICTOR! ALL OF YOU...
...YOU CHILDREN ARE BEING RIDICULOUS!
CONTROL YOURSELVES. NOW.

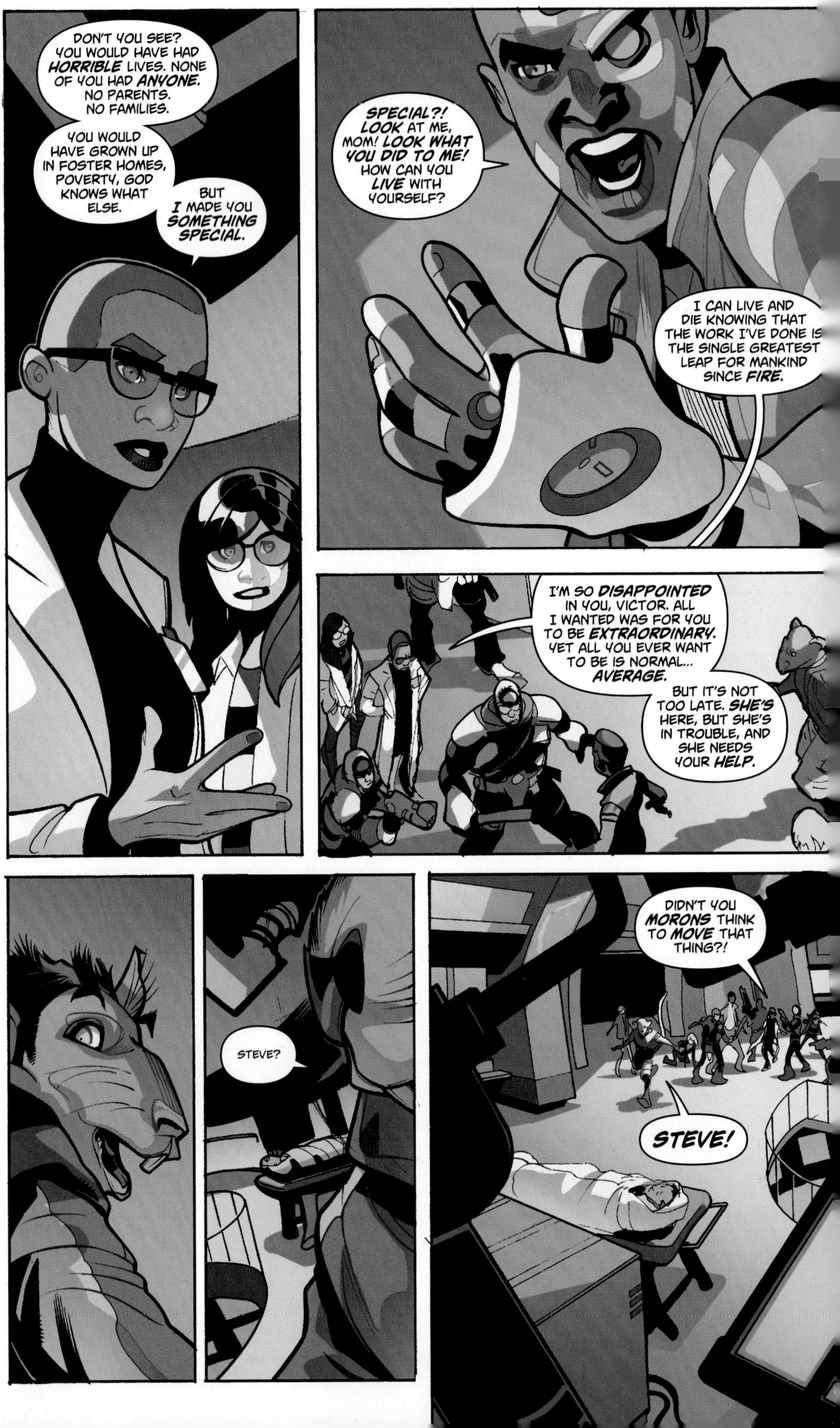
DON'T YOU SEE? YOU WOULD HAVE HAD HORRIBLE LIVES. NONE OF YOU HAD ANYONE. NO PARENTS. NO FAMILIES.
YOU WOULD HAVE GROWN UP IN FOSTER HOMES, POVERTY, GOD KNOWS WHAT ELSE.
BUT I MADE YOU SOMETHING SPECIAL.
SPECIAL?! LOOK AT ME, MOM! LOOK WHAT YOU DID TO ME! HOW CAN YOU LIVE WITH YOURSELF?
I CAN LIVE AND DIE KNOWING THAT THE WORK I'VE DONE IS THE SINGLE GREATEST LEAP FOR MANKIND SINCE FIRE.
I'M SO DISAPPOINTED IN YOU, VICTOR. ALL I WANTED WAS FOR YOU TO BE EXTRAORDINARY. YET ALL YOU EVER WANT TO BE IS NORMAL... AVERAGE.
BUT IT'S NOT TOO LATE. SHE'S HERE, BUT SHE'S IN TROUBLE, AND SHE NEEDS YOUR HELP.
STEVE?
DIDN'T YOU MORONS THINK TO MOVE THAT THING?!
STEVE!

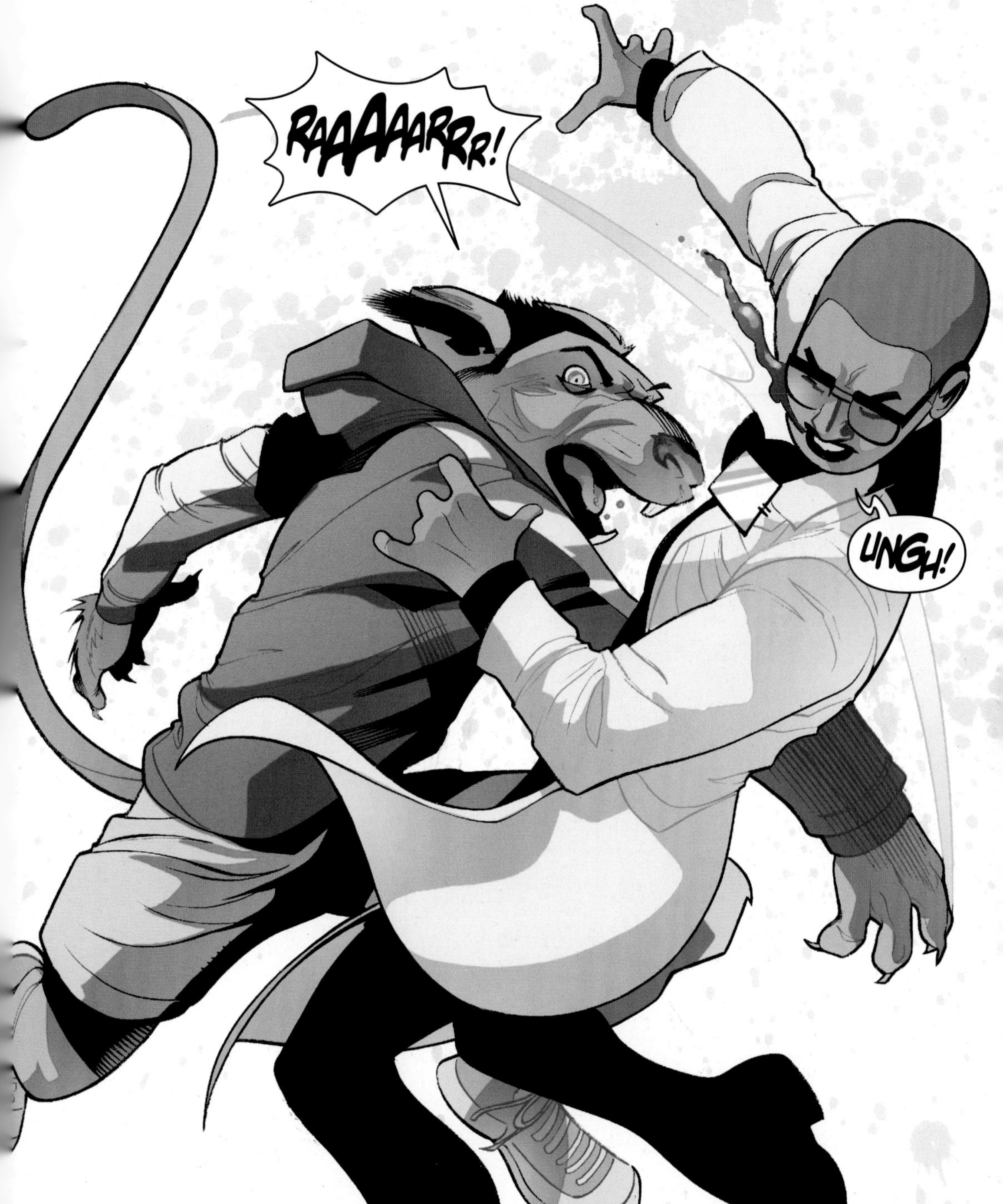
RAAAAARRRR!
UNGH!

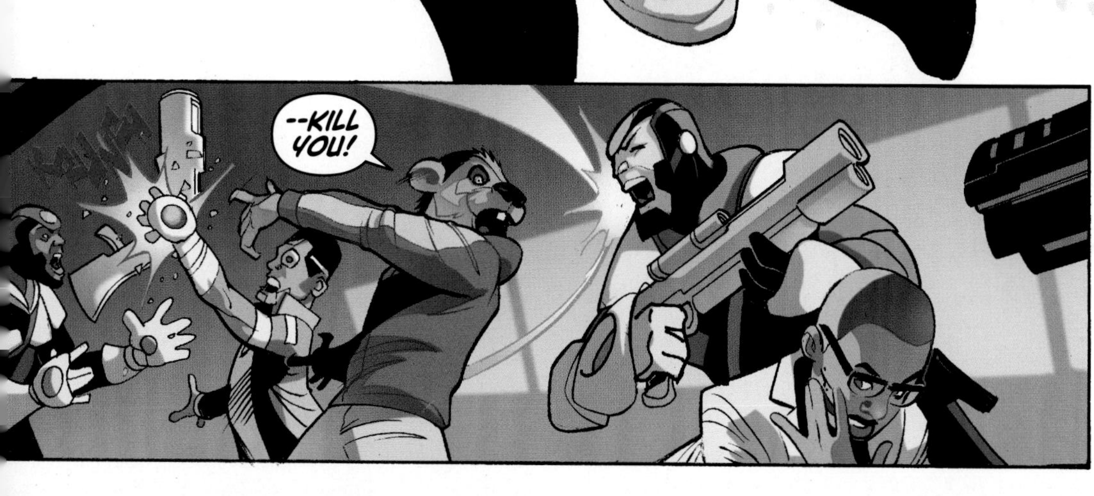
--KILL YOU!

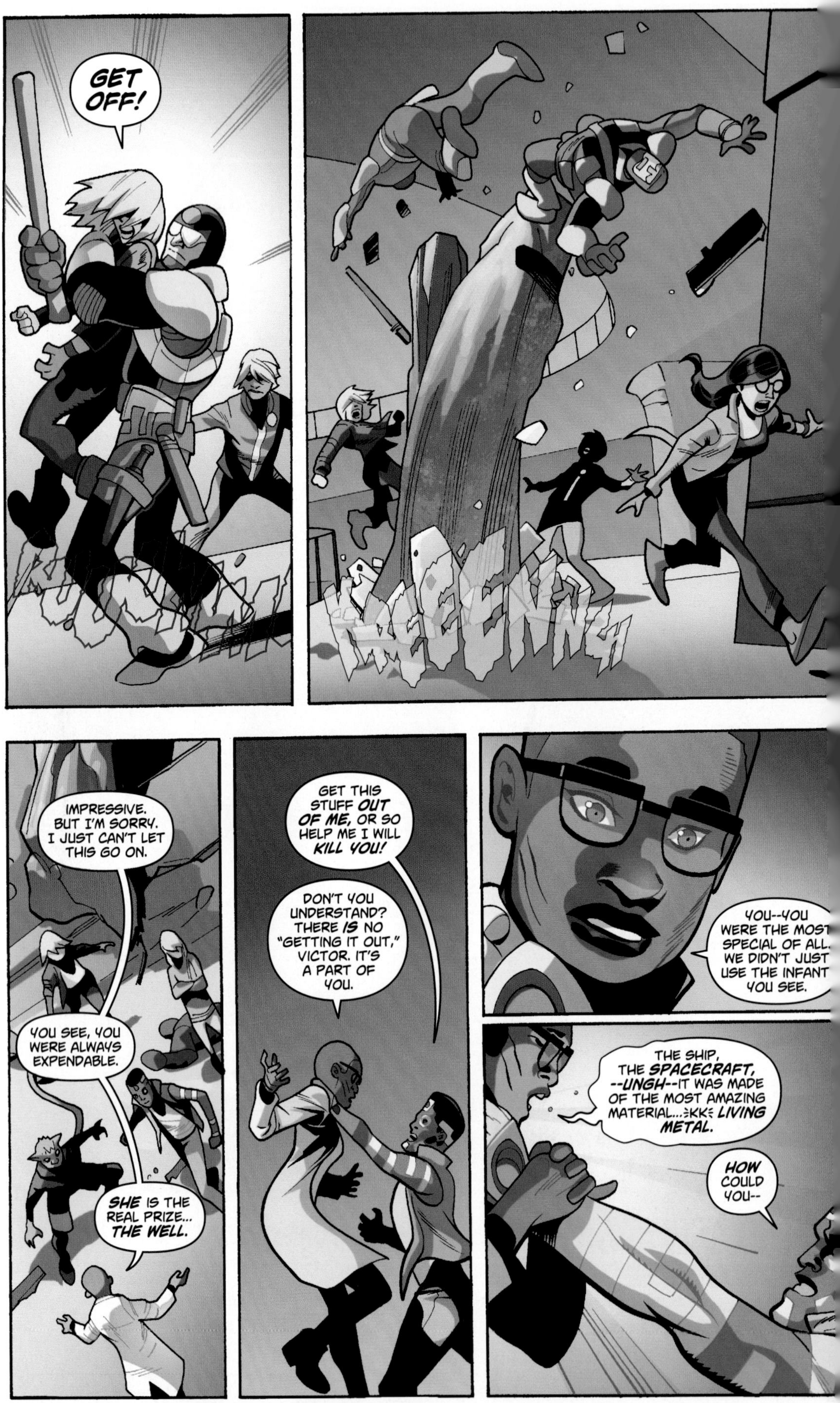
GET OFF!
RUMMMM
KRAASSHH
IMPRESSIVE. BUT I'M SORRY. I JUST CAN'T LET THIS GO ON.
YOU SEE, YOU WERE ALWAYS EXPENDABLE.
SHE IS THE REAL PRIZE... THE WELL.
GET THIS STUFF OUT OF ME, OR SO HELP ME I WILL KILL YOU!
DON'T YOU UNDERSTAND? THERE IS NO "GETTING IT OUT," VICTOR. IT'S A PART OF YOU.
YOU--YOU WERE THE MOST SPECIAL OF ALL. WE DIDN'T JUST USE THE INFANT YOU SEE.
THE SHIP, THE SPACECRAFT, --UNGH--IT WAS MADE OF THE MOST AMAZING MATERIAL...KK LIVING METAL.
HOW COULD YOU--

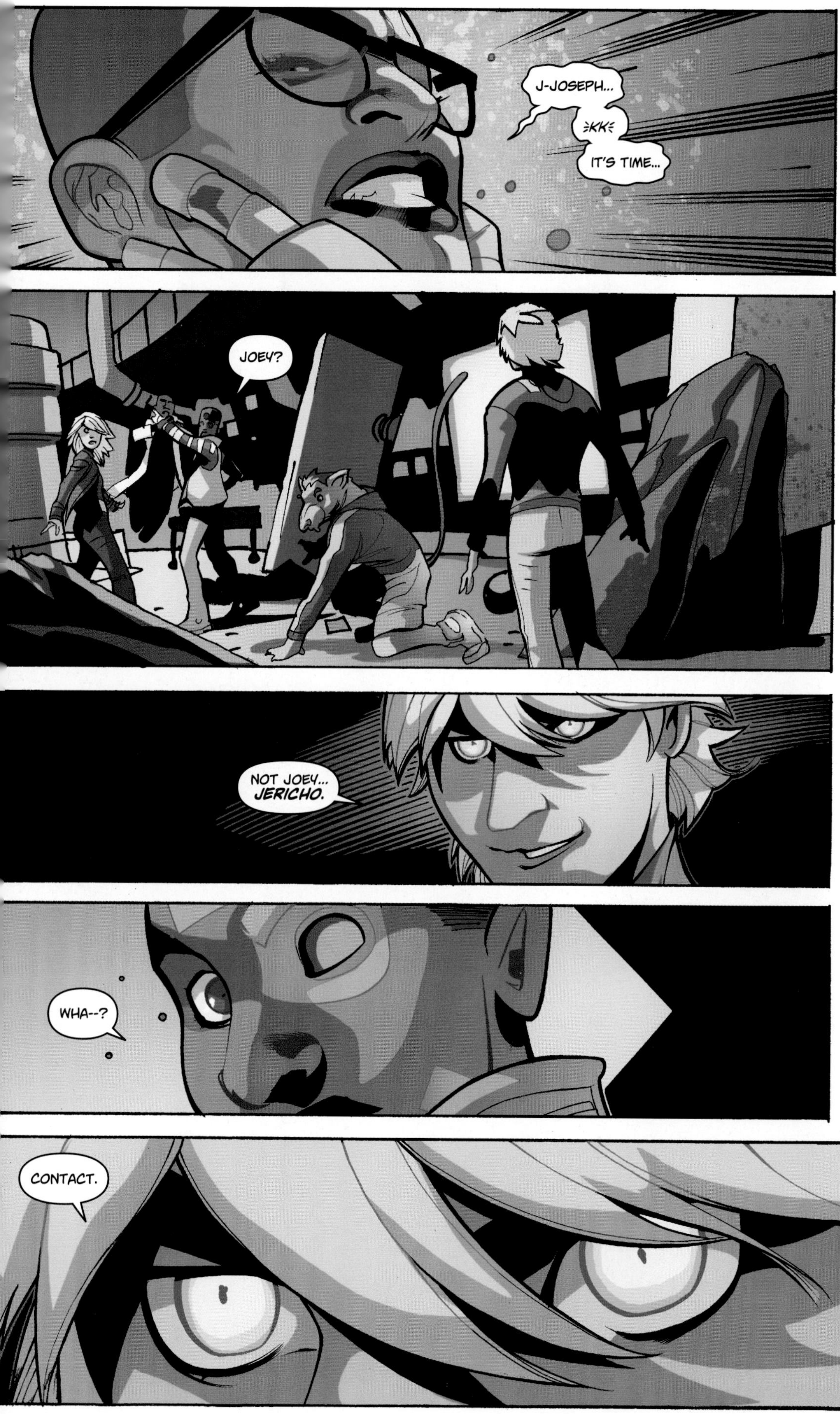
J-JOSEPH...
KK
IT'S TIME...
JOEY?
NOT JOEY...
JERICHO.
WHA--?
CONTACT.

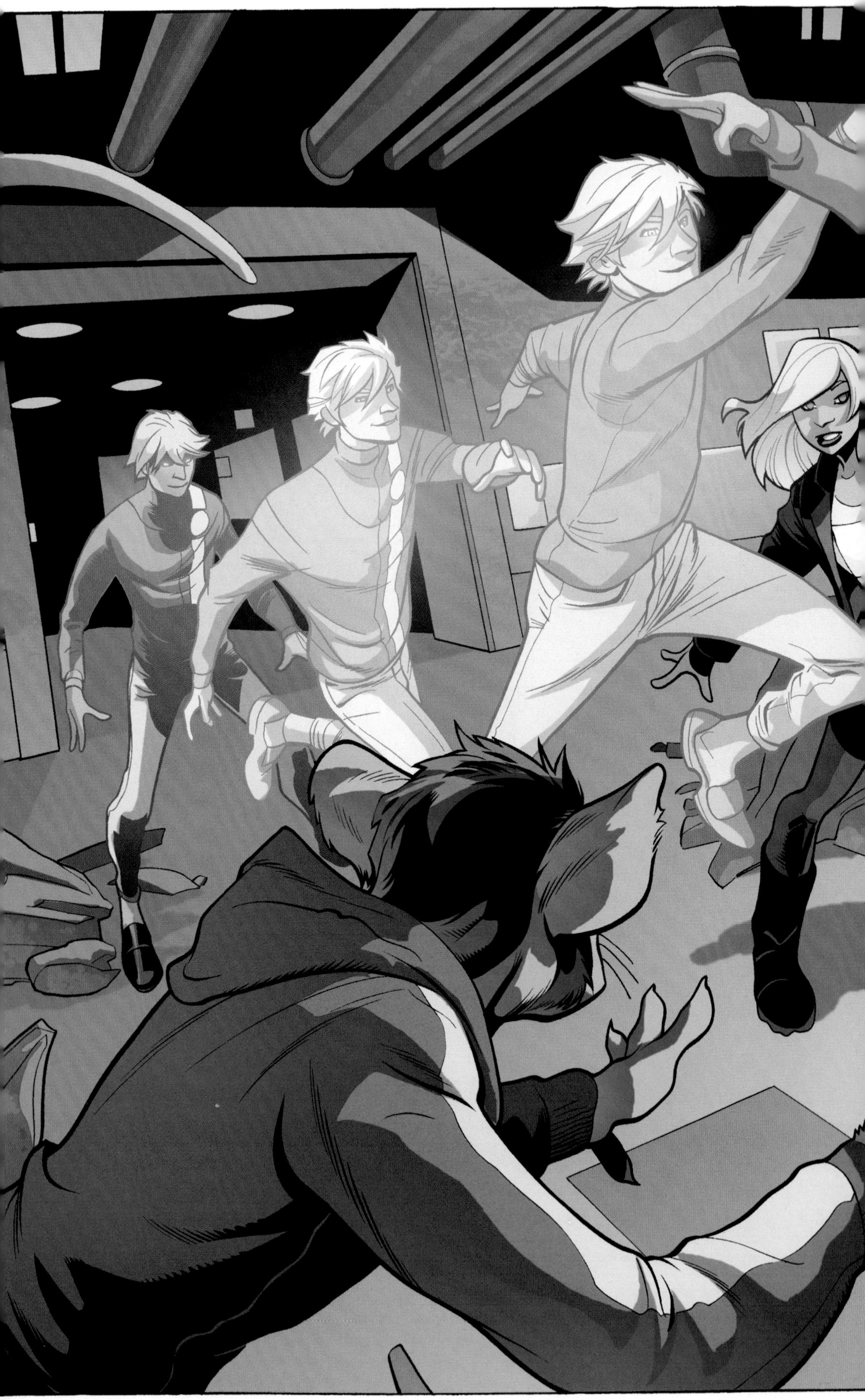

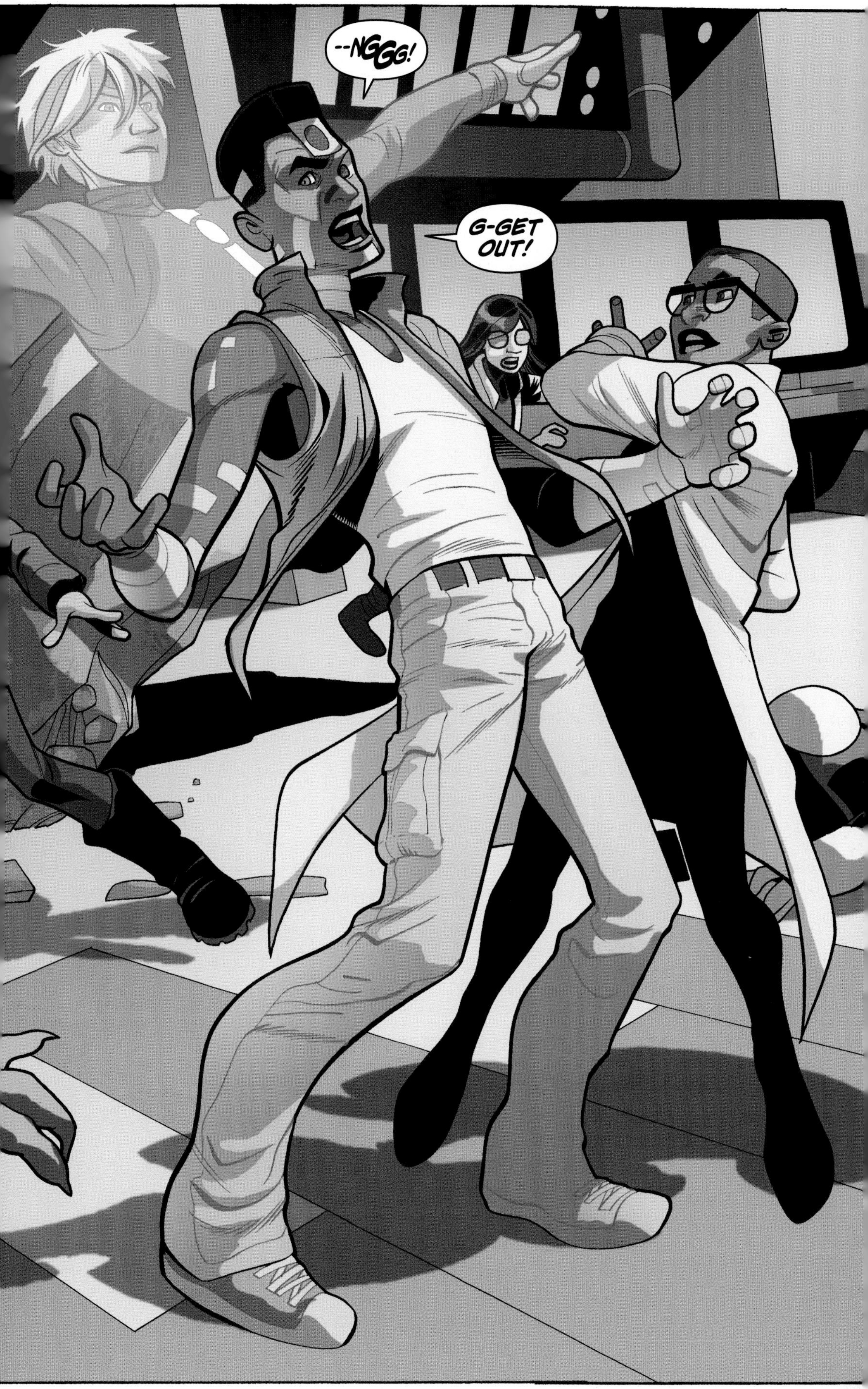
--NGGG!
G-GET OUT!

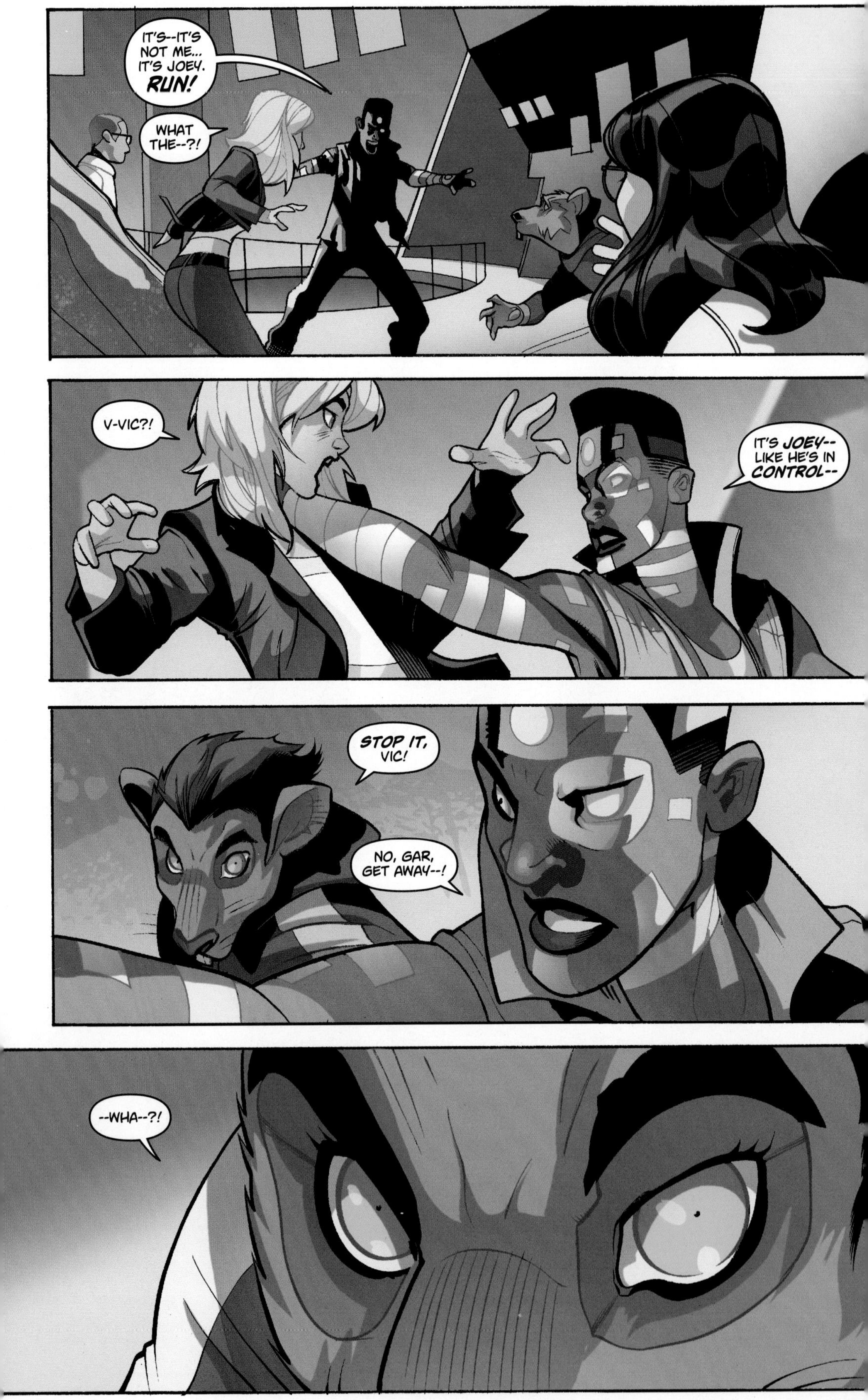
IT'S--IT'S NOT ME... IT'S JOEY. RUN!
WHAT THE--?!
V-VIC?!
IT'S JOEY-- LIKE HE'S IN CONTROL--
STOP IT, VIC!
NO, GAR, GET AWAY--!
--WHA--?!

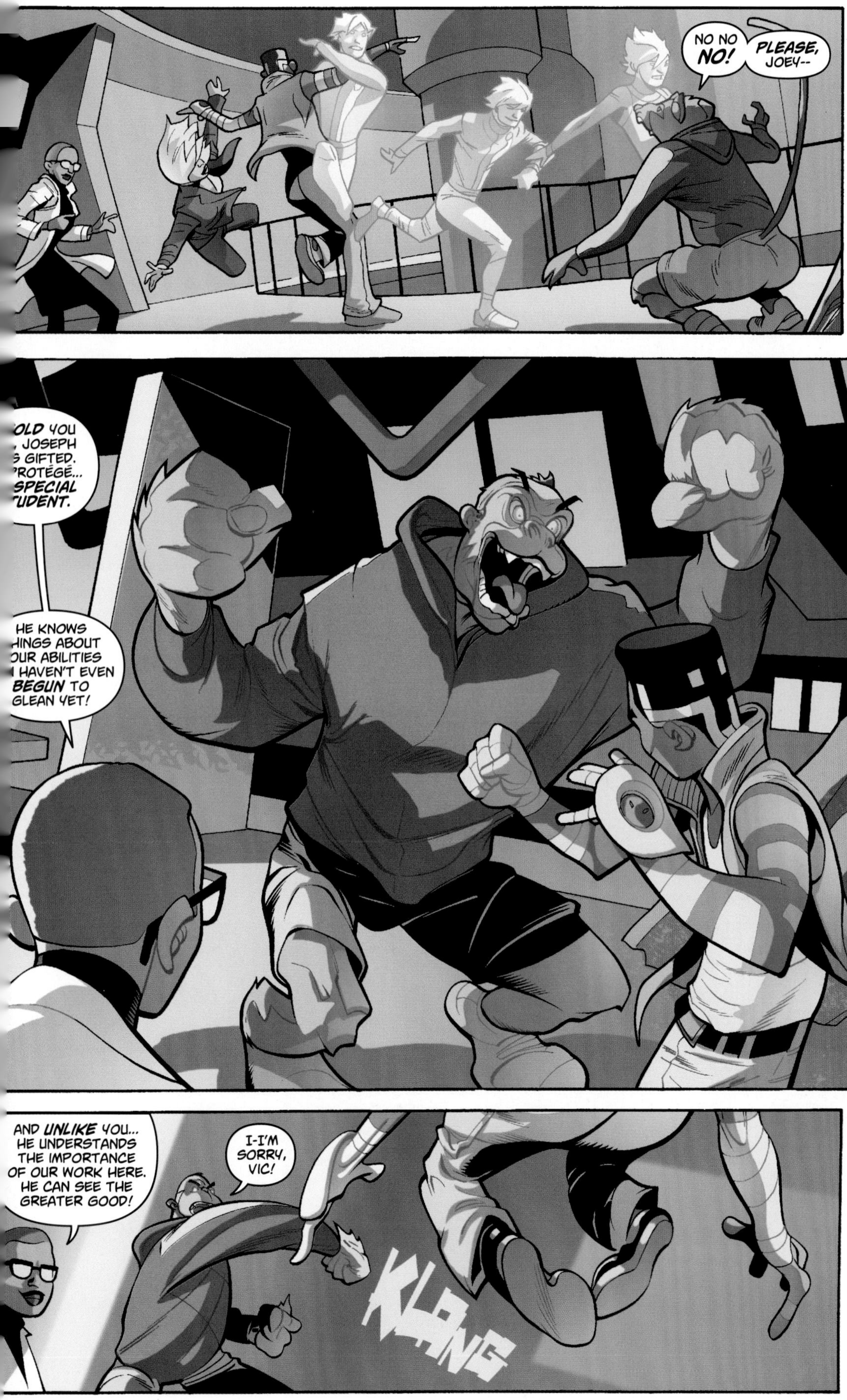
NO NO **NO!**
PLEASE, JOEY--
OLD YOU , JOSEPH S GIFTED. ROTÉGÉ... **SPECIAL TUDENT.**
HE KNOWS HINGS ABOUT OUR ABILITIES HAVEN'T EVEN **BEGUN** TO GLEAN YET!
AND **UNLIKE** YOU... HE UNDERSTANDS THE IMPORTANCE OF OUR WORK HERE. HE CAN SEE THE GREATER GOOD!
I-I'M SORRY, VIC!
KLANG

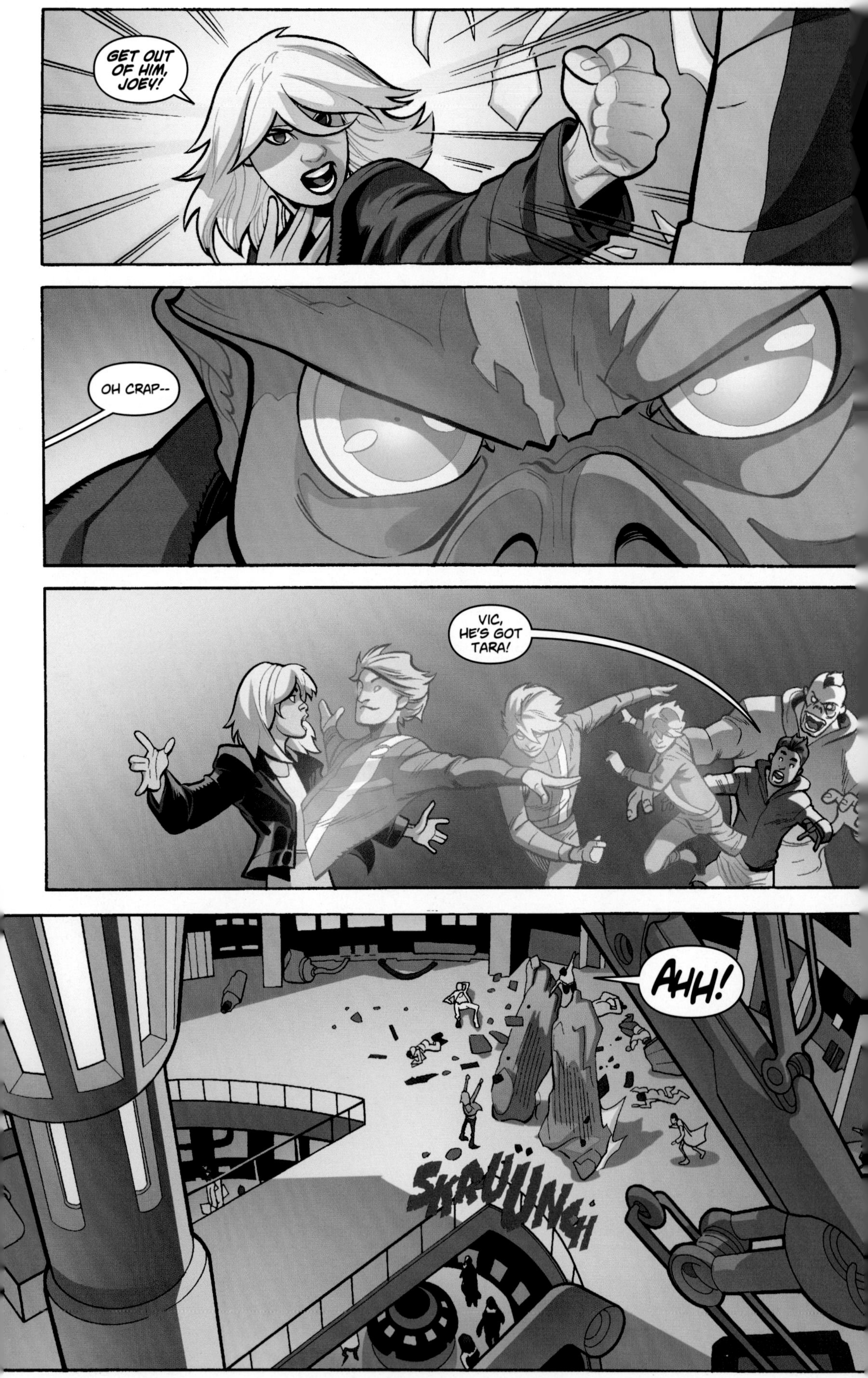
GET OUT OF HIM, JOEY!
OH CRAP--
VIC, HE'S GOT TARA!
AHH!
SKRUUNCH

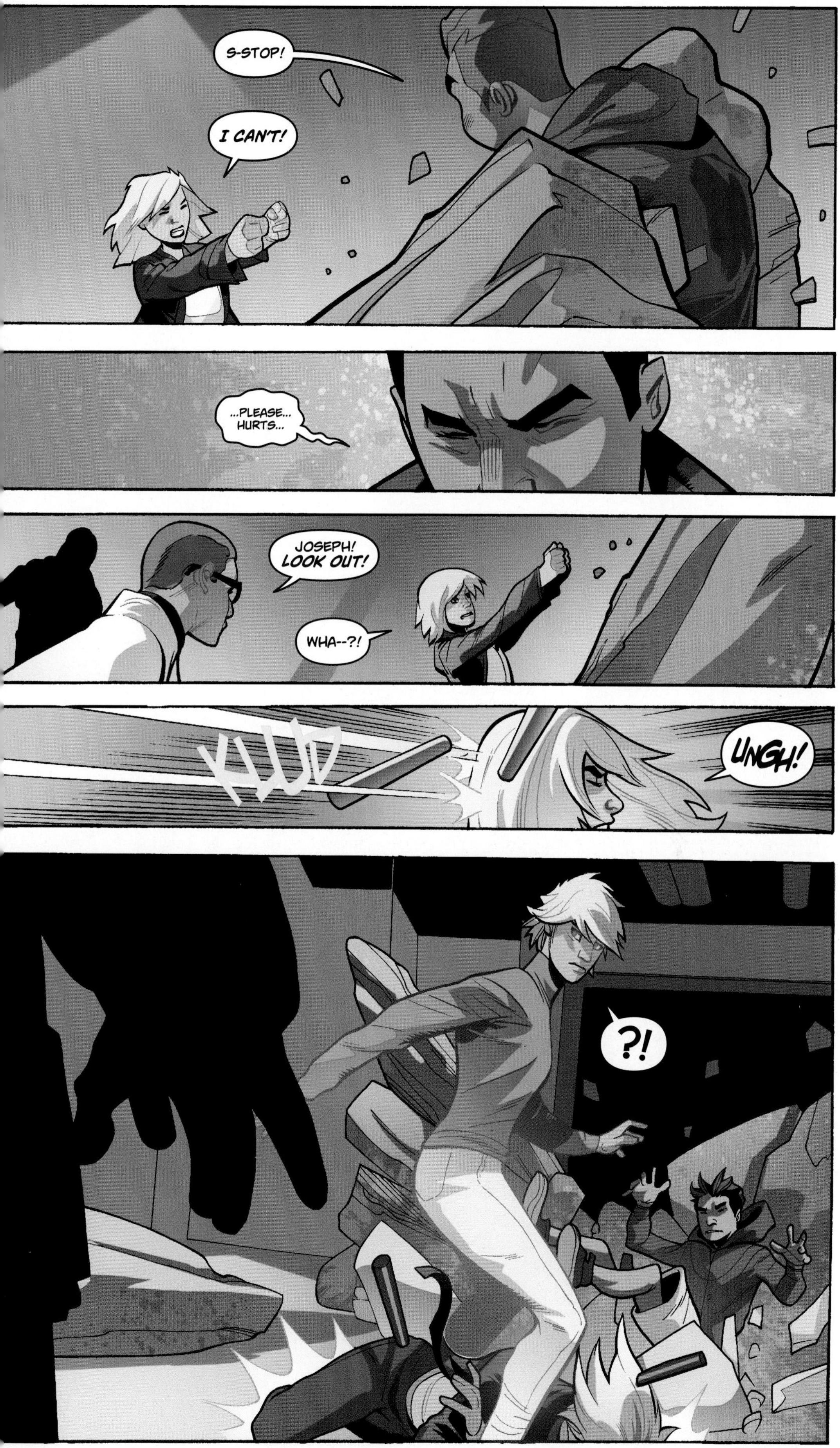
S-STOP!
I CAN'T!
...PLEASE... HURTS...
JOSEPH! LOOK OUT!
WHA--?!
KLUD
UNGH!
?!

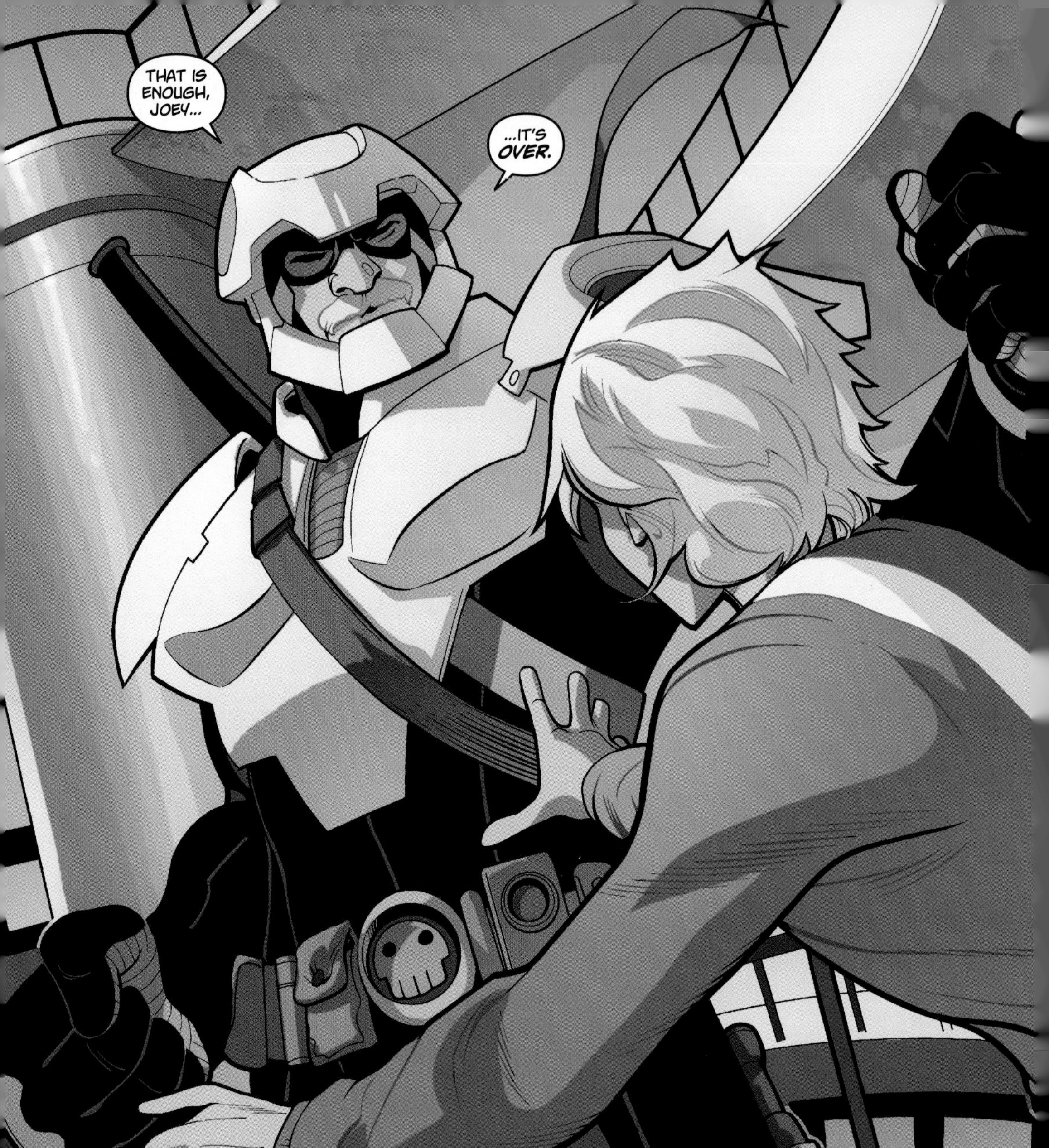
THAT IS ENOUGH, JOEY...
...IT'S OVER.

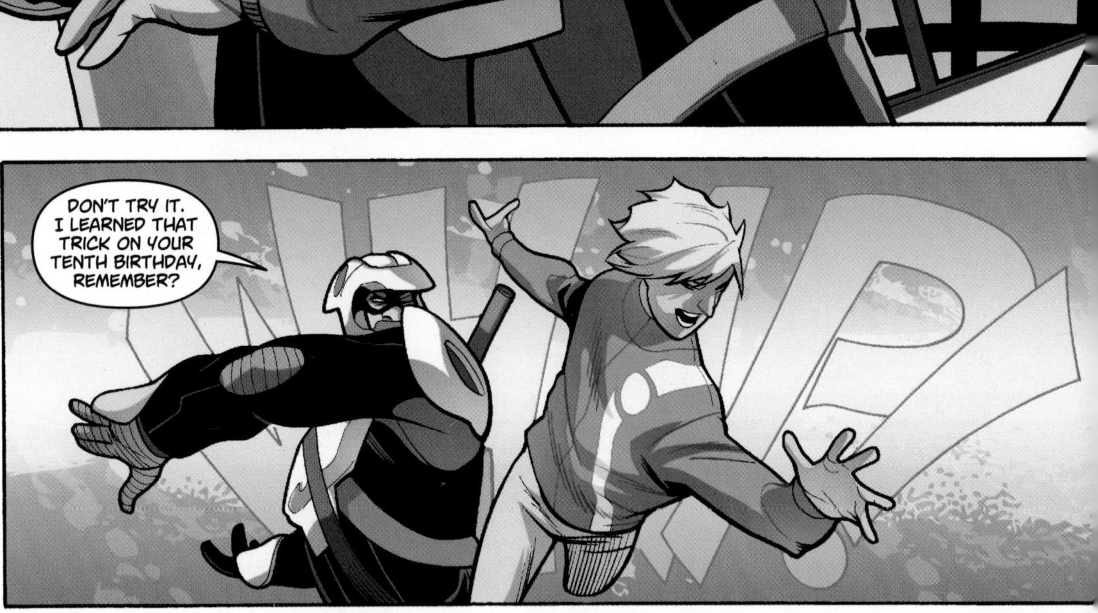
DON'T TRY IT. I LEARNED THAT TRICK ON YOUR TENTH BIRTHDAY, REMEMBER?

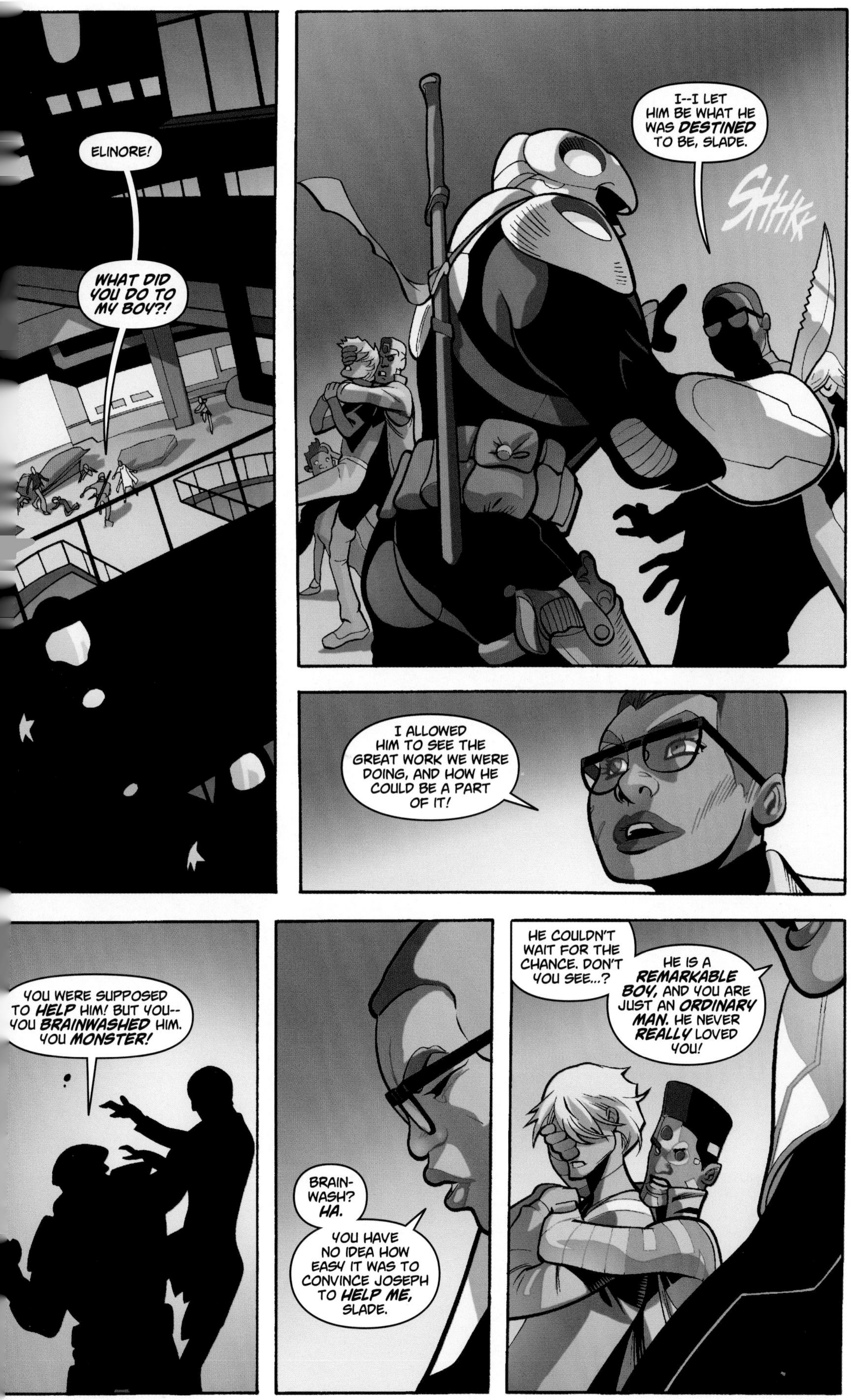
ELINORE!
WHAT DID YOU DO TO MY BOY?!
I--I LET HIM BE WHAT HE WAS DESTINED TO BE, SLADE.
SHHKK
I ALLOWED HIM TO SEE THE GREAT WORK WE WERE DOING, AND HOW HE COULD BE A PART OF IT!
YOU WERE SUPPOSED TO HELP HIM! BUT YOU-- YOU BRAINWASHED HIM. YOU MONSTER!
BRAIN-WASH? HA.
YOU HAVE NO IDEA HOW EASY IT WAS TO CONVINCE JOSEPH TO HELP ME, SLADE.
HE COULDN'T WAIT FOR THE CHANCE. DON'T YOU SEE...?
HE IS A REMARKABLE BOY, AND YOU ARE JUST AN ORDINARY MAN. HE NEVER REALLY LOVED YOU!

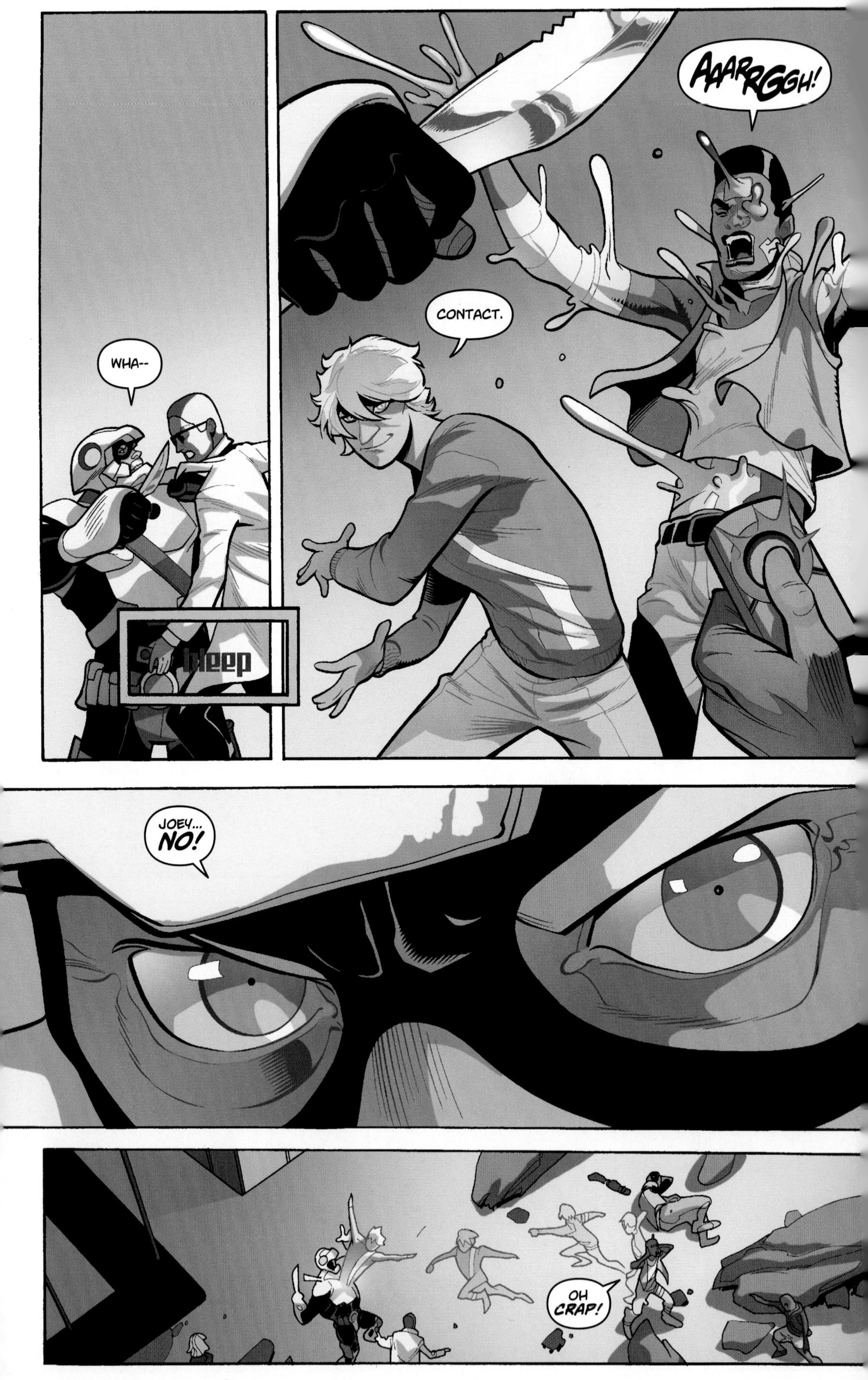
WHA--
bleep
AAARRGGH!
CONTACT.
JOEY... NO!
OH CRAP!

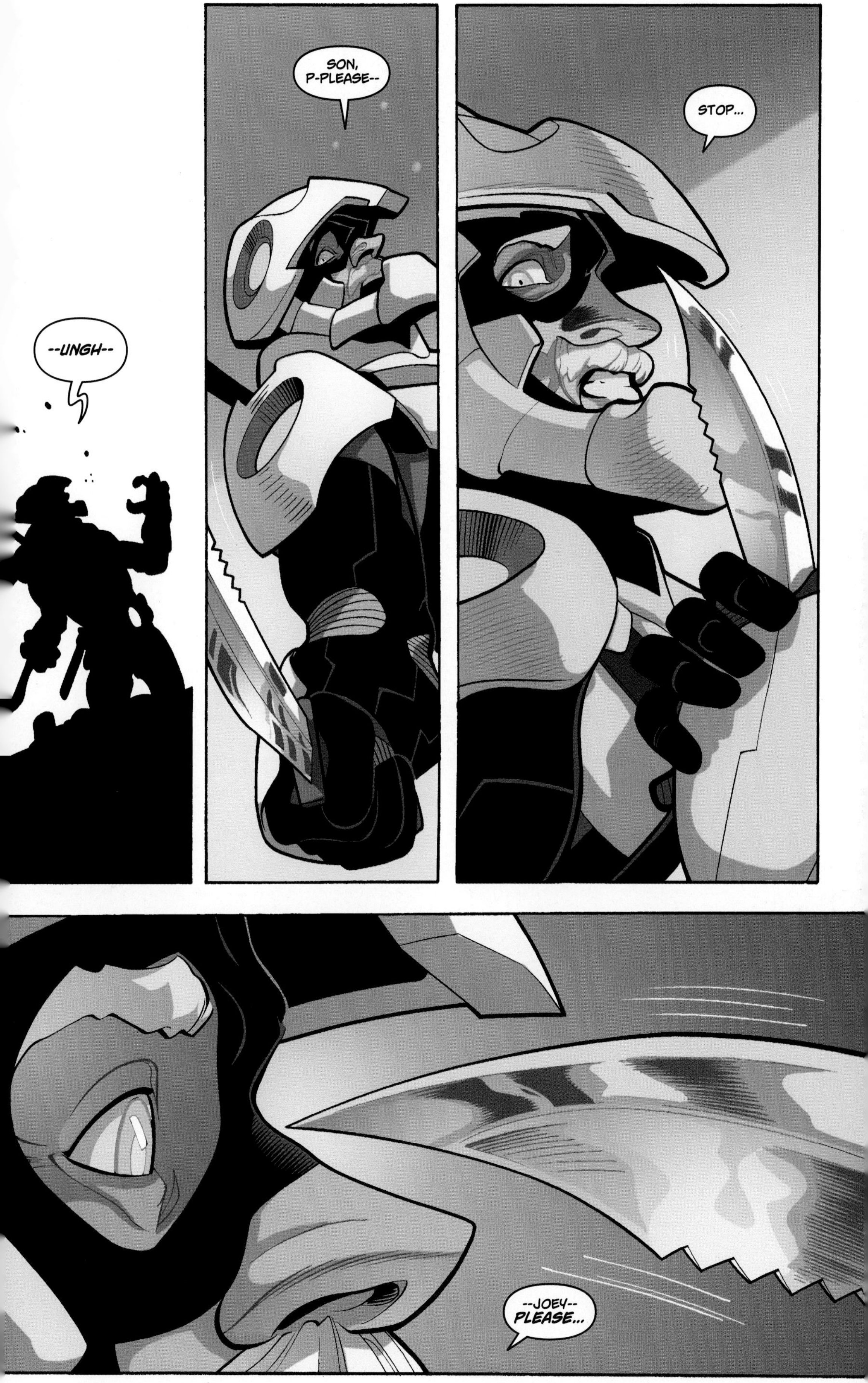

--UNGH--
SON, P-PLEASE--
STOP...
--JOEY-- PLEASE...

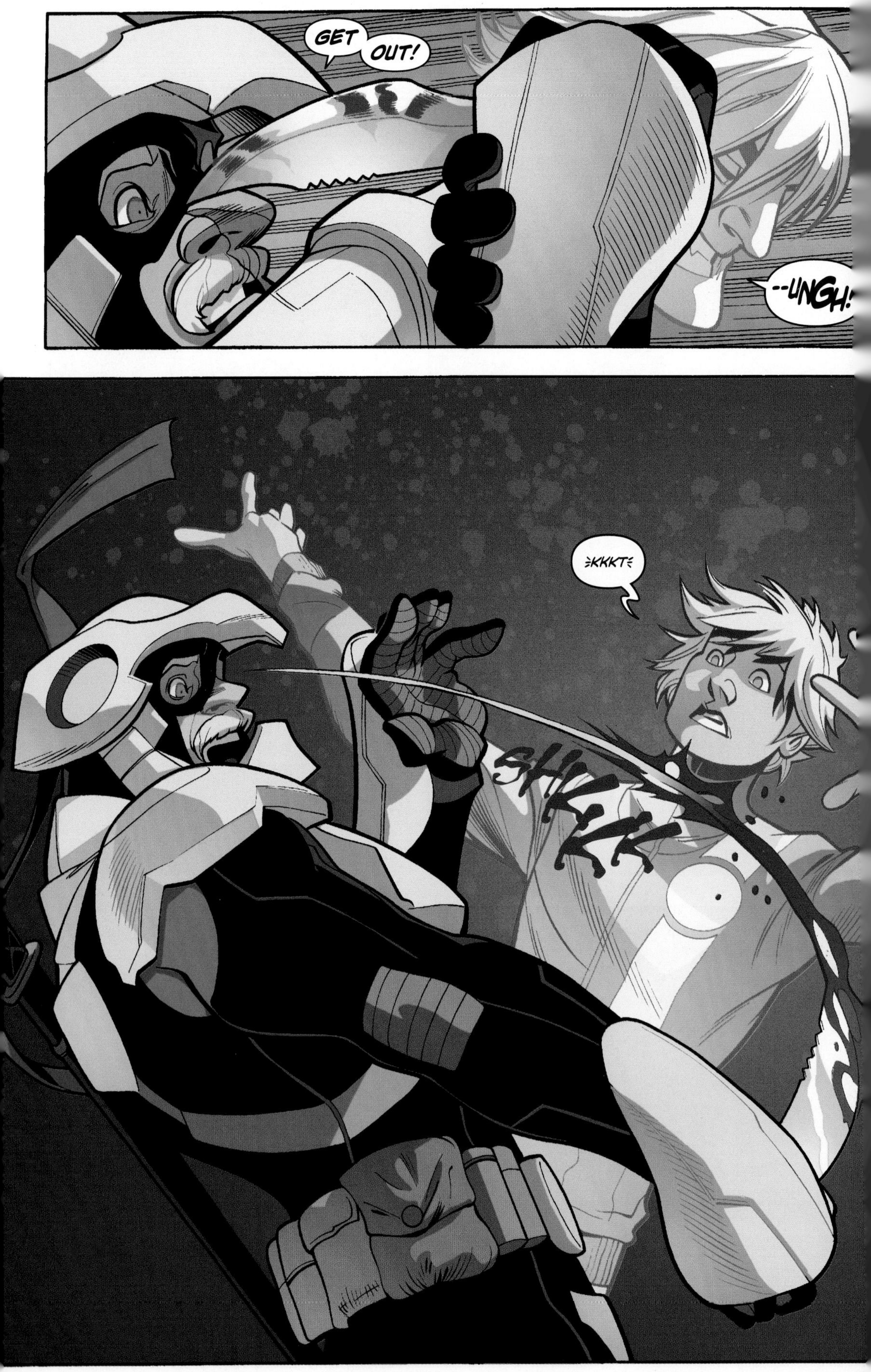
GET OUT!
--UNGH!
≠KKKT≠
SHKKK

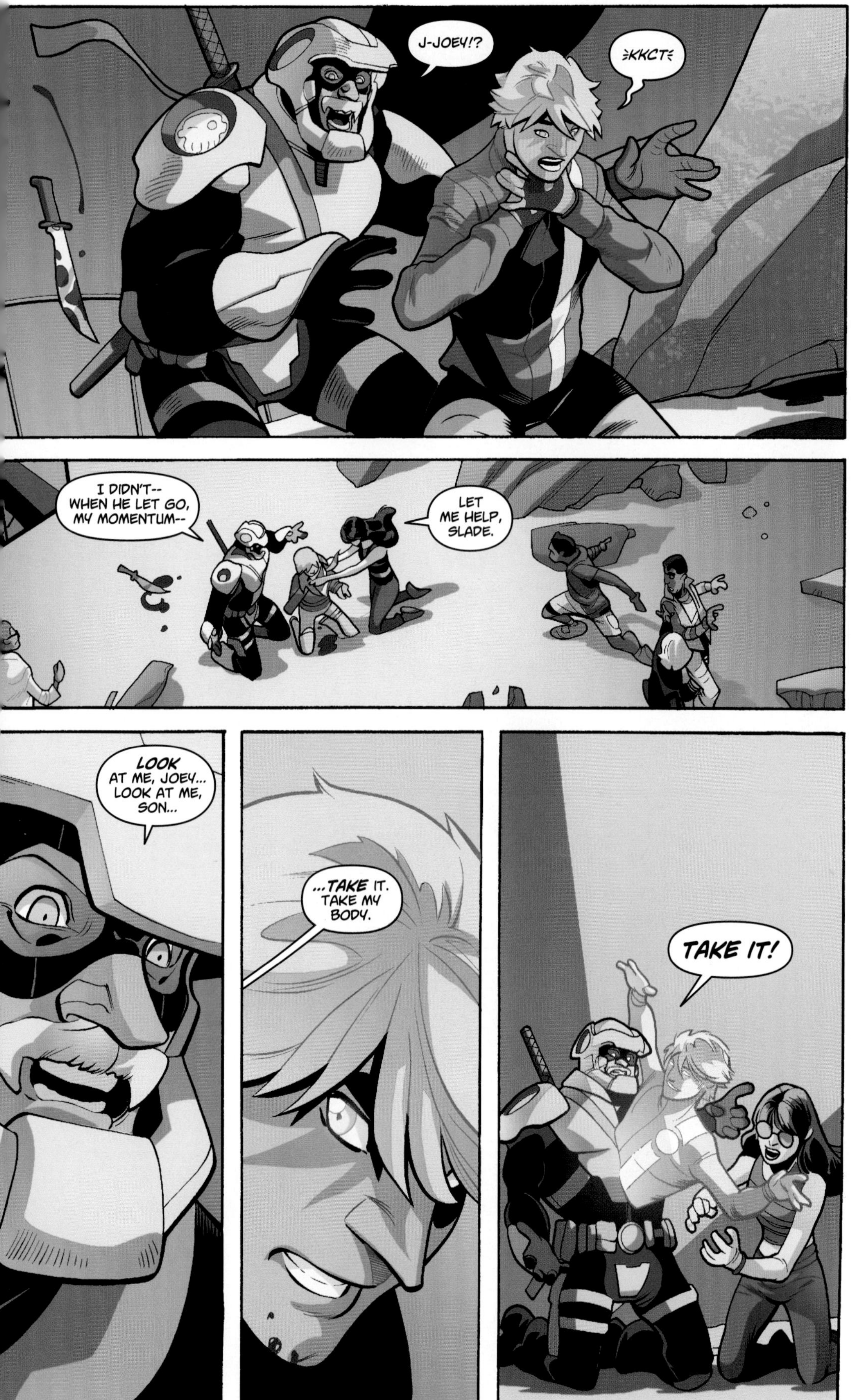
J-JOEY!?
KKCT
I DIDN'T-- WHEN HE LET GO, MY MOMENTUM--
LET ME HELP, SLADE.
LOOK AT ME, JOEY... LOOK AT ME, SON...
...TAKE IT. TAKE MY BODY.
TAKE IT!

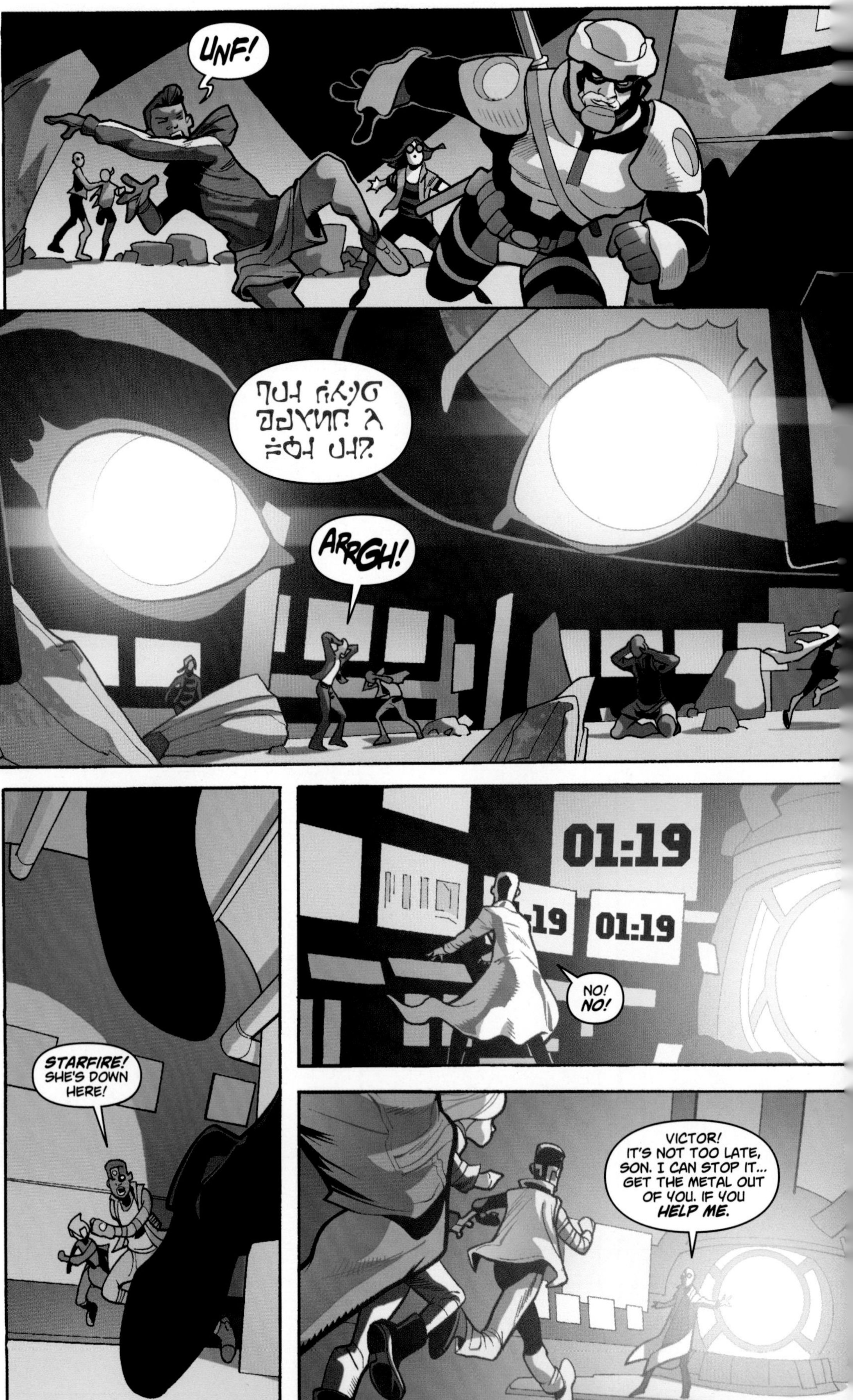
UNF!
ARRGH!
STARFIRE! SHE'S DOWN HERE!
01:19
01:19
NO! NO!
VICTOR! IT'S NOT TOO LATE, SON. I CAN STOP IT... GET THE METAL OUT OF YOU. IF YOU HELP ME.

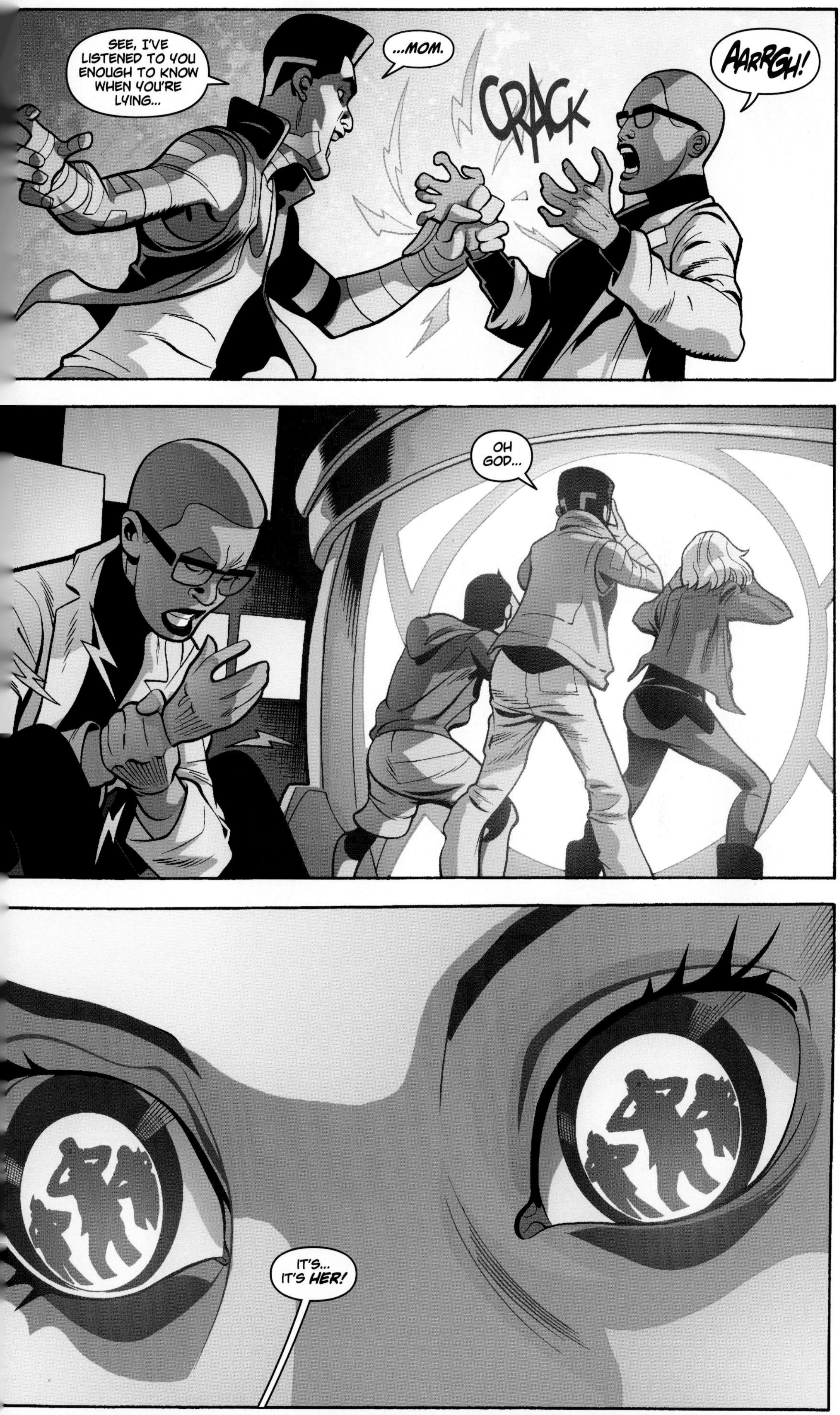
SEE, I'VE LISTENED TO YOU ENOUGH TO KNOW WHEN YOU'RE LYING...
...MOM.
CRACK
AARRGH!
OH GOD...
IT'S... IT'S HER!

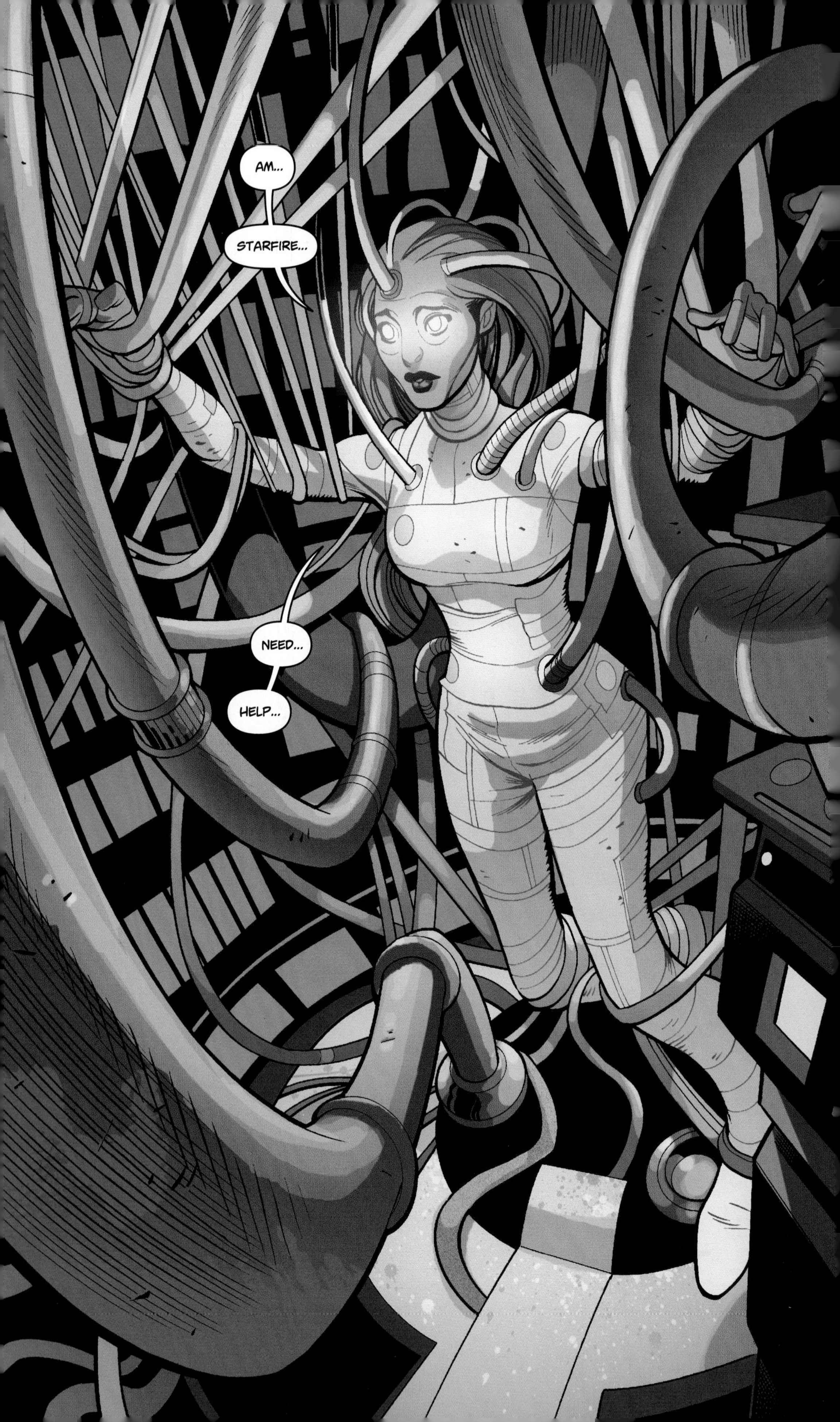
AM...
STARFIRE...
NEED...
HELP...

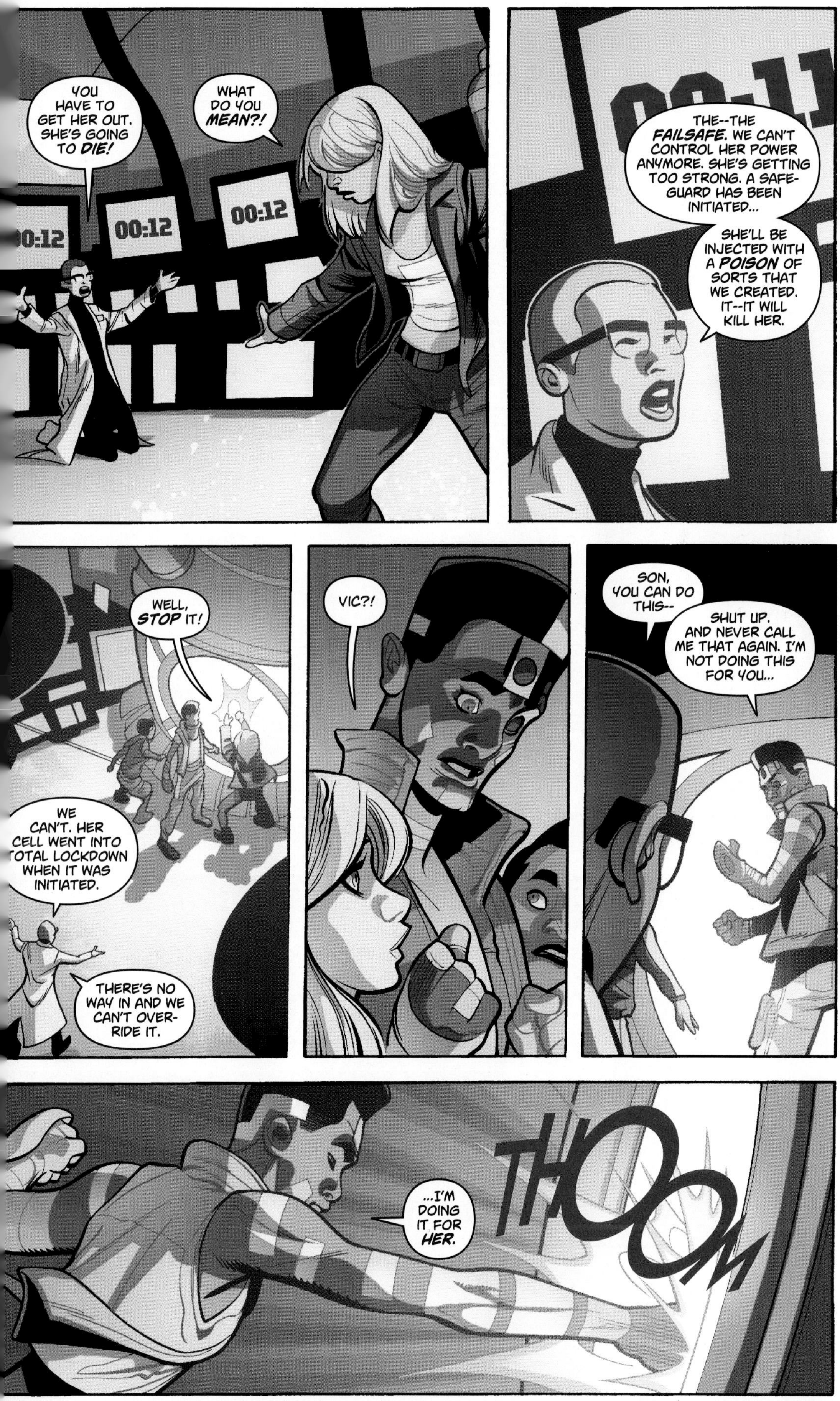
YOU HAVE TO GET HER OUT. SHE'S GOING TO DIE!
WHAT DO YOU MEAN?!
00:12
00:12
00:12
THE--THE FAILSAFE. WE CAN'T CONTROL HER POWER ANYMORE. SHE'S GETTING TOO STRONG. A SAFE-GUARD HAS BEEN INITIATED...
SHE'LL BE INJECTED WITH A POISON OF SORTS THAT WE CREATED. IT--IT WILL KILL HER.
WELL, STOP IT!
WE CAN'T. HER CELL WENT INTO TOTAL LOCKDOWN WHEN IT WAS INITIATED.
THERE'S NO WAY IN AND WE CAN'T OVER-RIDE IT.
VIC?!
SON, YOU CAN DO THIS--
SHUT UP. AND NEVER CALL ME THAT AGAIN. I'M NOT DOING THIS FOR YOU...
...I'M DOING IT FOR HER.
THOOOM

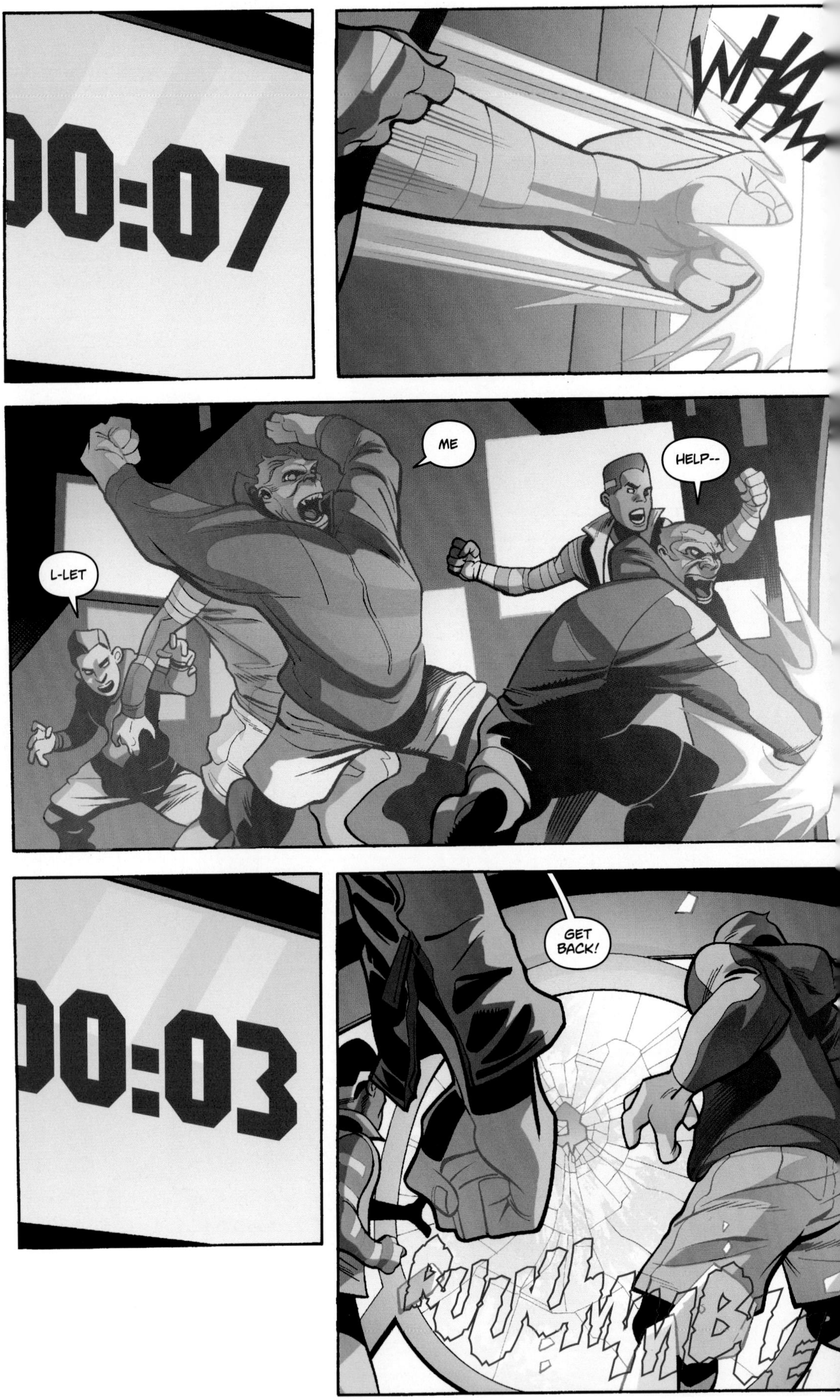
00:07
WHAM
L-LET
ME
HELP--
00:03
GET BACK!
RUUMMMBLE

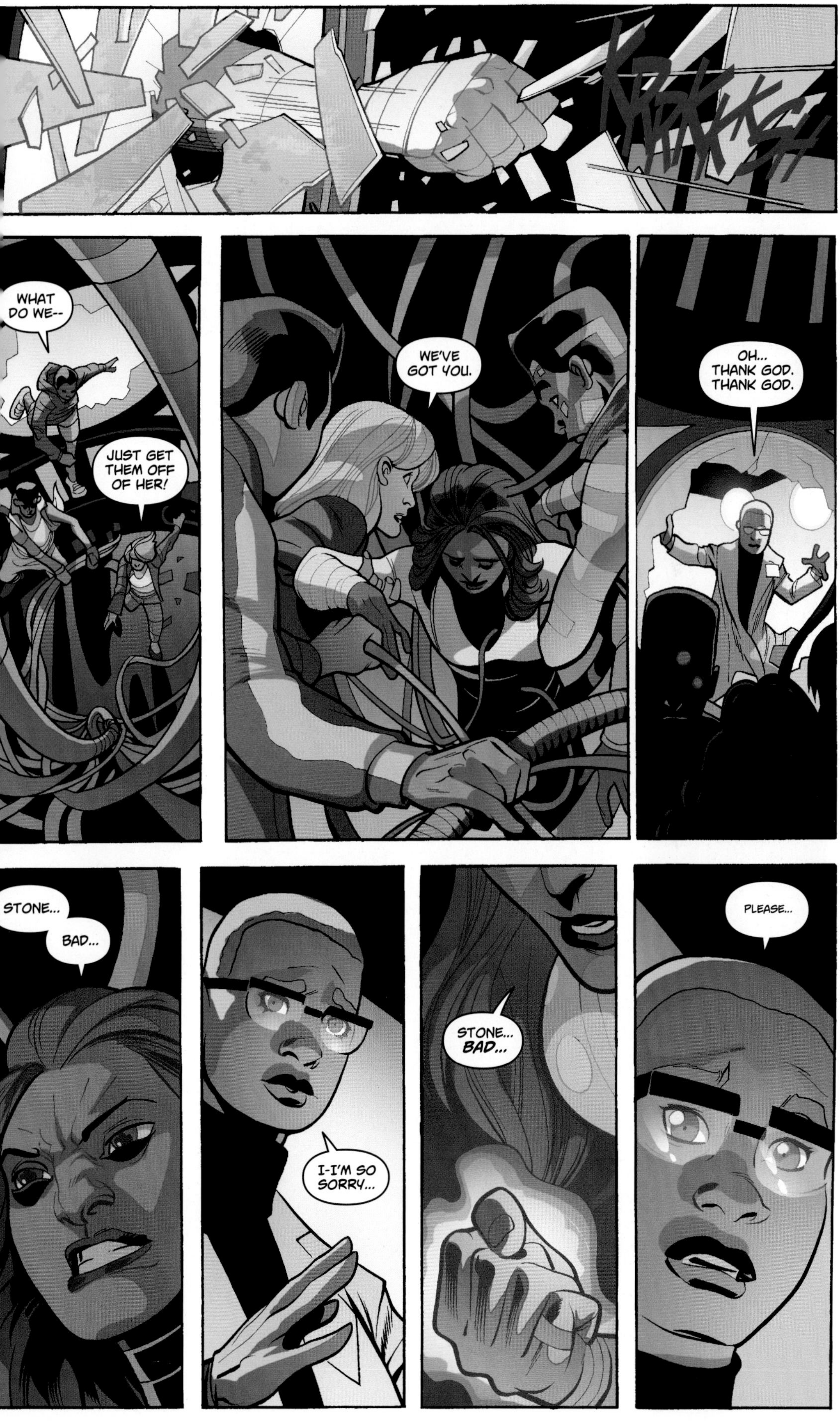
KRKKKSH
WHAT DO WE--
JUST GET THEM OFF OF HER!
WE'VE GOT YOU.
OH... THANK GOD. THANK GOD.
STONE...
BAD...
I-I'M SO SORRY...
STONE... BAD...
PLEASE...

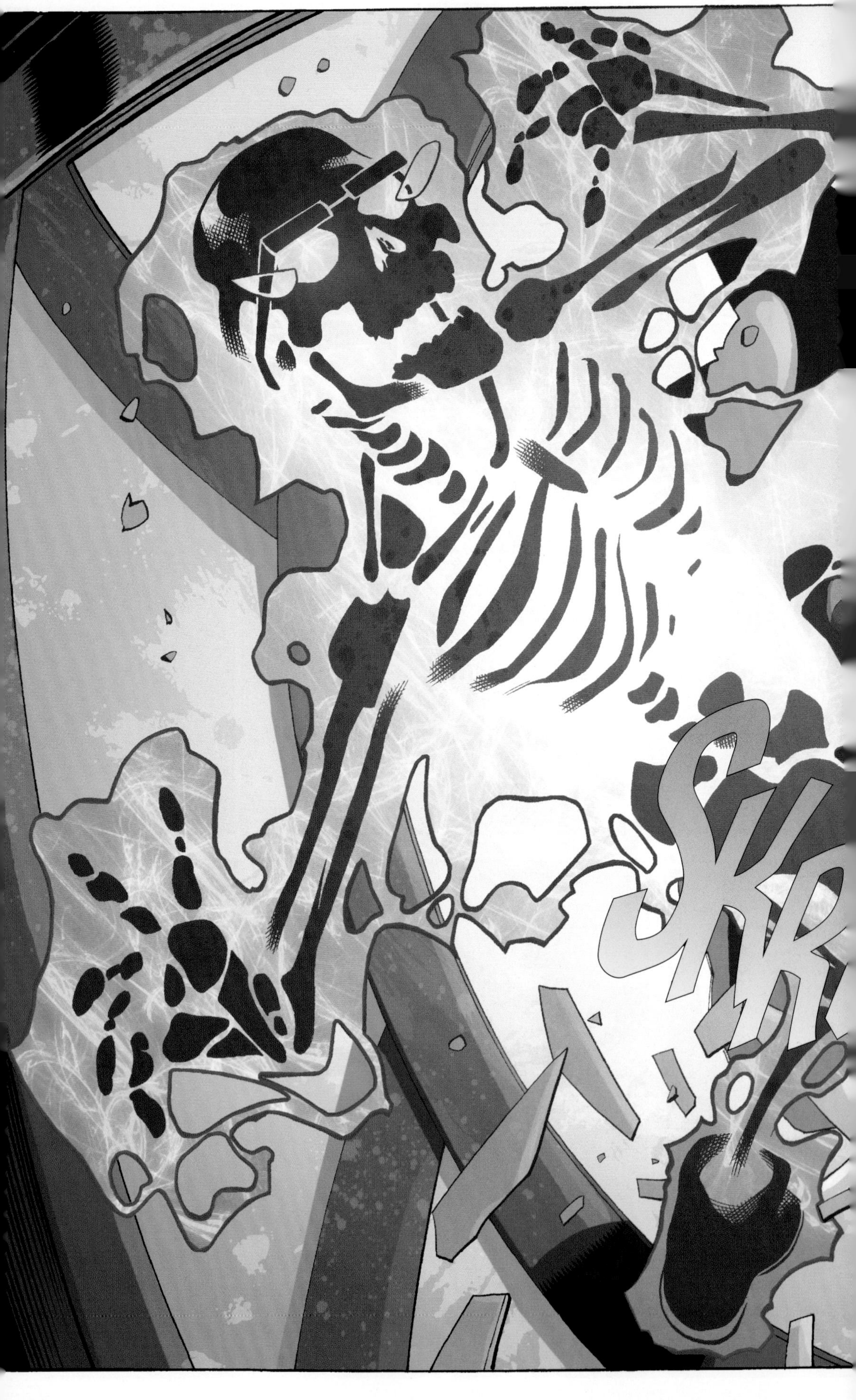

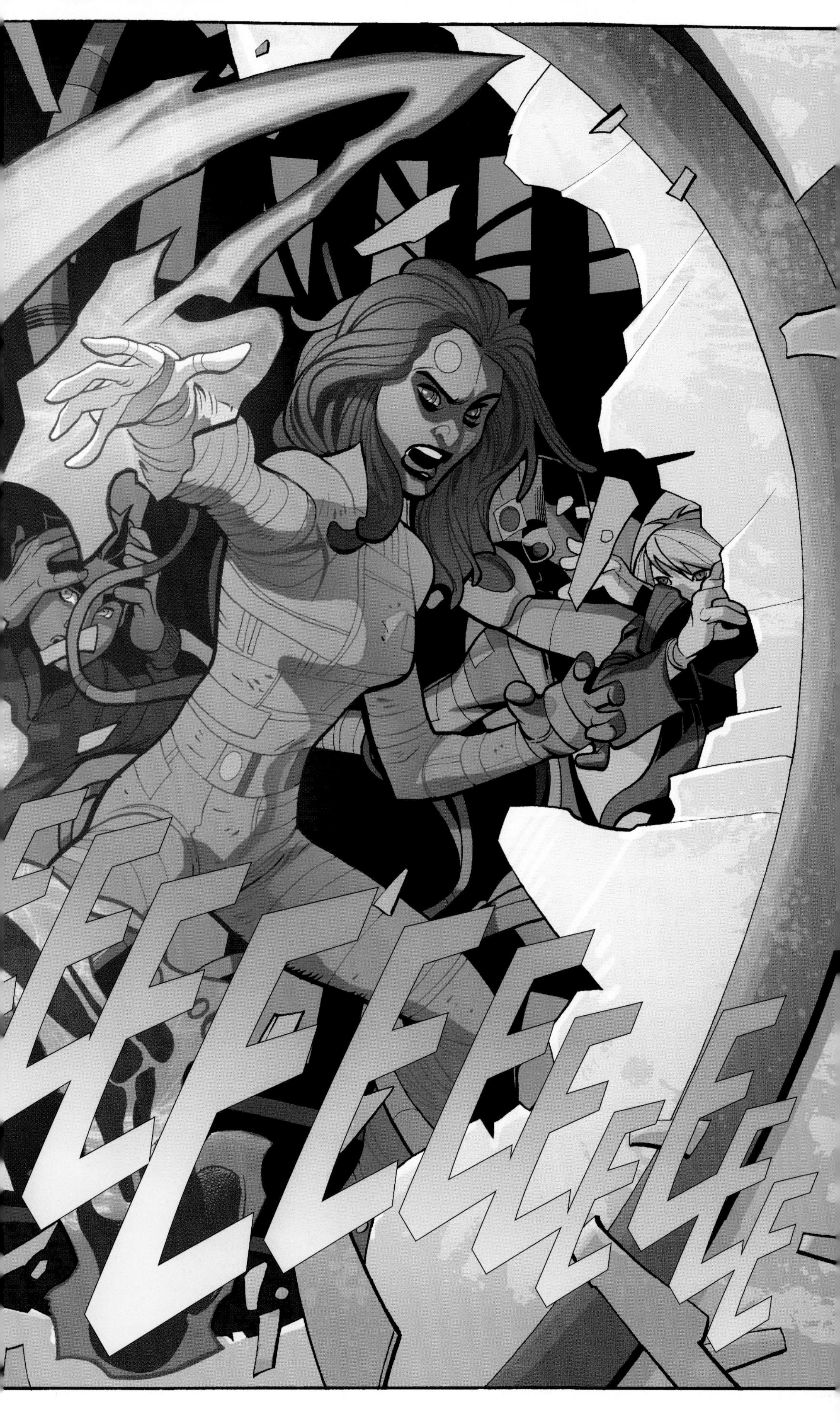
EEEEEEEEEE-

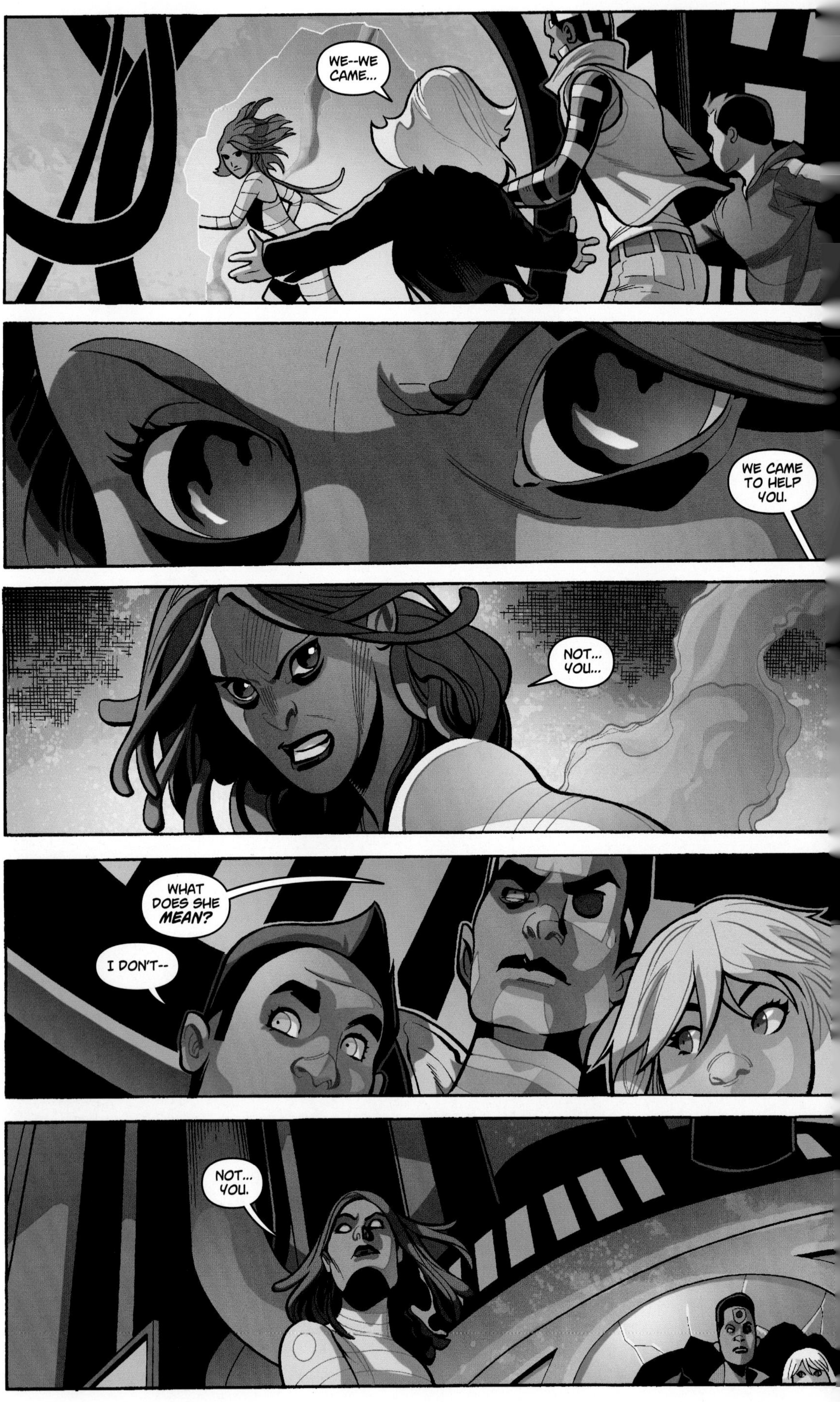

WE--WE CAME...
WE CAME TO HELP YOU.
NOT... YOU...
WHAT DOES SHE MEAN?
I DON'T--
NOT... YOU.

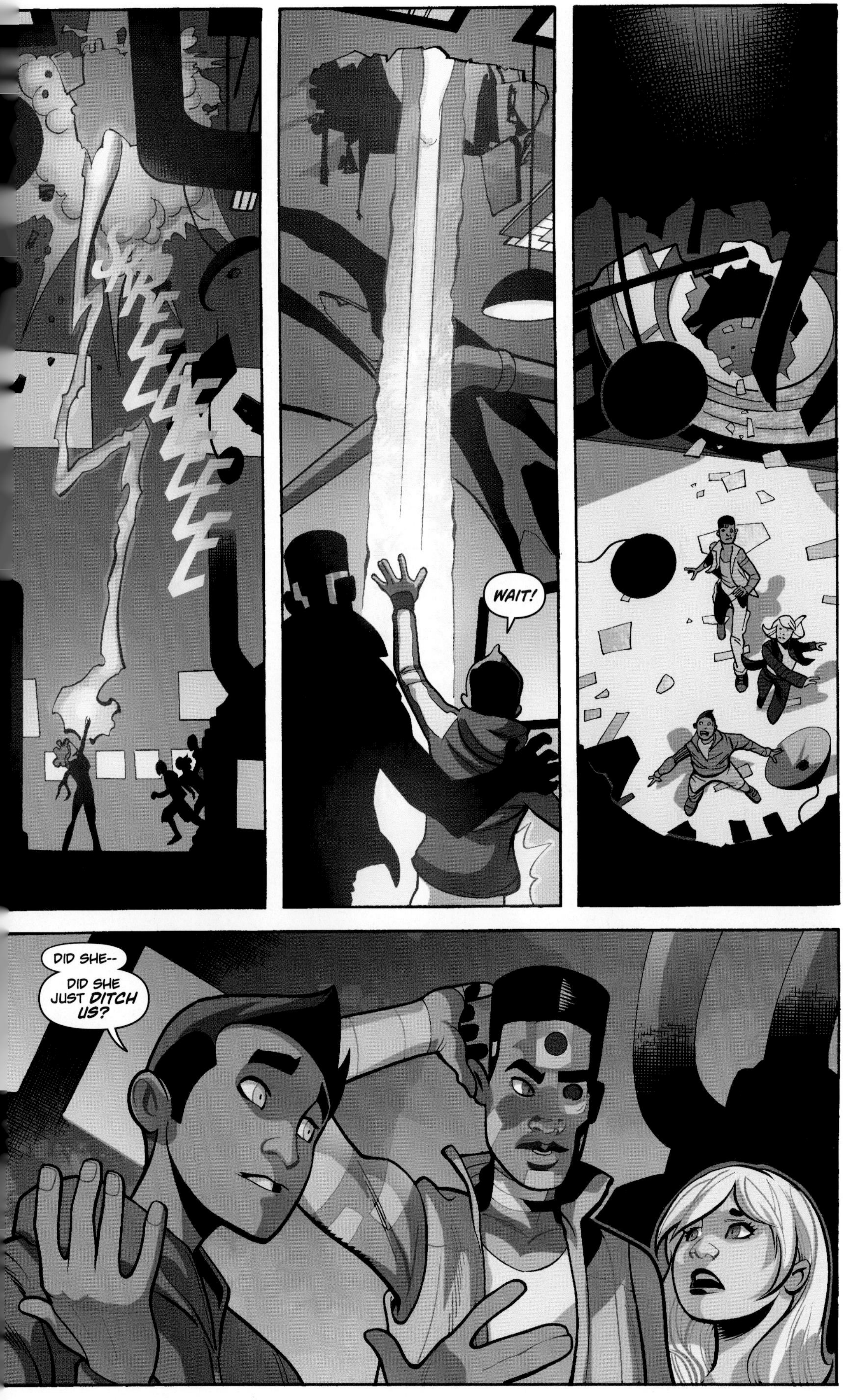
SKREEEEEEEE
WAIT!
DID SHE--
DID SHE JUST DITCH US?

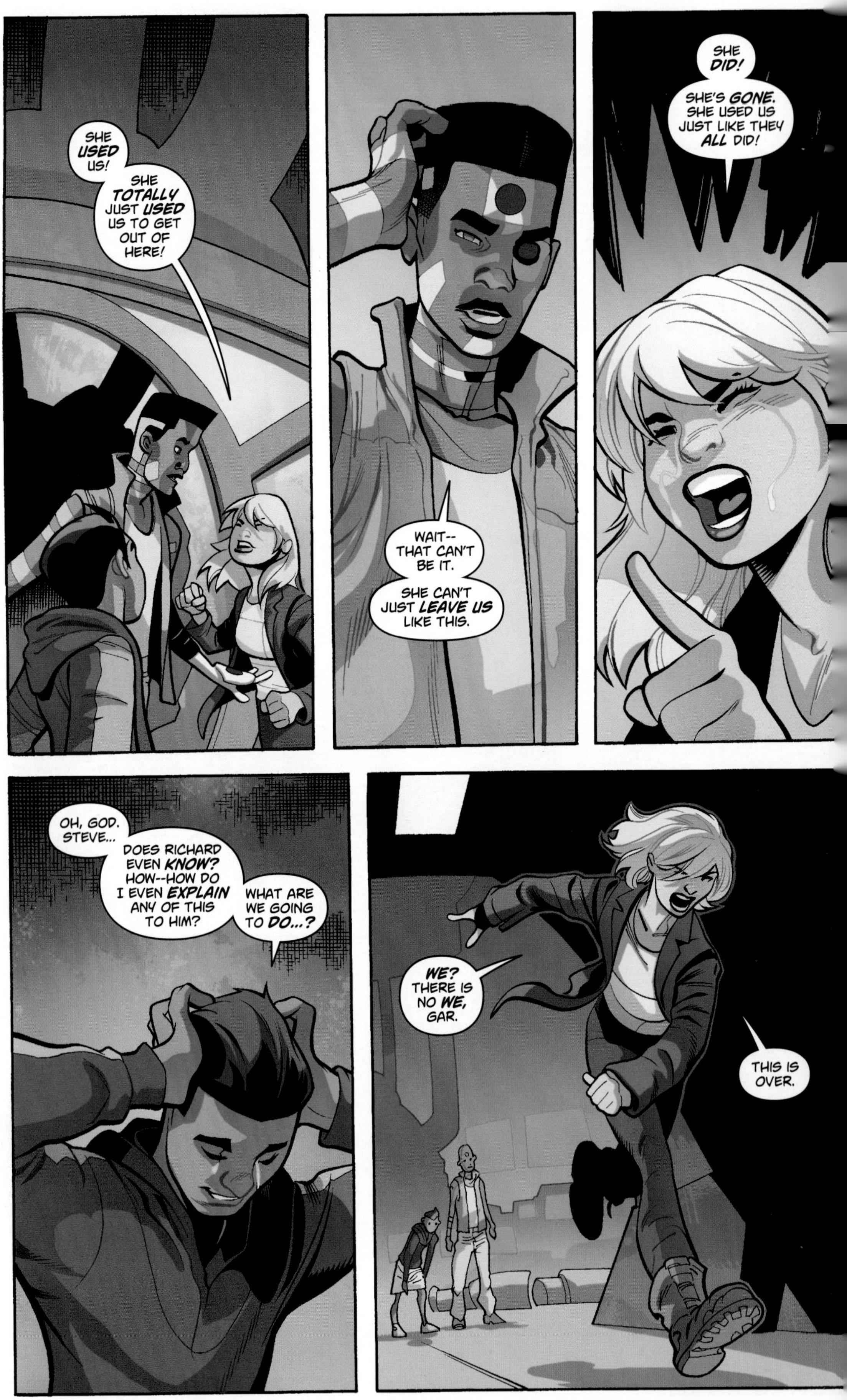
SHE USED US!
SHE TOTALLY JUST USED US TO GET OUT OF HERE!
WAIT-- THAT CAN'T BE IT.
SHE CAN'T JUST LEAVE US LIKE THIS.
SHE DID!
SHE'S GONE. SHE USED US JUST LIKE THEY ALL DID!
OH, GOD. STEVE...
DOES RICHARD EVEN KNOW? HOW--HOW DO I EVEN EXPLAIN ANY OF THIS TO HIM?
WHAT ARE WE GOING TO DO...?
WE? THERE IS NO WE, GAR.
THIS IS OVER.

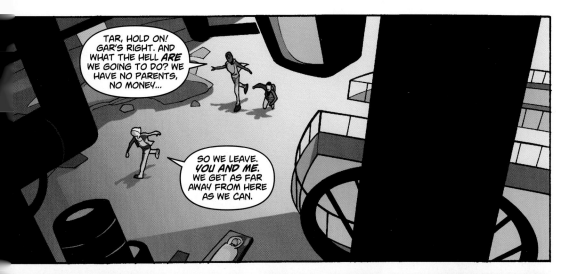

TAR, HOLD ON! GAR'S RIGHT. AND WHAT THE HELL *ARE* WE GOING TO DO? WE HAVE NO PARENTS, NO MONEY...

SO WE LEAVE. *YOU AND ME.* WE GET AS FAR AWAY FROM HERE AS WE CAN.

HOW AM *I* GOING TO GO ANYWHERE?! IF ANYONE *SEES ME,* THEY'RE JUST GOING TO LOCK ME UP AND STUDY ME.

WE'LL FIGURE IT OUT. BUT WE CAN'T STAY HERE. THERE MIGHT BE MORE OF THOSE GUARDS COMING. *WHO KNOWS* WHAT ELSE.

I--I CAN'T LEAVE HIM HERE. NOT LIKE THIS.

AND THAT KID IN THE TANK. HE'S ONE OF US. WE CAN'T LEAVE *HIM,* EITHER.

EVEN IF WE *CAN* GET HIM OUT OF THERE, WHERE THE HELL DO WE *GO,* THEN!?

UTAH.

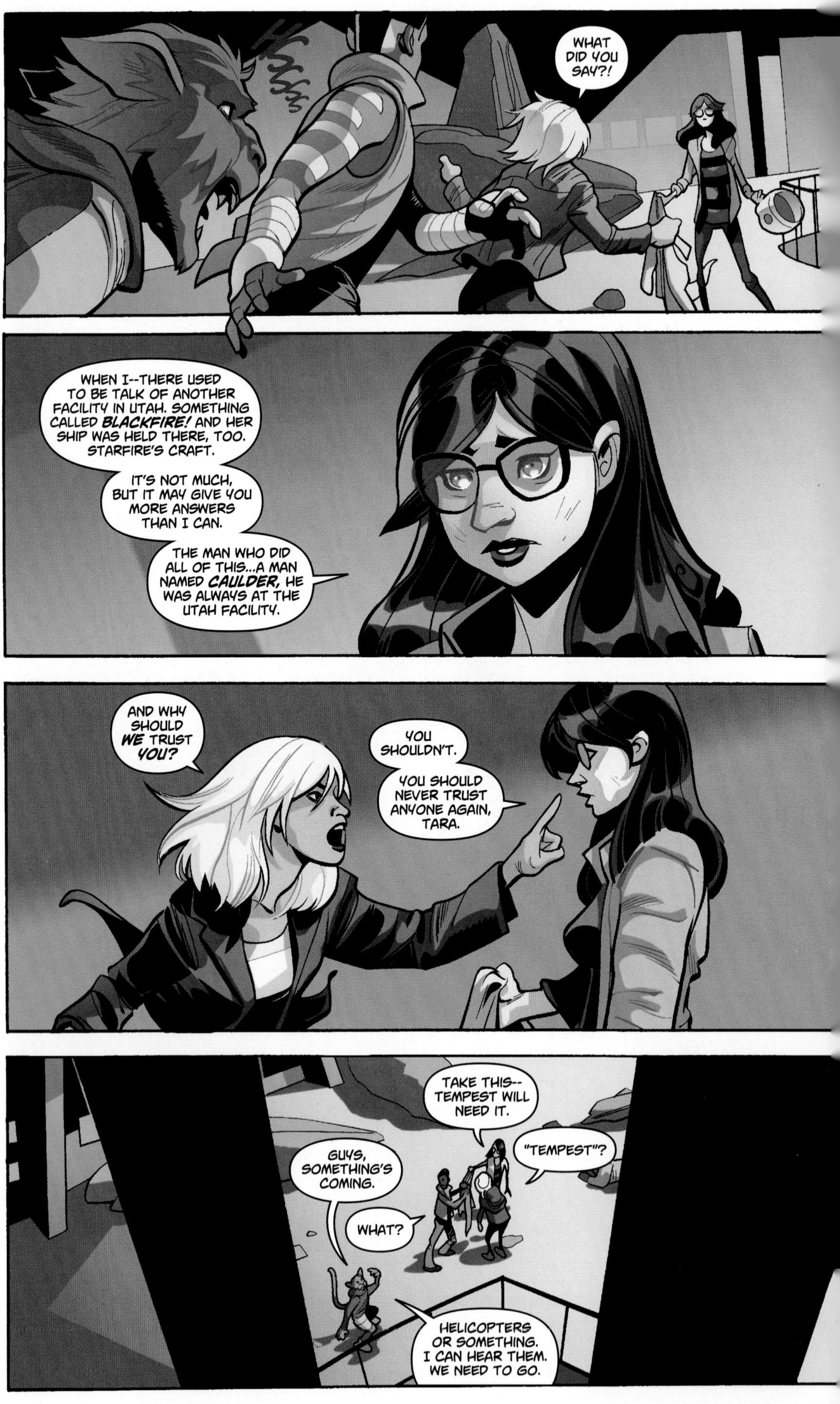

WHAT DID YOU SAY?!
WHEN I--THERE USED TO BE TALK OF ANOTHER FACILITY IN UTAH. SOMETHING CALLED *BLACKFIRE!* AND HER SHIP WAS HELD THERE, TOO. STARFIRE'S CRAFT.
IT'S NOT MUCH, BUT IT MAY GIVE YOU MORE ANSWERS THAN I CAN.
THE MAN WHO DID ALL OF THIS...A MAN NAMED *CAULDER,* HE WAS ALWAYS AT THE UTAH FACILITY.
AND WHY SHOULD *WE* TRUST *YOU?*
YOU SHOULDN'T.
YOU SHOULD NEVER TRUST ANYONE AGAIN, TARA.
TAKE THIS-- TEMPEST WILL NEED IT.
"TEMPEST"?
GUYS, SOMETHING'S COMING.
WHAT?
HELICOPTERS OR SOMETHING. I CAN HEAR THEM. WE NEED TO GO.

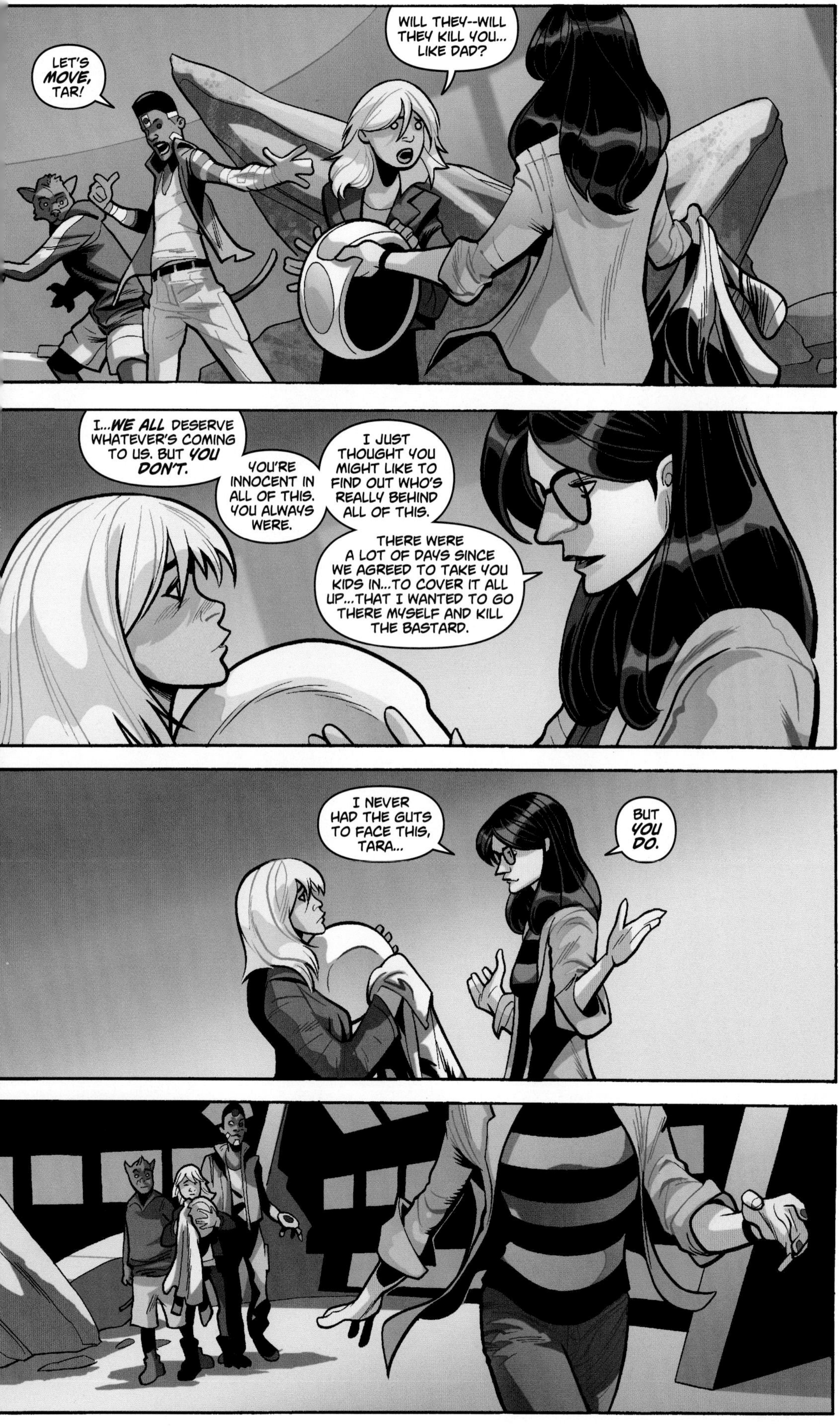
LET'S MOVE, TAR!
WILL THEY--WILL THEY KILL YOU... LIKE DAD?
I...WE ALL DESERVE WHATEVER'S COMING TO US. BUT YOU DON'T.
YOU'RE INNOCENT IN ALL OF THIS. YOU ALWAYS WERE.
I JUST THOUGHT YOU MIGHT LIKE TO FIND OUT WHO'S REALLY BEHIND ALL OF THIS.
THERE WERE A LOT OF DAYS SINCE WE AGREED TO TAKE YOU KIDS IN...TO COVER IT ALL UP...THAT I WANTED TO GO THERE MYSELF AND KILL THE BASTARD.
I NEVER HAD THE GUTS TO FACE THIS, TARA...
BUT YOU DO.

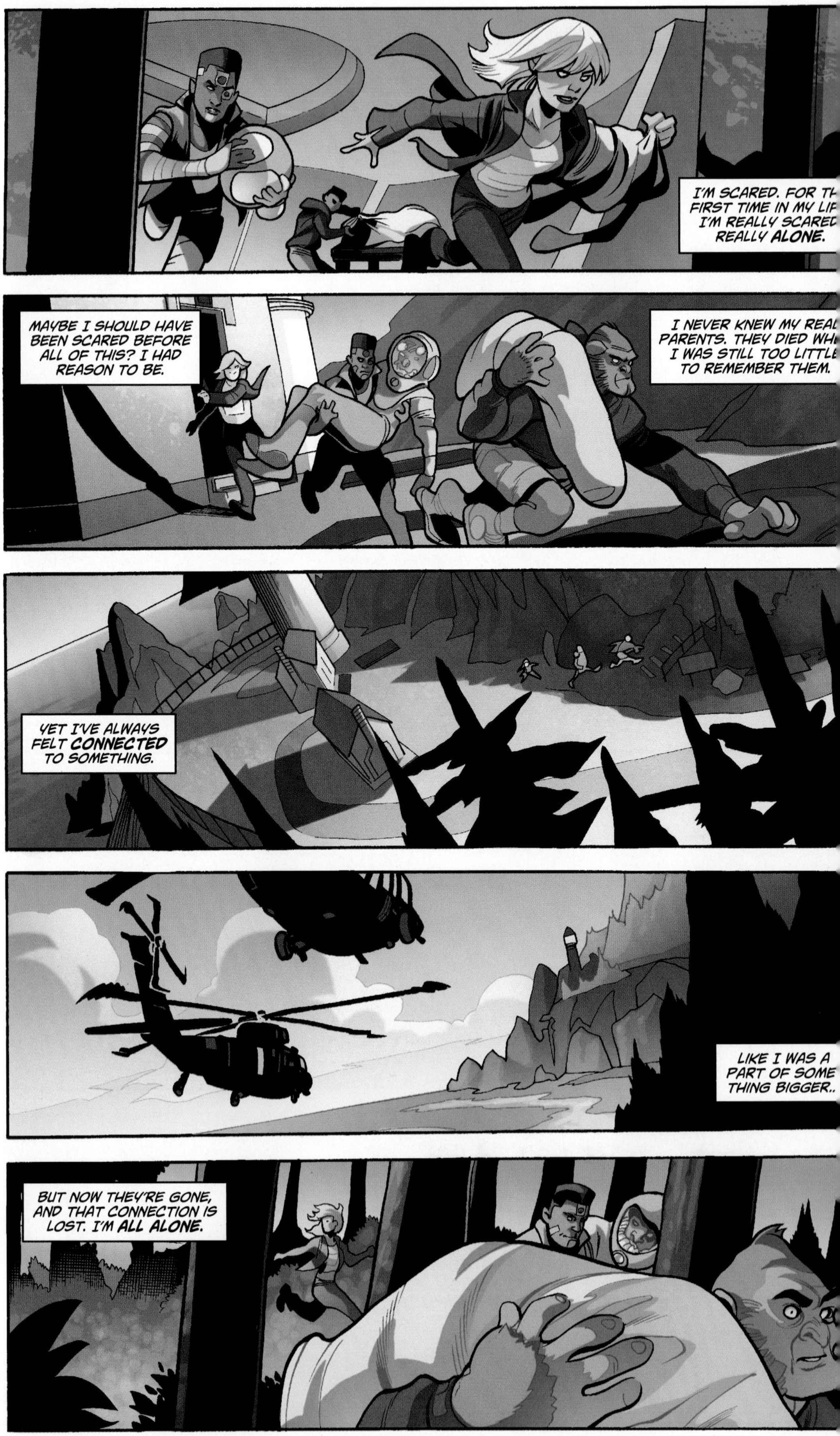
I'M SCARED. FOR TH
FIRST TIME IN MY LIF
I'M REALLY SCARED
REALLY ALONE.
MAYBE I SHOULD HAVE BEEN SCARED BEFORE ALL OF THIS? I HAD REASON TO BE.
I NEVER KNEW MY REAL
PARENTS. THEY DIED WH
I WAS STILL TOO LITTLE
TO REMEMBER THEM.
YET I'VE ALWAYS FELT CONNECTED TO SOMETHING.
LIKE I WAS A PART OF SOME THING BIGGER..
BUT NOW THEY'RE GONE, AND THAT CONNECTION IS LOST. I'M ALL ALONE.

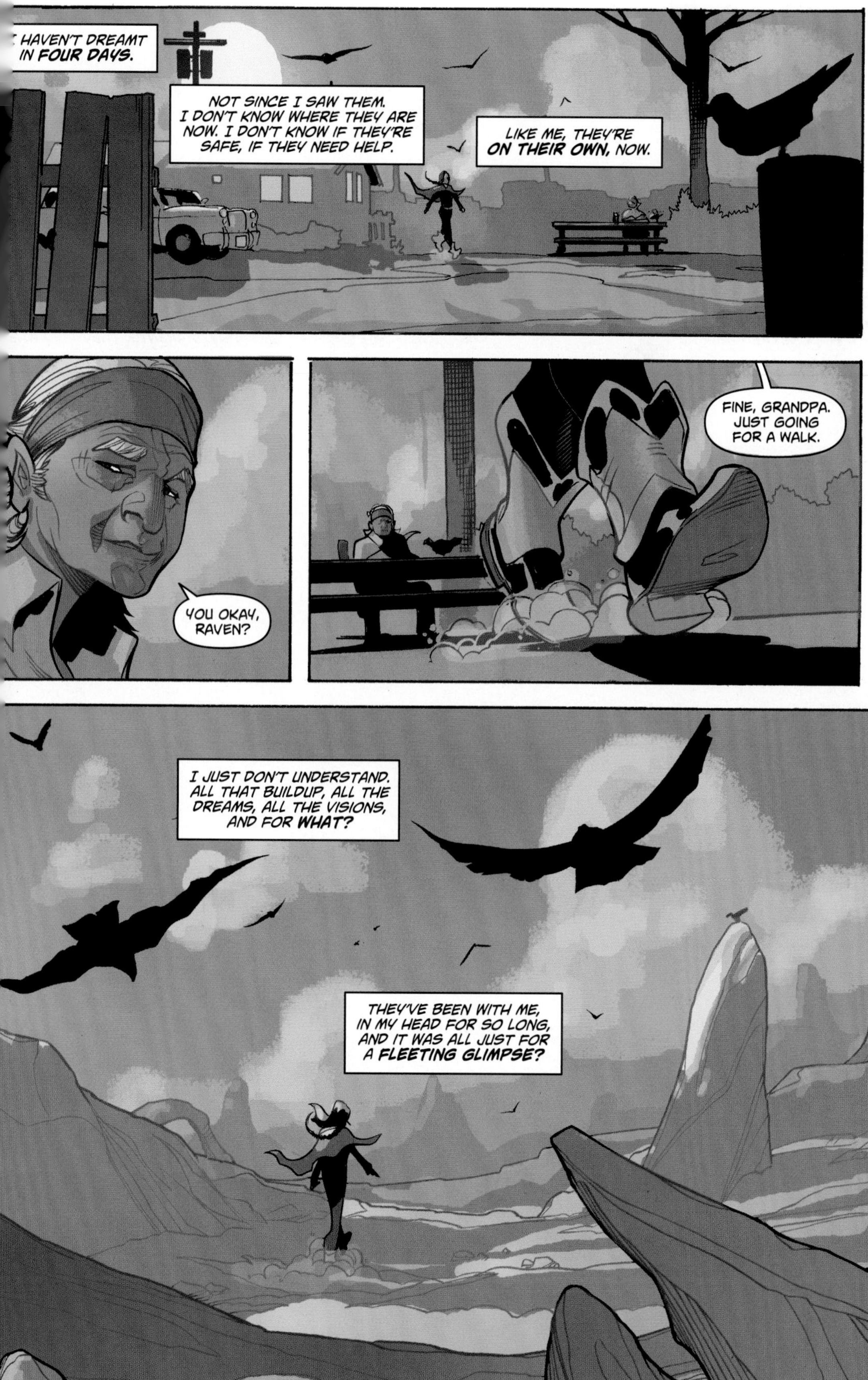
I HAVEN'T DREAMT IN FOUR DAYS.
NOT SINCE I SAW THEM. I DON'T KNOW WHERE THEY ARE NOW. I DON'T KNOW IF THEY'RE SAFE, IF THEY NEED HELP.
LIKE ME, THEY'RE ON THEIR OWN, NOW.
YOU OKAY, RAVEN?
FINE, GRANDPA. JUST GOING FOR A WALK.
I JUST DON'T UNDERSTAND. ALL THAT BUILDUP, ALL THE DREAMS, ALL THE VISIONS, AND FOR WHAT?
THEY'VE BEEN WITH ME, IN MY HEAD FOR SO LONG, AND IT WAS ALL JUST FOR A FLEETING GLIMPSE?

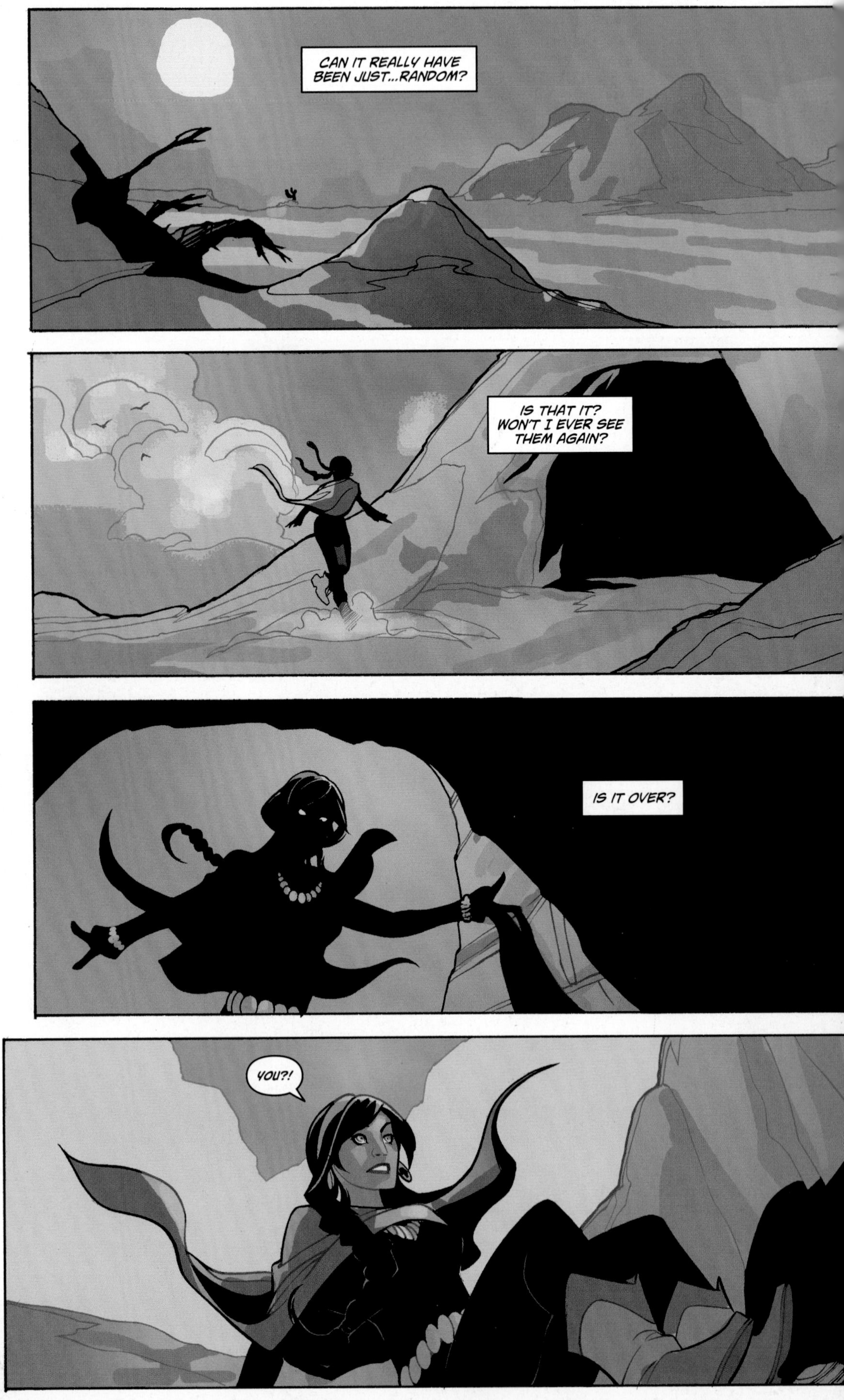
CAN IT REALLY HAVE BEEN JUST...RANDOM?
IS THAT IT? WON'T I EVER SEE THEM AGAIN?
IS IT OVER?
YOU?!

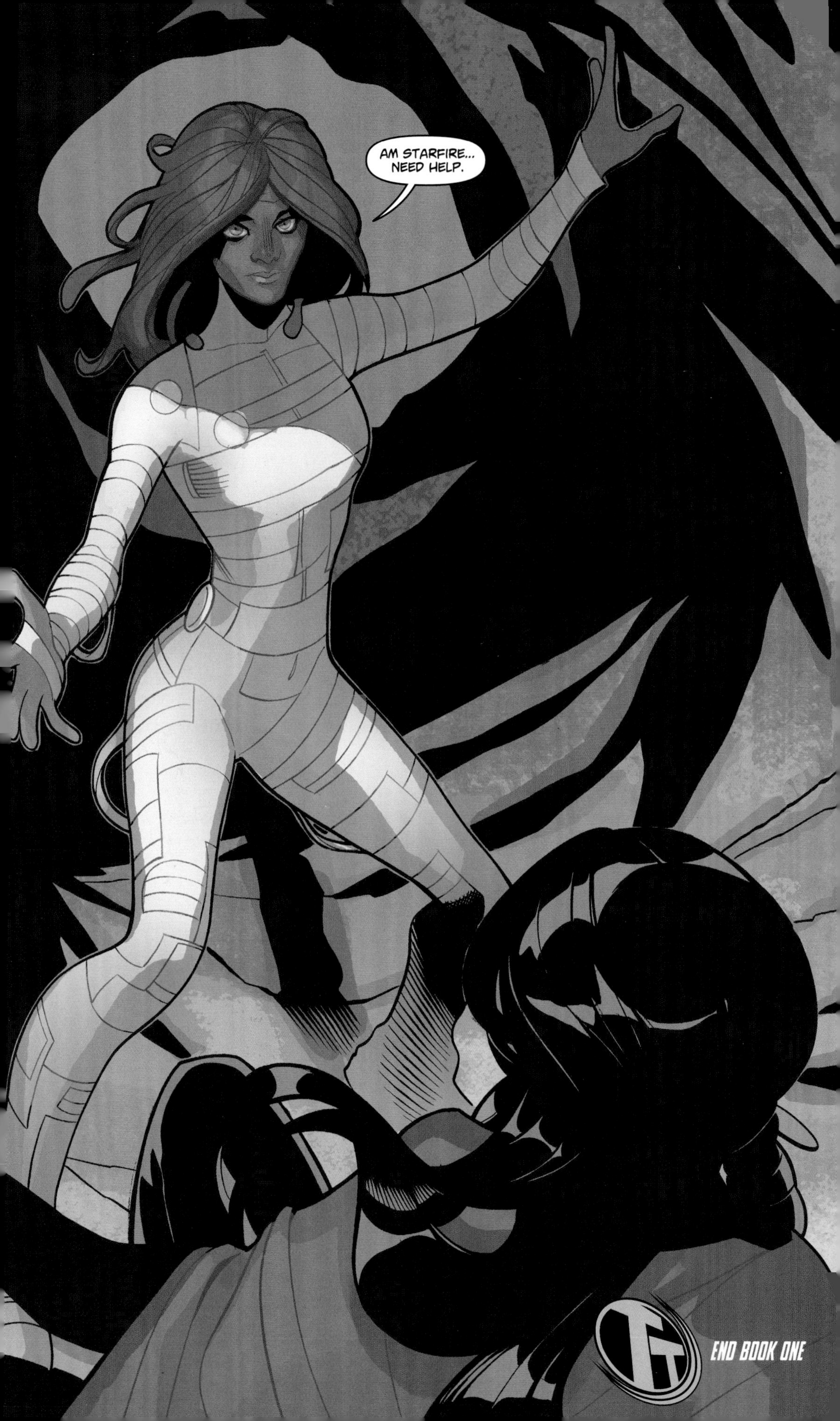
AM STARFIRE... NEED HELP.
END BOOK ONE

JEFF LEMIRE   New York Times Bestselling author Jeff Lemire is the creator of the acclaimed graphic novels SWEET TOOTH, *Essex County, The Underwater Welder* and the sci-fi love story, TRILLIUM. His next original graphic novel will be *Roughneck* from Simon and Schuster. Jeff is also a prominent writer for DC Comics where he currently writes the monthly adventures of JUSTICE LEAGUE UNITED. He has also written the monthly adventures of ANIMAL MAN and GREEN ARROW, among many others.

In 2008 and in 2013, Jeff won the Schuster Award for Best Canadian Cartoonist. He has also received The Doug Wright Award for Best Emerging Talent and the American Library Association's prestigious Alex Award, recognizing books for adults with specific teen appeal. He has also been nominated for 8 Eisner awards, 7 Harvey Awards and 8 Shuster Awards. In 2010, *Essex County* was named as one of the five Essential Canadian Novels of the Decade by the CBC's Canada Reads.

He currently lives and works in Toronto with his wife and son.

TERRY AND RACHEL DODSON   In 1993, Oregon-based Terry Dodson first gained industry attention with his distinctive illustrative style on *Mantra* for Malibu Comics. He next moved on to Marvel Comics where he worked on X-Men titles such as *Storm* and *Generation X,* where his wife, Rachel, began adding her masterly inking to his work. Shortly afterward, the Dodsons launched HARLEY QUINN for DC Comics with writer Karl Kesel, starring the Joker's deadly female sidekick.

The Dodsons collaborated with writer Mark Millar on the year-long blockbuster Marvel Knights *Spider-Man*, and then with writer/ filmmaker Kevin Smith on *Spider-Man and the Black Cat*. They returned to DC Comics to help re-launch WONDER WOMAN, working alongside noted writers Allan Heinberg, Gail Simone and Jodi Picoult.

Currently the Dodsons are splitting their time between working on company-owned universes and establishing new worlds of their own with creator owned projects such as *Songes*, *Red One* and more to come.

BRAD ANDERSON, a native of Kenora, Ontario, Canada, began his comic career after attending the Joe Kubert school in 1996. Shortly after returning to Canada, he began coloring comics at Digital Chameleon, where he cut his teeth on some of the top characters in the business. After leaving as Art Director, he began working independently on a long stint with Dark Horse on *Star Wars: Legacy*, as well as CATWOMAN, BATMAN: EARTH ONE, and many other series at DC.

Brad currently resides in Winnipeg, Canada, with his wife Kim and two children.